HEALTHCARE TECHNOLOGIES SERIES 40

Applications of Artificial Intelligence in E-Healthcare Systems

Other volumes in this series:

Applications of Artificial Intelligence in E-Healthcare Systems

Edited by
Munish Sabharwal, B. Balamurugan Balusamy,
S. Rakesh Kumar, N. Gayathri and Shakhzod Suvanov

The Institution of Engineering and Technology

Published by The Institution of Engineering and Technology, London, United Kingdom

The Institution of Engineering and Technology is registered as a Charity in England & Wales (no. 211014) and Scotland (no. SC038698).

© The Institution of Engineering and Technology 2022

First published 2022

The Institution of Engineering and Technology
Futures Place
Kings Way, Stevenage
Hertfordshire, SG1 2UA, United Kingdom

www.theiet.org

British Library Cataloguing in Publication Data
A catalogue record for this product is available from the British Library

ISBN 978-1-83953-449-2 (hardback)
ISBN 978-1-83953-450-8 (PDF)

Typeset in India by MPS Ltd
Printed in the UK by CPI Group (UK) Ltd, Croydon

Contents

About the editors

Munish Sabharwal is a professor and the dean of the School of Computer Science and Engineering at Galgotias University, India. He is a member of numerous engineering societies spanning USA, Singapore, India, and China and a fellow of the Centre for Education Growth and Research (India) and of the Institute of Electronics and Telecommunication Engineers (India). His research interests include Artificial Intelligence, Machine Learning, Biometrics, and E-Banking.

B. Balamurugan Balusamy is an associate Dean-Student Engagement Shiv Nadar University, Delhi-National Capital Region (NCR), India. He is a previous recipient of the IBM Developer Superstar Award and the CSC-VIT Best Faculty Coordinator Award. His current research interests include Internet of Things technologies and blockchain applications for healthcare. He is a member of Association for Computing Machinery, the Computer Society of India, and the International Association of Engineers.

S. Rakesh Kumar is an assistant professor of Computer Science at Galgotias University, India. His research interests include big data analytics, Internet of Things technologies, artificial intelligence and machine learning. He is a member of Association for Computing Machinery, the Computer Society of India, and the International Association of Engineers.

N. Gayathri is an associate professor of Computer Science and Engineering at Galgotias University, India. She is a member of Association for Computing Machinery, the Computer Society of India, and the International Association of Engineers.

Shakhzod Suvanov is a lecturer and research scholar in the Faculty of Digital Technologies at Samarkand State University, Uzbekistan. His research interests include machine learning, artificial neural network, mathematical modeling, and dynamical systems.

Chapter 1

Introduction to AI in E-healthcare

N. Suresh Kumar[1], D. Damodharan[1], K. Anandhan[1] and S. Jerald Nirmal Kumar[1]

Abstract

Artificial intelligence includes the improvement of computer frameworks that are suitable for performing assignments that regularly require human knowledge, for example, object detection, solving complex problems and so on. Nowadays, humans encounter various novel diseases, with symptoms that may not be identifiable at an early stage, causing high loss of life. AI can improve healthcare and so extend the human life span. Specifically, with rapid enhancements in computer handling, these AI-based frameworks are currently improving the accuracy and productivity in identifying and treating diseases across different specializations. AI is evolving in the e-healthcare industry in a number of areas, including: collecting medical records, AI-based diagnostics, automatic follow-up, etc. Data science (AI, machine learning, deep learning) has been extensively developed for the e-healthcare sector to provide improved quality in decision-making, finding daily infection patterns, identifying early risks and prediction, and so saving lives and promoting good health. Electronic health records enable the provision of better data-driven decisions, building good machine learning models for prediction, greater operational speed and accuracy, and reducing the amount of valuable time spent by patients and healthcare workers. In this chapter we discuss the complete road map to construct powerful artificial intelligence (AI) in e-healthcare systems using tools and intelligent algorithms. AI e-healthcare applications can be used to manipulate, transmit, and keep patient information, using medical records to enable fast access anywhere in the world. This works on the Internet which is able to monitor payments and maintain records through e-healthcare areas.

Keywords: Medical records; intelligent algorithms; framework; patient information

[1]School of Computing Science and Engineering, Galgotias University, UP, India

1.1   Introduction to artificial intelligence

Artificial intelligence (AI) is an extremely promising field of computer science, which has been used to develop highly intelligent machines and applications. AI is used to teach machines to learn, think, decide and act in the same ways that humans would [1]. It has left its mark in almost all fields including biology, neuroscience, sociology, psychology, computer science and philosophy. In 1956, a group of scientists from different backgrounds decided to organize a summer research project on intelligent machines. Four creative minds led the project, John McCarthy, Claude Shannon, Nathaniel Rochester, and Marvin Minsky. At this meeting, John McCarthy coined the phrase "artificial intelligence." Humans have natural intelligence as we learn from experience. For example, as children we were naturally curious about fire but may not have been aware of its dangers. However, when we placed our hands near fire and realized that it hurts, we gathered this information and stored it in our brain. The next time we went near fire we realized that we should be more careful. How do we do that? We retrieve the past information that is stored in the brain and analyze it, which helps us to decide and take the action of not going so near to the fire.

The term AI refers to three types of artificial intelligence (Figure 1.1). The first is artificial narrow intelligence (ANI), which refers to a computer's ability to do extraordinarily well at a single, well-defined task, such as playing chess or detecting tumors on CT scans in seconds, with precision equal to or better than that of humans. The second level is artificial general intelligence (AGI), which refers to a machine that can match a human's cognitive capacity and has the ability to understand and learn complex intellectual tasks in the same way as a human. In medicine, AGI can be the perfect assistant to physicians. The third level is artificial super intelligence (ASI), which, as its name implies, refers to a machine surpassing the cognitive capacity of all humanity. The ideal vision is to almost reach AGI but stop right before so that we can harness the benefits of AI without completely losing control. AI machine learning is a technique in which an algorithm learns from data, recognizes patterns, and makes decisions with little to no human intervention.

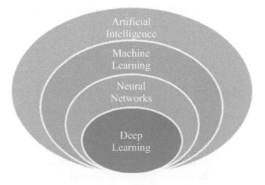

Figure 1.1   AI framework

1.2   Machine Learning

Machine Learning (ML) was introduced by Arthur Samuel in 1959. It is defined as a machine being able to "learn". In ML [2], the training time is comparatively less than with the deep learning (DL) models. When the amount of data is less, it is preferable to use a machine learning algorithm. The performance will be reduced when the data count increases beyond a certain saturation point. It is suggested to choose a deep learning algorithm for a huge number of varieties and unstructured data for analysis.

1.3   Deep Learning

Deep learning (DL) was first described in 2000, by Igor Aizenberg. DL is a subset of ML, which is under the framework of AI. DL uses algorithms inspired by the structure and functions of the human brain. The significant key factor about DL is that the training time is high and testing time is less as compared to ML. DL can address a large of amount input data to perform an analysis in a more efficient manner as compared to machine learning [3]. A DL performance graph is measurably high, with a tremendous amount of data. DL is a subset of machine learning that uses an unconventional approach to how AI should think. It uses a layered architecture of artificial neural networks modeled after the neural network of the human brain, while the other methods deal better with data arranged in a spreadsheet and can only execute narrow tasks. Deep learning can analyze images, sounds, and other high-dimensional data, and it can be used for more complex tasks.

1.4   AI timeline in the healthcare sector

1.4.1   AI discovery and the development of drugs

Basic drug development consists of five different phases: step 1, detection and development; step 2, preclinical examination; step 3, scientific development; step 4, Food and Drug Administration (FDA) review; and step 5, Food and Drug Administration post market protection scrutiny. AI can help to build structure-based drug discovery by predicting the effects of a compound and its safety. The developments costs of a new drug is almost $2.6 billion and it may take 15 years to reach the market. AI has a vital role in reducing this cost and speeding up the process. AI techniques, such as deep learning, are used for drug discovery, and bio companies planning to reinvent medicine by using artificial subsets and natural language processing (NLP) [4].

1.4.2   AI personalized healthcare

All humans have a unique genome, and understanding genome mutations to iden-tify illnesses earlier can save human lives. AI personalization refers to the labeling of dissimilar consumer datasets and mining useful insight from these datasets. These insights are fed into an automation engine that can carry out actions without human intervention. Personalized medicine has the potential to get better improve, saving more human lives, and AI is the driving force behind these future break-throughs. Wearable technologies such as Internet of Things (IoT) devices are helping to collect unique live datasets from individuals. AI will help both organizations and patients, providing efficient diagnoses and reducing errors. The following are examples of AI-based drugs companies: Pathi – enabling more accurate cancer diagnosis with AI; Buoy Health – AI-based symptom and cure checker; Freenome – Detecting cancer at an earlier stage; and Zebra Medical Vision – an AI-powered radiology assistant.

1.5   AI devices in healthcare

In healthcare, AI is a wide-ranging term used to label the use of ML algorithms and software to imitate human thought through investigation, appearance, and understanding of complex medical and healthcare information (Figure 1.2) [5]. AI is the ability of computer procedures to estimate decisions based uniquely on the input. This technology has traditionally been used in the healthcare field to gather facts, process them, and give an exact output to the stakeholders, but in the current era AI, through machine learning and deep learning skills, predicts behavior and creates its own model for processing. AI behaves differently in each scenario by means of accurate algorithms and extreme prediction accuracy. In order to achieve this we are in need of AI devices in healthcare for more accurate diagnosis of diseases. AI devices are applied to analyzing huge amounts of information through electronic health records for disease diagnosis and forecasting, and they also perform analysis processes, treatment procedures, drug development, personalized medicine, and patient monitoring [6]. The healthcare industry faces increasing issues around income, cost, and quality, so that AI is seen as the key to a better solution and also the

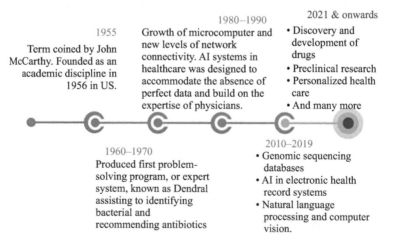

Figure 1.2   Timeline of AI in the healthcare sector (1955–2021)

margin of error is minimal. There has been huge growth of research into various areas of healthcare because of AI, with devices used in such areas as dermatology, radiology, screening, disease diagnosis, telemedicine, and electronic health records.

1.5.1   Role of AI in healthcare

AI is playing an important vital role in all industries nowadays. In healthcare, the number of patients has increased dramatically, and so the traditional methods are not sufficient to store patient information. Big data usage is rapidly increasing nowadays, with Hadoop Distributed File System (HDFS) and map reduce tools helping to store and process a huge amount of data in a short time using a distributed computing environment. The combination of big data and AI is another milestone for the healthcare industry, especially for doctors and the special design of healthcare products. AI will assist specialist physicians to make accurate decisions using intelligent machines. The different data types have been analyzed by artificial intelligent algorithms. These mechanisms enable AI systems to generate clinically useful results and can identify a variety of diseases handled by AI communities. AI can apply various algorithms to learn from existing huge amounts of data and assist doctors to make accurate decisions in a timely manner. AI systems derive useful information from HDFS datasets stored inpatient records to assist the physician in predicting any risks [7].

Figure 1.3 illustrates AI-based advancements in intelligent detection used to recognize the early stages of patient illnesses, as earlier detection of a disease mean treatment can be more effective. Patient data histories have been provided to AI algorithms to identify the risks and assist physician to take the correct actions. AI can help individual patients with different diseases and enable better treatment plans that could help expand access to medical services. Healthcare involves physicians, technicians, nurses, hospital staff, and pharmacists effectively monitoring the patient's disease which can be described as an ecosystem. AI can design the framework to identify patient risks. There are many types of wearable devices available in the market, which can help to measure the human heartbeat, pulse, and calories burned. They can also help AI systems to learn from past feedback to improve the whole system. AI devices can be divided into two categories: first, those that analyze

Figure 1.3   AI advancements in healthcare

structured data using a medical application, and second, natural language processing (NLP) derived from unstructured data for medical application [8].

1.6   Framework for AI in healthcare using AI devices

Different challenges have been addressed and difficulties overcome using the proposed framework for healthcare using AI devices.

1.6.1   Step 1: Analytic integration

This analytic integration tool helps us to integrate well with existing business intelligence tools [9] such as tableau and Qlik, and provides high-quality and closer perceptions to support business-critical issues. There is no longer the need to wait for a long time to train data, rather its insights enable correct, consistent, and precise data, and it also systematizes analytics tasks that take time during the integration of external tools.

The following are approaches that are faster and more precise as compare with tradition methods:

- Statistical process control
- Time series outlier detection
- Forecasting
- Multidimensional time series clustering

1.6.2   Step 2: Choose/build predictive models

The reason for selecting or building a predictive model is to meet a wide range of needs. In business, predictive models act as self-service tools because they are reasonable and increase revenues. There are also many challenges which can be rectified with the support of AI algorithms, and these are often applied to fit the essentials of local healthcare organizations. Different kinds of predictive models which help healthcare to be more effective using AI (Figure 1.4) include the following:

- Prescriptive – What should I do.
- Predictive – What will happen.
- Diagnostic – Why did it happen.
- Descriptive – What happened.

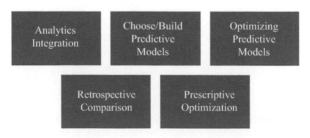

Figure 1.4   AI framework for healthcare in AI devices

1.6.3   Step 3: Optimizing predictive models

Step 2 is only the first part of the success in predictive models, whereas the second part of validating the models is also important and is achieved by optimizing predictive models to enhance their influence within the organization. This results in the following:

- Functional model understanding.
- Operational model understanding.
- Contextual model understanding.

1.6.4   Step 4: Retrospective comparison

The only way to acquire more information is to carry out a randomized trial. The majority of issues occur because of different standards of practice. In this procedure we can overcome these problems and can provide the best solution to our objectives, so that we can save time and reduce corporate friction [10]. To achieve the best result in this approach we use the following models: statistical modeling, group differences, causation, and sensitivity analysis.

1.6.5   Step 5: Prescriptive optimization

The planning requires in-depth knowledge of healthcare and its tools in a prescriptive optimization approach, where it is incorporated in to the AI devices to achieve success through demanding methods, and forecasted augmented intelligence (AI). The following steps help to make AI devices more popular in healthcare in through prescriptive optimization:

- Problem refinement;
- Learning design.

AI devices in healthcare will play a major role in slowing down the spread of infections in forthcoming pandemics and even in the current COVID-19 pandemic. They perform effective testing, which helps to control outbreaks [11]. The advancements in AI devices for healthcare can compromise the performance in better accounting of generalization errors, role-dependent XAI, interactive user interfaces.

1.7   Support smart devices and applications

Doctors are physically monitoring the patient and maintaining their medical records is one of the major roles for their services. AI reduces a load of physical monitoring by doctors as it engages with machines that monitor all activities and maintain all records such as pulse monitoring, sugar level, etc., with live tracking of the patient, with the report saved and sent to the physician. Health care department before doing the diagnosis they are practicing with simulation for the same so that it results in higher success rates. This type of process will mainly be used for heart surgery, brain surgery, and other difficult cases. The monitoring system is connected through a network including smart medical devices mapped with a smartphone app, so that display devices can gather medical records and other types of essential health data that are connected through smart devices and transfer the information to the surgeon. Applying AI to e-healthcare data has been used in various areas, for instance, multi-research, especially in medicine, where AI looks like a machine learning classification with electronic health records data to predict risks at an earlier stage and improve healthcare diagnoses.

1.8   IoT devices

IoT devices assemble and allocate health data such as blood pressure, oxygen and blood sugar levels, weight, and ECG signal monitoring.

1.9   Backend facilitator

The backend facilitator (BF) can control and maintain the work process, and if any issues are faced by the system, the authorized persons at the backend facilitator will resolve them. Medical records will be updated in the backend to maintain their privacy. The tools which are used for security management and application development are the building blocks for backend control and also it can be accessed and controlled by authorized remote access consultants.

1.10   Architecture design for an e-healthcare system

The architecture design for an e-healthcare system includes the interior design of these modules and the framework is split into four layers, including the user interface, information handling, message trade motor, and information vault, as shown in Figure 1.5.

1.10.1   UI layers

This layer contains the client, authentication, and support. It is accessible only by using an authenticate username and password. It approves client information depends on the client accreditation. As a result of the user interface, the user can easily access the connection's internal parts, which include patient records, unusual occurrences data, details reports, information dissemination, appraisal and valuation records, making phone decisions, and pictures.

1.10.2   Information-handling layer

This layer includes the data input module, segment, and HL7/LOINC library. The information module incorporates the consolidated data, client measurement data, and lacking access information [12]. Consolidated data contains biometric sensor information, clinical records information about the medical services in the architecture diagram. Medical records are processed manually in earlier but using this layer in AI provide the convenience to automate the data more fast and accurate through Google Weather API.

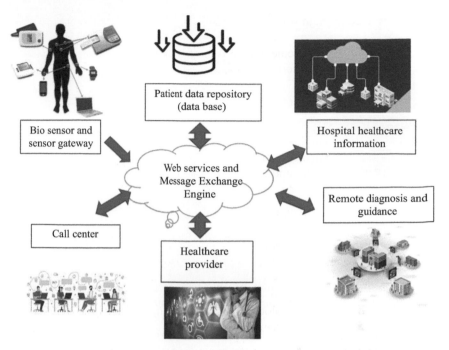

Figure 1.5   Architecture design of the e-healthcare information system

1.10.3   Remote diagnoses and guidelines

A remote diagnosis system is a new way for monitoring the patient using an IOT device. This platform is used to connect the patient at home to track the health merits such as heartbeat rate, pulse ECG rate, etc. The telehealthcare was responsible for collecting patient details and provide to the physician for analysis. The physician is responsible to verify each patient details analysis and provide proper guidelines for the patient using the mobile application interface.

1.10.4   Data exchange machine

Patient medical records are very important for the health care center. There are different types of medical records available their dataset stored in the digital platform such as cloud computing, big data, etc. The advanced technology will provide more secure, reliable, faster computing and processing purposes.

1.11   Bigdata devices (storage)

Big data technologies information is large in size, especially for medical services, and is a term used to describe huge volumes of information made by the selection of electronic information of patients' records and help in control emergency clinic execution. The real circumstances for the most information is utilized in the

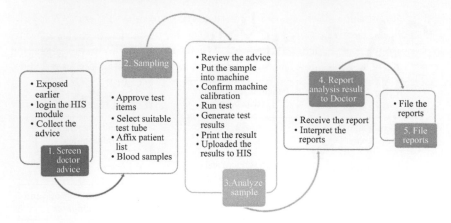

Figure 1.6   Challenging procedure for the despondent outline

e-medical care field. Each patient has his own record which involves well-being history, sensitivities and research capability test results. Data are shared by resources of safely secured frameworks such as a data framework. Each document contains once changeable records, which free from administrative work and threat. AI methods have been applied clinically to improving visual impurity conclusion, anticipating sickness movement, and hazard appraisal. A few sicknesses were concentrated in articles remembered for this survey including glaucoma, waterfalls, and AMD.

Figure 1.6 depicts the framework for all risk variables into the step-by-step process of initially monitoring all patient records without the failure mode. The first and second steps include acquiring patient data and storing it in a database that is accessible to the health information system. The third step is to construct an operational high-risk analysis flow stage that evaluates the operations, for example, blood model placed into the machine for challenging, approve that the mechanism is standardized, track all trial and monitoring data, and publish the findings.

The likelihood of failure involves comparable damage to computer hardware, testing time misreading access to other patient records, patent records not imported in the right way to the database, and misunderstanding the findings. The latter two steps, analysis and seeing the report, have a lower risk factor, hence the third stage will have a higher danger factor. Figure 1.5 illustrates this.

1.12   Data mining

Data mining is planning data using a structured method which improves access to information for medical services. Uniform e-medical care is a beneficial approach for increasing consideration access for collectors; there are three stages to measure the sufficiency of the nature of e-medical services administration. In architecture, an example of e-medical care design arises, in which three levels of administrations can be coordinated with the equipment. Organizational level: terminal gadget (crucial sign sensor, POC identifier), information specialize gadgets (Bluetooth, Zegbee, Wi-Fi, 3G+, Web) [14], middle gadgets (passage, information trade, and so on), maintenance framework finish (call focus, e-medical services IS, HIS, etc.). Worker interface, information processing, information sharing, and information repository are examples of structure levels. Sensor data, HIS, illness IS, and physician interviews are all examples of information sources.

1.13   AI assistance for surgical robotics

The main goal of AI applications in surgery is to help the physician to navigate complex operations using different kinds of designer robotics. There are four major phases, as shown in Figure 1.7, which are used in robotic and autonomous systems (RAS): Phase 1, insights; Phase 2, mapping and localization; Phase 3, system control and modeling; and Phase 4, human–robot communication. The captured image is identified by instrument tracking, and segmentation tasks are divided into three stages, multiclass segmentation, segmentation background, and segmentation, for various different instruments [15].

The architectures are supported by deep learning for segmentation, for example: U-Net, LinkNet based on ResNet architecture, Ternaus Net-VGG16, and DCNN architecture.

In AI, surgical task segmentation is used to construct a framework containing kinematic data for suturing, needle passage, and knot tying. The identification of surgical subtasks was presented using a hidden Markov model and linear dynamic systems. AI subsets, such as machine learning and deep learning, are more powerful in surgical robot's design for system modelling and control [16].

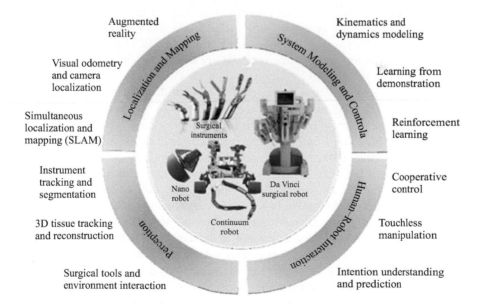

Figure 1.7   AI assistance for robotic and autonomous systems

1.14 AI e-healthcare risk factors

AI provides a portion of the medicare strategy as well as advantages over traditional analytics and medical executive procedures. Finding and practicing the appropriate algorithms only becomes more specific and accurate as they interact with training data, allowing people to get amazing insights into diagnosis, maintenance procedures, treatment variations, and long-term results. AI plays an important role, without human assistance, a supercomputer that interacts and interconnects with a system network, based on the training model of how the human will act as the same the performances and/or action will play the role of the application in that need to use keyboard, mice, speakers, sensors, and monitors in the cutting edge of research that has important application for the role of patients. AI-based IoT devices and hardware, such as sensors, are widely used for producing, collecting, and securely sending e-healthcare data to other locations. The transfer's health records, such as blood pressure, sugar level, and oxygen level management in blood, ECG information, and weight records, are also kept in the system depository, and this stored information will be utilised for future surveys and research, which will benefit the physician. AI might help to increase and improve the quality of the clinical staff by taking over some of the diagnostic duties typically allocated to humans. Electronic health records are constantly monitored, providing patients access to all information, staying up to date on live and fresh lab tests, and tracking medications to see whether a patient is also following the doctor's orders.

1.14.1 Risk factors in supporting AI e-healthcare

Although an e-Healthcare system foundation is required to create an exceptional awareness, a few states genuinely struggle to tackle this type of issue and completely carry out these modules. According to this HITECH research, the EU is likewise interested in a large jump, with 94% of centers executing electrical health records (EHRs), but the EU really lags behind. Healthcare data are extremely important unique information that must be kept confidential. If any data is lost it can have serious implications for the individual, and so the security of healthcare data is crucial. If the information falls into the hands of an unwelcome individual, he or she will be abused and threatened with a monetary penalty for any favor. Therefore, healthcare data are transferred online allowing rapid access anywhere in the world. AI will help to increase the accuracy level and reduce the time for data collection. All patient and medical information goes online, so if a hacker has access to the patient information or medical combination alterations are made, the danger elements in AI the e-healthcare conveyed are also substantial.

All forms of data are very vulnerable to hackers who are preoccupied with the arrangement and collaboration of personal health information of collectively affected people with physicians. Risk factors include hackers misappropriating patient information to buy medicines, stealing equipment they plan to sell later, or temporarily creating demand to increase the cost of equipment [17]. Hackers can create fake IDs, document files, and also fake insurance claims in the patient's name.

1.14.2   Patient e-record security applications

To secure an AI system, first policies would be protected from access by using proper locking techniques.

To secure an AI system, first policies would be protected from access by using proper locking techniques. Wide and wireless connections and devices, as well as numerous technological characteristics such as IoT, Big Data, Cloud, and so on, which are more products and secure, are necessary. The default password must be modified, and a hard and unexpected strong password should be used for production. Information exchange between multipurpose programmes and various gadgets is enabled by tools like broad and distant association; as a result, information should be encoded throughout correspondence in any case, and local traffic will be released [18]. The mobile application should use TLS/SSL and validate the device's TLS endorsements, which will protect the communication against a man-in-the-middle attack. TLS/SSL should be used to enable communication between mobile or web apps and cloud administrations by allowing its use from the cloud administration. Correspondence among portable applications [19] and gadgets is completed as remote communication. The last necessity of the IoT framework is the entrance instrument for the IoT administrations, which is refined by utilizing the entrance application. The entrance application might be introduced on brilliant gadgets or on working area frameworks. For example, modeling exercise calculation about health process through smart strength element can be accessible as tracks:

Usually, the strength units are,

$$SSU = f(Dc, iGW, Bf, AA) \tag{1.1}$$

The following are the strong strength unit (SSU) factors in Eq. (1.1): f is for reason; Dc stands for data authority gadgets; iGW stands for the IoT gateway in the smart healthcare unit; Bf stands for the backend facilitator, which provides backend administrations to the clever well-being framework; and AA stands for the entrance access application. Condition (1.1) illustrates the entire perceptual comfort unit, which is dependent on each component of the medical care significant model.

$$SSU = (a + bBC + yiGW + \&Bf + 0AA + u) \tag{1.2}$$

Condition (1.2) depicts the smart health unit as follows: where, for each part, DC is a capacity that represents information gathering and is used to acquire information and convey it to the IoT entrance gadget for assessment.

1.15   Challenges to the use of AI devices in healthcare

- AI integration with current tools.
- Integrating AI experts in business.
- Demonstrating the positive impact of AI.

1.16   AI devices and managing healthcare data

- PathAI—It is more accurate to diagnose cancer using AI.
- Buoy health—This device is an intelligent symptom checker.
- Zebra medical vision AI—This device is used to aid the radiology assistant.
- Cloudmedx—This helps to manage the patient history using machine learning.
- H2o.AI—This health system data is managed through AI devices.
- Google Deepmind Health—This device notifies doctors when patients are in distress.
- AI robot—This is a specially designed machine to assist with surgery and manages related data.

1.17   AI in e-healthcare applications

AI is improving in its ability to perform tasks more efficiently, quicker, and at less cost than humans. Examples of how this transition is currently taking place are keeping safe, early warning, diagnostic judgment, counseling, end-of-life treatment, research, and planning.

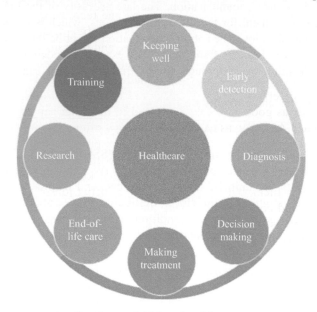

Applications of AI in e-healthcare

AI could advance or outright revolutionize medicine at every level. There are many tasks within medicine where humans will not be able to compete with AI. AI will be able to mine medical records to take in all the information from more than 31 million medical papers available in the big data coming from studies and have all that knowledge readily available for its human counterparts with that vast knowledge deep learning algorithms that will be able to design treatment plans in oncology. They will analyze huge data sets of genomic profiles and combine them with attributes from a patient's medical file to identify targeted personalized treatments. Those treatment plans will include precision medicine unlike the classical method where drugs and treatments are based on the needs of the average person obtained from statistics.

AI will be able to analyze how an individual's body would react to a treatment plan and advise accordingly before any medication. Moving away from the one-size-fits-all medical solutions toward these targeted personalized therapies is one of the biggest advantages we could gain by using AI. A further advanced revolution in AI will include drug design and finding efficient drug combinations. It could analyze data from patients in real time, which would help with cheaper and faster clinical trials in e-healthcare. Drugs are still tested on humans, instead AI would run millions of simulations on virtual patients to break through into a new world for the healthcare industry. The next big step for AI would be every medical decision is supported and cross-checked by an algorithm to reduce human error. Before we could reach these visions, first of all, there is no AI revolution without a lot of data, and that data can only come from medical records, sensors, and apps. An AI algorithm is just as good as the data it is fed, and while medical institutions and tech companies can keep data private, in some cases, individual profiles can be traced back. Confidence remains an issue; we will need a lot more time and trust in a driverless car to see how it behaves under familiar situations, and medical practitioners also will need a lot more time to trust AI with a medical diagnosis. This should be considered when determining whether or not to introduce AI in the healthcare setting. AI is just as good as the data we feed it, but what happens if the data are skewed? When AI [20] was used to predict how often prisoners would reoffend in the United States, researchers found that the program predicted a relatively high risk of black people committing future crimes, regardless of how minor their initial offence was. AI programmers must know about these issues and actively combat them, but the ultimate fear is losing jobs by replacing humans in healthcare and consequently losing the art of medicine. AI will not take the jobs of physicians, nor will it monopolize medicine. It's not the use of technologies that has been taking the art away from physicians, already it is the administrative tasks and the monotonous day-to-day assignments that take physicians away from patients and away from their primary role. Fortunately, those are tasks that will be taken over by AI, and autonomous systems will thus free up medical professionals to finally fulfill the mission they signed up for (Figure 1.8).

To help patients with compassion, creativity, and care there will never be a situation where either a robot or an algorithm will take the place of a doctor. When AI discovers a drug or remedy that hasn't been discovered before, the true art of medicine would be to reverse engineer to explain how it arrived at that point. This would be the most difficult task that doctors have ever encountered. How should we think about all of this? AI will only support, elevate, and advance those who know how to use and harness this new tool that we are creating, but the time when you can still decide if you want to be in control in that future is today.

Figure 1.8   AI visualizing application

1.17.1   Overview of AI applications in e-healthcare

In next few years AI will involve various fields, in e-health care will involve to handled the physician and patient data to diagnosies. To fulfill the basic patient and physician requirement using AI e-healthcare.

The key drivers for application of AI in e-healthcare:

- Different types of surgery have been feasible because of advances in robotics solutions.
- AI will reduce the human labor for uncomfortable work in the hospital surrounding.
- Existing technology infrastructure has facilitated the integration of AI applications in hospitals.
- AI application has reduced medical errors due to the usage of automation systems.
- Extensive and real-time analysis of the health needs of the patients has been feasible and evidence-based policies for the cure of the diseases.

AI applications can reduce the costs and time involved in detecting and treating disease states, in order to improve health care quality and efficiency.

References

[1]   R. Hajjo, "The ethical challenges of applying machine learning and artificial intelligence in cancer care", 2018 1st International Conference on Cancer Care Informatics (CCI), 2018, p. 231, doi: 10.1109/CANCERCARE. 2018.8618186.

[2]   W. Liu, E.K. Park, U. Krieger, and S.S. Zhu, "Smart e-health security and safety monitoring with machine learning services", 2020 29th International

Conference on Computer Communications and Networks (ICCCN), 2020, pp. 1–6, doi: 10.1109/ICCCN49398.2020.9209679.

[3]   D.I. Dogaru and I. Dumitrache, "Big data and machine learning framework in healthcare", 2019 E-Health and Bioengineering Conference (EHB), 2019, pp. 1–4, doi: 10.1109/EHB47216.2019.8969944.

[4]   F. Jiang, Y. Jiang, H. Zhi, *et al.,* "Artificial intelligence in healthcare: past, present and future", *Stroke Vasc Neurol* 2017. doi: 10.1136/svn-2017-000101.

[5]   J. Waring, C. Lindvall, and R. Umeton, "Automated machine learning: review of the state-of-the-art and opportunities for healthcare", Art Intell Med 2020;104:101822, doi: 10.1016/j.artmed.2020.101822.

[6]   A. Rajkomar, J. Dean, and I. Kohane, "Machine learning in medicine", *N Engl J Med* 2019;380(14):1347–1358.

[7]   Y. Zang, F. Zhang, C.A. Di, and D. Zhu, "Advances of flexible pressure sensors toward artificial intelligence and healthcare applications", *Mater Horiz* 2015;2:140–156.

[8]   R. Shankar, B.K. Sarojini, H. Mehraj, A.S. Kumar, R. Neware, and A. Singh Bist, "Impact of the learning rate and batch size on NOMA system using LSTM-based deep neural network", J Defense Model Simul *2021,* doi:10.1177/154851292110497822021.

[9]   W.R. Hersh, "Caveats for the use of operational electronic health record data in comparative effectiveness research", *Med Care* 2013;51(803):S30.

[10]   G. Luo, "PredicT-ML: a tool for automating machine learning model building with big clinical data", *Health Inf Sci Syst* 2016;4(1):5.

[11]   R. Shah and A. Chircu, "Iot and AI in healthcare: a systematic literature review", *Issues Inf Syst* 2018;19(3):33–41, doi: 10.48009/3_iis_2018_33-41.

[12]   C. Guerra Tort, V. Aguiar Pulido, V. Suárez Ulloa, F. Docampo Boedo, J.M. López Gestal, and J. Pereira Loureiro, "Electronic health records exploitation using artificial intelligence techniques", *Proceedings* 2020;54(1):60, doi:10.3390/proceedings 2020054060

[13]   L.-C. Chen, C.W. Chen, Y.C. Weng, *et al.,* "An information technology framework for strengthening telehealthcare service delivery", *Telemed J e-Health* 2012;18(8):596–603.

[14]   A. Sureshkumar and R. Samson Ravindran, "Swarm and fuzzy based cooperative caching framework to optimize energy consumption over multimedia wireless sensor networks", Wireless Pers Commun 2016;90:961–984, https://doi.org/10.1007/s11277-016-3274-0.

[15]   X.Y. Zhou, Y. Guo, M. Shen, *et al.,* "Application of artificial intelligence in surgery", Front Med 2020;14:417–430, https://doi.org/10.1007/s11684-020-0770-0.

[16]   A. Bohr and K. Memarzadeh, "The rise of artificial intelligence in healthcare applications", Artif Intell Healthcare 2020:25–60, doi:10.1016/B978-0-12-818438-7.00002-2.

[17]   A. Mehbodniya, A. Suresh Kumar, K. Pitambar Rane, K. Kumar Bhatia, and B. K. Singh, "Smartphone-based mHealth and Internet of Things for diabetes

control and self-management*",* J Healthcare Eng *2021,* Article ID 2116647, 10 pages, https://doi.org/10.1155/2021/2116647.

[18]   W.-C. Lin, J.S. Chen, M.F. Chiang, and M.R. Hribar, "Applications of artificial intelligence to electronic health record data in ophthalmology", *Trans Vis Sci Tech* 2020;9(2):13,https://doi.org/10.1167/tvst.9.2.13.

[19]   E.A. Alweshail and H. Brahim, "A smartphone application to provide the health care services at home", 2020 3rd International Conference on Computer Applications & Information Security (ICCAIS), 2020, pp. 1–5, doi: 10.1109/ICCAIS48893.2020.9096758.

[20]   N.S. Kumar, A.K. Goel, and S. Jayanthi, "A scrupulous approach to perform classification and detection of fetal brain using Darknet YOLO v4", 2021 International Conference on Advance Computing and Innovative Technologies in Engineering (ICACITE), 2021, pp. 578–581, doi: 10.1109/ICACITE51222.2021.9404656.

[21]   C. Ruggiero, R. Sacile, and M. Giacomini, "Home telecare", J Telemed Telecare 1999;5(1):11–17.

Chapter 2

The scope and future outlook of artificial intelligence in healthcare systems

M. Arvindhan[1], Rajkamal Gupta[1],
S. Dayana Priyadharshini[2] and
Kalaiarasi Sonai Muthu Anbananthen[3]

Abstract

The goal described in this chapter is to imitate human cognitive functions in the context of artificial intelligence. This translates into healthcare, enhanced by the availability of health data and the rapid advancement of analytical technology. This chapter discusses and addresses the current scenario of AI in overall healthcare applications. Different forms of healthcare data may be used. Machine learning for complex information, namely, classical vector support and neural network systems and current dedicated knowledge as well as linguistic processing for unstructured data are common AI techniques. Cancer, neurology, and cardiology are the key fields of health issues that could be analyzed and predicted using AI methods. AI transforms the healthcare area, providing guidelines for the diagnosis and treatment, communication with, and collaboration of patients. Exploring AI and big data analytical applications provides users with insights and enables users to prepare and use resources, particularly to meet unique health challenges.

Keywords: Artificial intelligence; machine learning; deep learning; healthcare; cancer; COVID-19

2.1 Introduction

Artificial intelligence (AI) has been used in a wide range of healthcare technologies, including high-quality clinical decision-making, automated helpers for healthcare practitioners, image-processing diagnosis, sanitization, and treatment, as

[1]Galgotias University, Noida, India
[2]National Institution of Technology – Trichy, Trichy, India
[3]Faculty of Information Science & Technology Multimedia University, Melaka, Malaysia

well as socially assistive robotics in hospitals. As a result, healthcare providers are increasingly interested in implementing AI-based clinical decision support systems (clinicians, caregivers, health authorities, etc.). Techniques focused on education and understanding have been widely and often used to improve patient decision support. AI enables a deeper understanding of the medical processes that humans are incapable of handling considering the scale, heterogeneity, and/or difficulty of these areas. Additionally, it results in the acquisition of new experiences and information. The volume of health-related data produced spans the entire life cycle "from cradle to grave," including self-monitoring data from wearable devices and non-medical resources, in addition to clinical health data. In a broader sense, all data that have an effect on people, such as environmental data or employment records, may be considered health data, and the word "exposome" has been used to denote its significance for health. Not only are healthcare experts using data, but patients – or rather, the general public – are gradually using it for health literacy and self-management, as well as legislators interested in decision-making around public health, treatment adherence reform, and insurance plan creation (Figure 2.1) [1,2].

2.1.1 Importance of AI in healthcare

AI has reformed markets worldwide and has the ability to reshape the field of healthcare dramatically. It has the ability to review data on hospital visits to clinics, prescriptions taken, lab testing conducted, and operations performed, and also includes data from sources from outside health systems–including social media, credit card transactions, census reports, and online search log files containing useful health-related information. Globally, the use of AI in healthcare systems has increased, with various technologies being tested and implemented across various facets of the health system architecture and implementation. The COVID-19 pandemic has resulted in an increase in the introduction of AI-based information technology in healthcare at both the national and regional levels. Even then, the

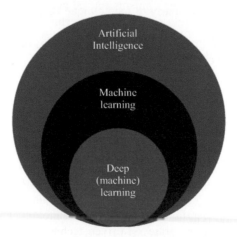

Figure 2.1   Latest technology view with the depth structure

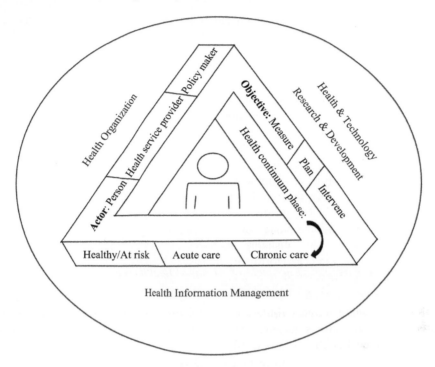

Figure 2.2   Pyramid structure of healthcare phases with AI

advancement of AI-driven technologies in healthcare is outpacing the growth of supportive policy mechanisms and legislation (Figure 2.2) [3,4].

2.1.2   Life cycle approach to AI

Any regulatory guidelines or mechanisms for the use of AI-driven innovations in healthcare must address the full lifecycle of the technology.

Figure 2.3 shows the AI life cycle, which includes:

1.   Business and use case development;
2.   Design of an algorithm and product;
3.   Procuring training and test data;
4.   Building the algorithm and/or product;
5.   Testing and validating the algorithm;
6.   Deploying the AI;
7.   Monitoring its performance.

As defined previously, the implementation of AI-driven technologies involves an iterative process that includes scoping, planning, and constructing, accompanied by implementing the AI-driven technology and tracking it continuously. To effectively integrate AI-driven technology into a health system, countries must understand and embrace each stage of the AI life cycle.

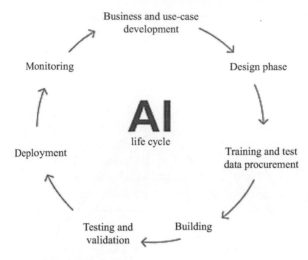

Figure 2.3   Life cycle of AI-based healthcare analysis

This chapter, which covers the AI lifecycle, discusses four strategic areas and related policy guidelines to assist policymakers in integrating AI-driven technology into their health systems [5,6].

2.2   Leadership and oversight

Effective utilization of AI-driven technology in healthcare systems requires leadership capability to ensure the health system's digital sophistication, regulatory environment, and professional workforce are all in place to make the best of an AI-driven healthcare system. Additionally, leaders must be able to articulate compelling use cases for integrating AI into healthcare environments. The diversity of health systems in the Global Digital Health Partnership (GDHP) countries, along with their digital sophistication, has necessitated a wide variety of oversight processes over the use of AI, and indeed technology in general, in hospital environments. Although all countries have claimed that they had an agency or body responsible for digital health, there was no continuity in the organization, remit, or statutory powers. GDHP members agreed that health system stakeholders would have a strategic vision for the use of AI in healthcare, with space for local understanding and execution. It was emphasized that a country's high-level strategy should be founded on specifically defined areas within the health sector where AI-driven innovations have the ability to improve population health the most [7,8].

2.2.1   Standards and regulation

To ensure the protection and efficiency of AI-powered technology, robust standards must be developed that allow thorough regulation and are consistent across the international landscape. In the absence of standardization, a variety of problems may arise, including quality assurance, legal challenges, and patient care concerns. For instance, there is no certainty that an AI model developed and trained for in one country or environment would perform equally well in another. Additionally, AI developers may be required to produce products tailored to specific national conditions, potentially impeding market competitiveness, and may select the most suitable location to build their product based on the lowest degree of expectations. Adequate regulatory supervision is required for the implementation of these requirements, as well as the establishment of sufficient mechanisms and personnel to oversee compliance both before and after deployment. Each country interviewed described experiencing challenging issues while attempting to control AI-driven healthcare technologies. The issues ranged from defining the nature of AI regulation, to uncertainty about who would bear responsibility for each point, to ensuring that the regulatory staff possessed the necessary skills. Not only would regional policymaking in this area relieve national governments of burdens, it would also add consistency, allowing countries to use one another's regulatory approval mechanisms to supplement their own [9,10].

2.3   AI and machine learning are entering a new era

The usage of machine learning in diagnostic imaging is not new; furthermore, algorithms are far more effective today than they were in the past. The artificial neural networks (ANNs) used in deep learning often have several functional layers, sometimes over 100, and can contain thousands of neurons with millions of connections. (In comparison, simple ANNs with just one intermediate layer are referred to as "shallow" networks.) All of these relations are modified incrementally during an ANN's training phase by varying their respective parameters— in statistical words, their weights. Thus, deep networks provide an almost infinite number of possible computing combinations and can also model extremely complex, nonlinear contexts. Throughout the training phase, the various layers of an ANN gradually arrange the input data, resulting in a more abstract "understanding" of the data. Naturally, such deep ANNs are only feasible due to sophisticated mathematical techniques and the availability of more computer resources and faster graphics processing units (GPUs) for computing the countless steps involved in the learning process. For image recognition, "deep convolutional neural networks" (a form of ANN) have been shown to be particularly effective. Similar to the visual cortex in the brain, these networks begin by extracting fundamental image characteristics such as corners, borders, and shading from the input data. They then decide individually on more complex image patterns and artifacts via various abstraction stages. When the majority of these networks are evaluated on nonmedical image databases, their error rate drops to a few percent. Additionally, various network models and techniques (e.g., deep learning and "reinforcement learning") can be combined to obtain the desired outcome for the given problem (Figure 2.4) [11–13].

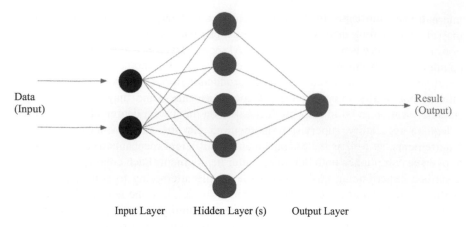

Figure 2.4   Network model in deep learning for a training image data pattern

2.4   Exploring the clinical value of AI

The potential of AI in medical imaging is not only in increased automation, efficiency, and standardization, but also in an unparalleled use of quantitative data that transcend human cognition's limitations. This will allow more accurate and customized diagnostics and therapies. Today, artificial intelligence plays a significant role in the routine collection, encoding, and analysis of images. Siemens Healthineers, for example, has developed a pattern recognition algorithm for its 3D diagnostic software "syngo.via" that detects body parts, individually numbers vertebrae and ribs, and even assists in precisely superimposing diverse check-up dates or different modalities. This significantly contributes to the simplification of medical imaging workflows. Similarly, award-winning algorithms such as "CT Bone Reading" for simulated rib cage unfolding (2D reformatting) and "eSie Valve" for simultaneous 3D simulation of heart valve anatomy and blood flow are applicable (Figure 2.5) [14,15].

Countries must view the vision and direction for the use of AI-driven technology in their health systems from a "needs-based" perspective. The application of AI by a country can be determined by the challenges and opportunities in the health sector, where AI-driven technologies have the most potential to enhance people's health outcomes. There should be oversight from the beginning to the end: a health system's oversight of AI-driven technology must be comprehensive. The lifecycle of artificial intelligence as well as associated practices such as testing, finance, and workforce development plays a crucial role in developing an effective AI approach in healthcare. Regulatory clarification should be provided: regulatory clarity is essential both within and between countries to allow AI developers to comprehend and handle the risks associated with integrating AI-driven technology into a health system [16,17].

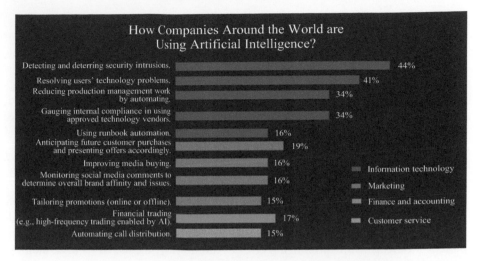

Figure 2.5   Various domain usages of artificial intelligence

2.4.1   Ecosystem

Creativity should be aligned with healthcare needs: prioritizing AI studies and allocating funds accordingly should be driven by the needs of patients and the health system. There should be access to high-quality data: countries should work to aggregate and connect data from around their health and social care systems, to establish high-quality archives for review by qualified experts, to provide reliable analytics environments and/or to implement effective data extraction mechanisms. There should also be a pipeline of deployment: a comprehensive integration pipeline can be used to facilitate the transformation of AI research into digital healthcare applications. Collaboration should take place across sectors: public–private collaborations can be explored to solve critical expertise and financing shortages impeding and stalling AI-driven technology growth, while protecting the needs of patients and the health system [18].

2.5   How is AI transforming the healthcare industry?

AI is having a profound effect on the healthcare market, redefining healthcare and its fundamental roles. Five areas in which artificial intelligence has altered the healthcare sector are now considered.

2.5.1   Digital consultation

The implementation of artificial intelligence in healthcare has allowed patients to communicate with physicians in real time. While the idea of remote consultation is not recent, the older consultation applications have considerable limitations. Numerous problems were resolved as a result of new and advanced advances in artificial intelligence. To begin with, advances in deep learning have allowed users to make more educated choices. Rather than answering questions impulsively, these AI-driven programs learned from many real-world use cases to ask pertinent questions about the patient's health record. Second, the advanced natural learning method has simplified responding to the patient's questions. By effectively learning and comprehending complex sentences, it has transformed the way computers are used to answer questions dramatically. Both of these advances have impacted the healthcare sector significantly [19].

2.5.2   Smart diagnosis

Remember the old days when diagnosing diseases was a time-consuming process? Since the advent of artificial intelligence in healthcare, this has become a piece of cake. AI software has aided physicians in diagnosing patients more efficiently and accurately. AI and emerging technologies assist with identifying and resolving patient problems while minimizing errors. Additionally, the use of AI in cardiology and radiology departments has allowed the early detection of serious issues. For example, AI-based applications have enabled the early detection of cancer cells and the development of strategies to inhibit their growth. The cardiology department has similarly benefitted. In short, AI has revolutionized the way doctors identify diseases and significantly minimized their diagnostic errors [20].

2.5.3   Drug discovery

In addition to providing accurate diagnoses, AI systems are now addressing the needs of pharmaceutical production. They are using massive datasets and vital knowledge to identify novel therapeutic targets. These medical advances could be very useful in the treatment of serious diseases such as Ebola, cancer, among many others. Also, AI in medication production could aid in the discovery of medicines that could be useful in more successfully treating deadly diseases. It is capable of analyzing subtle patterns in medicine, enabling scientists and researchers to monitor drug discovery more precisely. In sum, the incorporation of AI into medicine will speed up the pace of drug development and could reintroduce fresh hope to the healthcare industry [21].

2.5.4   Robotic assistance

AI in healthcare does not necessarily imply that robotics will eventually take the place of all physicians; it simply involves combining the robustness of robotics with the converging abilities of surgeons. Recent advancements in AI have resulted in a growth in the use of AI-driven robots that efficiently imitate human work, but with fewer errors. Likewise, this is the case for the healthcare industry. Robotics in healthcare has the potential to greatly increase the quality and stability of the treatment of patients. It can provide critical knowledge about a patient's well-being and can even make diagnostic recommendations. Additionally, AI can aid in microsurgery, ensuring a shorter healing time for patients. It will assist the surgeon by providing accurate information about the relevant problem and the appropriate steps to be taken [22].

2.5.5   *Virtual follow-up system*

Doctors are always in high demand, and this becomes a major issue for patients who need routine treatment and examinations. That is when AI applications come into action. AI-powered chatbots assist in resolving this problem by delivering ongoing assistance to patients who need regular care. Patients facing issues must first join instantly, and within seconds, the chatbots can have an appropriate response. Additionally, with advanced developments, patients no longer need to type their symptoms; chatbots can effortlessly analyze handwritten messages and photographs. Additionally, these AI-powered bots are capable of diagnosing patients and prescribing appropriate drugs based on their symptoms. Above all, these AI systems will address patients in the same way that a person can [23].

2.6   Potential of AI in various fields of healthcare systems

The future of AI in healthcare is very optimistic and exciting. Over the next few years, we are likely to see an increase in hybrid models that seek to enhance diagnosis, assist in risk identification, and also promote the growth of medicine. Additionally, these AI-driven solutions will assist healthcare facilities in mitigating data risks, while increasing operating quality and significantly improving patient recoveries. Although there remain many problems in the AI healthcare market, including patient comfort, AI device preparation and skills, and compliance with government requirements, once these obstacles are overcome, it has the potential to significantly improve the future of the healthcare industry. In sum, while AI-based programs have made great strides toward transforming the healthcare sector, they also have a long way to go before they have a meaningful effect on future health-care. It requires access to a huge volume of data, which it can do by collaborating with experts who are familiar with the relevant information, such as data scientists. One can evaluate whether the data are of sufficient quality for AI by utilizing a combination of the following:

1. Precision;
2. Thoroughness;
3. Individuality;
4. Adequacy of timing;
5. Validity;
6. Sufficiency;
7. Pertinence;
8. Representability;
9. Repetition.

2.6.1   *Comparison of various fields of healthcare using AI technology*

Currently, the major availability of AI technologies are made public and monitored. The major strength towards this technology is made towards Machine learning

Table 2.1   Comparison of various machine learning (ML) applications

Techniques used in ML	Description	Examples
Classification	The model acquires knowledge about the features of a given category, enabling it to assign uncertain data points into pre-defined groups	Determining whether a consignment of merchandize is subject to boundary screening Determining whether or not an email is spam
Regression	Calculates the importance of an unspecified data point	Estimating the market value of a home based on its size, area, or age Predicting air pollution levels in cities
Clustering	Recognizes clusters of related information within a dataset	Classifying retail consumers in order to identify subclasses with distinct shopping patterns By clustering data from smart meters, we can classify classes of electrical appliances and produce itemized energy bills
Reduced dimensionality or multi-dimensional learning	Reduces the data to the most important variables in order to improve the accuracy of simulations or to make the information more visually appealing	Evaluating and developing various algorithms for ML
Level	Develops a model for classifying additional data based on previously viewed lists	Whenever a person conducts a search on a website, the search engine returns pages in the order of their relevance

Algorithm. The machine learning methods that have the most insight vary according to the problem that is attempting to be solved (Tables 2.1 and 2.2).

2.6.2   Good at-risk phase

This phase encompasses all healthier individuals and those who have reported risks but have not received a diagnosis. It emphasizes primary and secondary protection by offering lifestyle counseling to help people sustain or improve their health and handle risks. Government campaigns would emphasize avoidance of risks, encouraging individuals to take ownership over their lifestyle decisions. The primary focus of service providers will be on well-being and well-being counseling,

Table 2.2   Different machine learning applications

Applications	Description	Examples
Natural language processing (NLP)	Natural language is processed and analyzed, understanding words, their significance, context, and narration	Converting speech into text for automatic subtitles generation Generating an automated response to a customer's email
Computer vision	Capacity of a computer or software to reproduce human vision	Identifying road signs for self-driving vehicles Facial recognition technology for automatic passport checks
Identification of anomalies	Discovers anomalies in the data set	Detecting fraudulent bank account users
Time-series analysis	To perform forecasting and reporting, it is essential to understand how data change over time	Budget reviews Economic predictor forecasting
System recommendation	Detects an item to make recommendations by rating it	Suggestion of related webpages based on the posts already read by a customer

with an emphasis on defined risks during health check-ups. Early identification (or, if possible, prediction) of disease onset would be advantageous at this point, as it will allow healthcare to be more proactive.

2.6.3   Acute care phase

As signs indicate the presence of a likely illness, the individual is registered in the healthcare system and becomes a patient. Medical examinations will be performed on the patient in order to arrive at a diagnosis. A recovery plan will be established, and the patient will be monitored when necessary. Usually, qualified medical providers lead the intensive care process, and the patient follows a care course tailored to the diagnosed condition. Although primary care will suffice for the majority, some patients will be referred to secondary care, which could require hospitalization. Health procedures such as surgery and the use of prescription medications can be used to treat the condition. Treatment can take place in a hospital or other setting. However, if the condition is incurable, progressive, or needs long-term therapy or recurrent therapies, the patient enters the chronic care process (for the purposes of this categorization).

2.6.4   Chronic care process

A person who requires ongoing medical attention for a longer period of time due to a diagnosed (chronic) illness, recovery from a disease, or overall declining health enters the chronic care phase. This person can be referred to as a "career," although the term is not often used. Rehabilitation is treatment that aims to restore an individual's fitness and, preferably, facilitate complete recovery from illness.

Additionally, health improvement may be required to enhance a patient's quality of life or to prepare them for treatment, which would benefit both outcome expectations and patient well-being. Chronic diseases necessitate on-going treatment aimed at disease prevention and patient well-being, but without the prospect of recovery. Palliative treatment is solely concerned with relieving suffering and enhancing quality of life. Elderly people also receive care to assist them in coping with illnesses and everyday problems. Although many older adults suffer from chronic diseases and even multimorbidity, aging is not a disorder, and treatment can require elements addressing general age-related functional decline. This treatment is primarily given at home, rather than in assisted-living centers for the elderly. Certain illnesses and conditions (e.g., mental) necessitate long-term treatment in specialist hospitals [24].

2.7   Analyzing the priority areas in healthcare systems

When we plot the areas described in Figure 2.6 and their associated votes in our three-dimensional main area matrix, certain trends emerge. However, caution

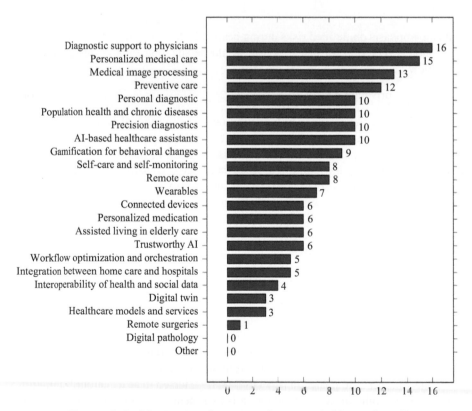

Figure 2.6   Monitoring the status of various fields used in AI

should be exercised when evaluating the data, as the mapping is not necessarily perfect (e.g., a diagnostic service to doctors may require both assessment and planning) and the participants may be unaware of the categorization (i.e. they may easily miss out on some less obvious areas).

- The balance of votes is for medical assistance in diagnostic and recovery planning (acute care/healthcare provider/plan). This often encompasses individualized medicine.
- The second highest vote concentration is for help for personal well-being in the form of preventive treatment, personal diagnostics, or health coaching through gamification or AI-based assistants (healthy and at risk/individual/plan).
- Optimization of health services, both at the community level and within hospital workflows, is often listed as having significant potential (acute care/policy maker/plan).
- Medical image recognition is a specific priority area for metrics (acute care/health service provider/measurement), but self-monitoring (e.g., with wearables) earned some votes (health and at risk + chronic care/individual/measure).

2.8   Challenges associated with the implementation of an AI-driven healthcare system

2.8.1   Regulatory challenges

In addition to privacy security, there are concerns over data ownership. Information management is a country-specific requirement whereby data obtained or preserved must adhere to the rules of the nation in which it is collected or handled and must reside within its borders. Patients and residents are creating increasing amounts of personal data, and so legislation should be implemented to establish who owns that data. Additionally, the manner in which such data are sent to health establishments should be limited. With the implementation of the EU's GDPR and the accompanying massive penalties, organizations have started to examine their data sovereignty standards and capability even more seriously. The GDPR mandates that all data gathered on people must be retained either within the EU, where it is subject to European privacy legislation, or in a jurisdiction that provides comparable safeguards. Additionally, this extends to all data controllers and data processors, which means that an entity is impacted regardless of whether it requires or delivers a cloud service that processes data belonging to EU residents [25].

A novel regulatory feature associated with the widespread introduction of AI is related to a technology's ethical implications. High-level governing bodies such as the Food and Drug Administration (FDA) have begun to regulate AI/ML and advise best practices to be used, such as in the case of templates that are constantly evolving. Another critical factor is the manner in which models should be used, particularly in light of whether additional consent can be sought from patients associated with the source data.

2.8.2   Standardization challenges

When developing a potential regulatory system for AI, it would be important to determine the kinds of mandatory legal standards that should be enforced on related actors. To ensure data portability, completeness, and usability, these specifications can be further defined by standards.

Standards facilitate technological transition by facilitating interoperability across disparate structures while maintaining protection. Standards can aid in the coordination of increasingly dynamic processes across several industries and manufacturers.

2.8.3   Ethical and social challenges

At the outset of a technology rollout, the first step is to demonstrate the tools' full capacity as an assistant and facilitator. This demonstrates the full importance of technology and how it can aid practitioners in their work. The tools that offered should be adaptable, personalized, and readily accessible. It is not a good idea to implement something that was not deemed necessary by the relevant expert. If value is recognized, teamwork occurs: humans and tools begin to cooperate effectively, and the wheel begins to spin more smoothly and quickly; the magic takes place, and inventions and humans act in unison. Although technology will expedite certain procedures, such as diagnosis and examination, and can execute certain routine tasks, freeing up healthcare practitioners to care for patients, it can never completely replace practitioners. It would then boost the delivery of effective and reliable care [26].

The majority of medical records are incompatible with one another due to their being in isolated files, incompatible structures, and proprietary applications, making them impossible to share, analyze, and interpret. Indeed, as previously mentioned, healthcare data are famously complicated. Proprietary software is often used to collect data compiled in siloed databases that are part of essentially incompatible programs. In that context, standardization, interoperability, and data collection and conversion on a large scale are not necessarily realized in practice. Interoperability, whether technological, procedural, or textual, is highly dependent on the consistency, precision, and completeness of data, since these characteristics have an effect on the performance and capabilities of AI tools. In that vein, many projects in the healthcare sector are currently underway to standardize data formats, namely, Health Level Seven International (HL7) or Integrating the Healthcare Enterprise (IHE), which define health information technology requirements and their implementation across networks.

2.8.4   Challenges for a transforming discipline

Resulting images from currently available scanners are constantly improving, resulting in an ever-increasing amount of images. Indeed, the projected total amount of health data increases every 3 years, making it increasingly difficult for radiologists to make effective use of existing data without the assistance of computerized automated analysis. It is required in radiological and clinical diagnostics to be able to quantitatively evaluate this increasingly untapped reservoir of data and, for example, to determine disease development and prognosis using novel detectable imaging biomarkers. Furthermore, it is well established that radiologists vary in their image interpretations; and even the same examiner can reach a different opinion after repeating a reading. If the error analysis is limited to photographs that specifically demonstrate pathological improvements, the error rate increases to about 30%, implying that in three out of 10 cases, pathological systems are either misinterpreted or completely ignored. This is unsurprising given the distractions and heavy workloads encountered in daily clinical practice, as well as the physiological conditions required for successful vision.

2.9 Vision and future potential of AI in healthcare

Numerous publications over the last decade have addressed the critical issue of how artificial intelligence could benefit healthcare. "The greatest benefit we could obtain from very simple and user-friendly gadgets capable of collecting a large amount of data about an individual" and "I see the greatest potential for AI in enabling precision medicine based not only on -omics data integration and analytics, but also on patient-generated data and IoT data integration, including complex event processing and other analytics that capture data in real time."

In some countries, the pressure on health systems is enormous, owing to the vast number of patients in general, and seriously ill patients in particular. While the crisis may have delayed noncritical investments in data collection and development of AI tools in some health systems, it may have intensified other practices. For example, the advancement of AI solutions for chest radiology has accelerated, as has the number of related studies. A more important increase that health systems are seeing is in the introduction of technologies that allow remote treatment, such as AI-based chat-bots, remote diagnosis, and automated risk assessment. Notably, these changes were not captured in the data gathered for this chapter and had little effect on participants' vision since the data were gathered previous to the pandemic [27].

In the next 5–10 years, it is extremely likely that sophisticated AI approaches will become the norm in diagnostic imaging. These upcoming advancements would not supplant physicians' roles, but will equip them with extremely precise methods for detecting illness, risk stratification in an easily understandable way, and optimizing patient-specific care and additional tests. Cardiovascular diagnostics is a textbook example of how imaging can evolve as a result of robotics and AI. Naturally, achieving the technical benefits of AI would necessitate the fulfillment of a number of preconditions. To begin with, neural networks – especially deep neural networks with their numerous learning parameters – require a large amount of training data in order to improve their "intelligence." As a result, developing and validating diagnostic AI requires the establishment of meticulously annotated and organ-specific image databases. Public–private collaborations between vendors, research institutions, and data-sharing programs would be critical in this endeavor. Siemens Healthiness, for example, which has collaborations with all 15 of the top

Processing	Assessment	Scaling up	Customized benefit
Automatic extraction of all image parameters	Fully quantitative diagnostic and risk stratification scores	Machine-learning-based metrics incorporating a large number of clinical and imaging variables in real time beyond the limits of human cognition	Personalized risk assessments and tailored management plans

Figure 2.7   Processing status of implementing machine learning assessments

hospitals in the United States, provides a robust testing platform that includes an increasing data pool of over 100 million selected disease diagnosis and four data centers with one set of flop of processing capacity (Figure 2.7).

AI implementation has the potential to revolutionize customized diagnostics and care. For example, with the use of interoperable information systems, clinical patient data may be connected to imaging algorithms to enable the development of individualized scanning strategies. Additionally, by aggregating large amounts of data, AI implementations are likely to allow more accurate diagnoses and realistic risk ratings. As a recent major multicenter analysis demonstrated, the long-term probability of mortality for patients with suspected cardiovascular disease can be measured with significantly greater accuracy when several clinical and CT angiogram parameters are incorporated into a customized prognosis model using machine learning procedures. Such AI-based interventions may improve the identification of high-risk patients in the future, but they may also help avoid needless procedures, thus involving diagnostic radiology more directly in outcome-driven clinical decisions.

2.10   Conclusion

Artificial intelligence (AI) is being used in a variety of fields and markets to assist policy makers in making better choices and anticipating potential challenges and pitfalls. We, as representative members of the Big Data Value Association (BDVA), have presented our vision for how AI can be used to successfully enhance health systems' services in this chapter. Our approach is founded on an analysis of relevant literature, a study, and participation in a workshop. Audience members from a variety of backgrounds (e.g. users, caretakers, healthcare professionals, and infrastructure providers) shared their thoughts on the efficiency of artificial intelligence, the challenges facing health coverage, and the implementers for advancement. These stakeholders indicate that AI has tremendous promise in healthcare, both in terms of cost savings and quality growth.

References

[1]   A Hosny, C Parmar, J Quackenbush, LH Schwartz, and HJWL Aerts. Artificial intelligence in radiology. *Nature Reviews Cancer*, 18(8):500–510, 2018.

[2]   CO Chris, C Euan, R Anand, and W Danish. Disinfection Robots Save Lives in the Fight Against the Corona Virus. https://ec.europa.eu/digital-single-market/en/news/danish-disinfection-robots-save-lives-fight-against-corona-virus, 2020.

[3]   G Litjens, T Kooi, BE Bejnordi, *et al.* A survey on deep learning in medical image analysis. *Medical Image Analysis*, 42:60–88, 2017.

[4]   JA Doucette, A Khan, R Cohen, D Lizotte, and HM Moghaddam. A framework for AI-based clinical decision support that is patient-centric and evidence-based. *In International Workshop on Artificial Intelligence and NetMedicine*, 2012, p. 26.

[5]   Deloitte Insights. Predictive Analytics in Health Care, Emerging Value and Risks. https://www2.deloitte.com/us/en/insights/topics/analytics/predictive-analytics-health-care-value-risks.html, July 2019.

[6]   AI How and Machine Learning are Helping to Fight COVID-19. https://www.weforum.org/   agenda/2020/05/how-ai-and-machine-learning-are-helping-to-fight-covid-19/, 2020.

[7]   R Vaishya, M Javaid, IH Khan, and A Haleem. Artificial intelligence (AI) applications for COVID-19 pandemic. *Diabetes & Metabolic Syndrome: Clinical Research & Reviews*, 14(4):337–339, 2020.

[8]   Secure and Private Health Data Exchange, Grant Agreement id: 826404 Topic: Su-tds-02-2018. call: H2020-sc1-fa-dts-2018-1. funding scheme: Ria – Research and Innovation Action. Funded Under: H2020-eu.3.1.5.1. https://curex-project.eu, 2020.

[9]   MI Jordan and TM Mitchell. Machine learning: trends, perspectives, and prospects. *Science*, 349(6245):255–260, 2015.

[10] A Rajkomar, J Dean, and I Kohane. Machine learning in medicine. *New England Journal of Medicine*, 380(14):1347–1358, 2019.

[11] Toolkit for assessing and reducing cyber risks in hospitals and care centres to protect privacy/data/infrastructures, grant agreement id: 826183 call:su-tds-02-2018. funding schema: Ria – research and innovation action. https://sphinx-project.eu, 2020.

[12] Safeguard of Critical Health Infrastructure, Grant Agreement id: 787002 funding schema: H2020-eu.3.7.4.

[13] Advanced Secure Cloud Encrypted Platform for Internationally Orchestrated Solutions in Healthcare, Grant Agreement id: 826093 call:h2020-eu.3.1.5.1. topic: Su-tds-02-2018. https://www.asclepios-project.eu/.

[14] BDVA. Data Protection in the Era of Artificial Intelligence. Trends, Existing Solutions and Recommendations for Privacy-Preserving Technologies, October 2019.

[15] M Zazzi, R Kaiser, A Sönnerborg, *et al.* Prediction of response to anti-retroviral therapy by human experts and by the EuResist data-driven expert system (the eve study). *HIV Medicine*, 12(4):211–218, 2011.

[16] Z Obermeyer and EJ Emanuel. Predicting the future—big data, machine learning, and clinical medicine. *The New England Journal of Medicine*, 375 (13): 1216, 2016.

[17]   A Akselrod-Ballin, M Chorev, Y Shoshan, *et al.* Predicting breast cancer by applying deep learning to linked health records and mammograms. *Radiology*, 292(2):331–342, 2019.

[18]   SM McKinney, M Sieniek, V Godbole, *et al.* International evaluation of an AI system for breast cancer screening. *Nature*, 577(7788):89–94, 2020.

[19]   J Born, N Wiedemann, G Brandle, C Buhre, B Rieck, and K Borgwardt. Accelerating Covid-19 differential diagnosis with explainable ultrasound image analysis. arXiv preprint arXiv:2009.06116, 2020.

[20]   DD Miller and EW Brown. Artificial intelligence in medical practice: the question to the answer? The *American Journal of Medicine*, 131(2):129–133, 2018.

[21]   I Ekman, R Busse, E van Ginneken, *et al.* Health-care improvements in a financially constrained environment. *The Lancet*, 387(10019):646–647, 2016.

[22]   PJ Slomka, D Dey, A Sitek, *et al.* Cardiac imaging: working towards fully-automated machine analysis and interpretation. *Expert Review of Medical Devices* 14: 197–212, 2017.

[23]   E Sokolovskaya, T Shinde, R Ruchman, *et al.* The effect of faster reporting speed for imaging studies on the number of misses and interpretation errors: a pilot study. *Journal of the American College of Radiology* 12: 683–688, 2015.

[24]   *The Economist*. The Future of Healthcare – Realities or Science Fiction, 2017. http://thefutureishere.economist.com/thefutureofheathcare-infographic.html (accessed October 9, 2017).

[25]   RJ Gillies, PE Kinahan, H Hricak. Radiomics: images are more than pictures, they are data. *Radiology* 278: 563–577, 2016.

[26]   B van Ginneken. Fifty years of computer analysis in chest imaging: rule-based, machine learning, deep learning. *Radiological Physics and Technology* 10: 23–32, 2017.

[27]   SS Venkatesh, BJ Levenback, LR Sultan, *et al.* Going beyond a first reader: a machine learning methodology for optimizing cost and performance in breast ultrasound diagnosis. *Ultrasound in Medicine and Biology* 41: 3148–3162, 2015.

Chapter 3

Class dependency-based learning using Bi-LSTM coupled with the transfer learning of VGG16 for the diagnosis of tuberculosis from chest X-rays

G. Jignesh Chowdary[1], G. Suganya[1], M. Premalatha[1] and K. Karunamurthy[2]

Abstract

Tuberculosis is an infectious disease that leads to the death of millions of people across the world. The mortality rate from this disease is high in patients suffering from immunocompromised disorders. early diagnosis can save lives and avoid further complications. However, the diagnosis of TB is a very complex task. The standard diagnostic tests still rely on traditional procedures developed in the 20th century. These procedures are slow and expensive. Therefore, this chapter presents an automatic approach for the diagnosis of TB from posteroanterior chest X-rays. This is a two-step approach, in which in the first step the lung regions are segmented from the chest X-rays using the graph cut method, and then in the second step the transfer learning of VGG16 combined with bidirectional LSTM is used for extracting high-level discriminative features from the segmented lung regions and then classification is performed using a fully connected layer. The proposed model is evaluated using data from two publicly available databases, namely the Montgomery County set and the Schezien set. The proposed model achieved accuracy and sensitivity of 97.76%, 97.01% and 96.42%, 94.11% on the Schezien and Montgomery County datasets, respectively. This model enhanced the diagnostic accuracy of TB by 0.7% and 11.68% on the Schezien and Montgomery County datasets, respectively.

Keywords: Deep learning; transfer learning; VGG16; tuberculosis; health informatics

[1]School of Computer Science and Engineering, Vellore Institute of Technology, Chennai, India
[2]School of Mechanical and Building Sciences, Vellore Institute of Technology, Chennai, India

3.1 Introduction

Tuberculosis (TB) is an infectious disease caused by the bacillus *Mycobacterium tuberculosis*, which affects the lungs. After HIV, TB is the leading cause of death across the world due to infectious diseases. According to one estimate, nine million new cases of TB are reported each year [1], of which 1.2 million people die [2]. TB is a highly contagious disease that spreads through the air when an infected person speaks, sneezes, or coughs. Most TB cases are found in southeast Asia and Africa as more people living there have less resistance to the disease due to malnutrition and poverty. The situation is even worse in patients suffering from immunocompromised disorders like HIV/AIDS [3]. Several antibiotics are available for the treatment of TB. The mortality rate of TB is high when it is not treated, but during clinical trials it was reported that the survival and cure rates were improved with antibiotics treatment [1]. Unfortunately, the diagnosis of TB remains a major challenge. The definitive test for diagnosing TB is by the detection of *Mycobacterium tuberculosis* in pus samples or clinical sputum [2,3]. However, this test takes several weeks to months to identify these slow-growing bacteria in labs. Another diagnostic test for TB is sputum smear microscopy. This is a 100-year-old procedure in which sputum samples are observed under a microscope for traces of *Mycobacterium tuberculosis*. In addition, there are immune response-based skin tests that are available to determine whether a person is infected with TB. These tests are reporting promising results but they require advanced equipment, which increases the diagnostic cost and also the time taken. Greater financial support is required to make these procedures commonplace for TB diagnosis. These tests cannot be used for the rapid screening of huge populations.

In addition to these procedures, there is another screening examination based on posteroanterior chest X-rays[4] that can be used for the rapid diagnosis of TB. Chest X-rays show the thoracic anatomy of the patient. In this procedure, an experienced radiologist is required to manually examine the X-rays for the presence of a TB infection. This examination is highly cost-effective and takes less time compared to other tests in TB diagnosis. However, there is one drawback with this examination, which is that it requires human intervention, which gives the scope for human error. Therefore to reduce the problem of human error, computerized methods like deep learning and machine learning are used for automatic diagnosis of TB from chest X-rays. These computerized methods have shown promising results in the field of medicine, especially for the diagnosis of pneumonia [5–7], cardiac diseases [8], various types of cancers [9–11], and brain tumors [12,13]. An overview of these methods is presented in Refs. [14] and [15]. Researchers across the globe are developing automatic methods for the diagnosis of TB using these computerized techniques. The recent advancements in the computerized diagnostic methods of TB are presented in Ref. [16]. In one study [17], the authors created a template to diagnose miliary TB in an African setting.

With this motivation, in this chapter, we propose an automatic approach for the diagnosis of tuberculosis manifestations in chest X-rays (Figure 3.1). This is a two step approach, in the first step, the lung regions are segmented from the chest

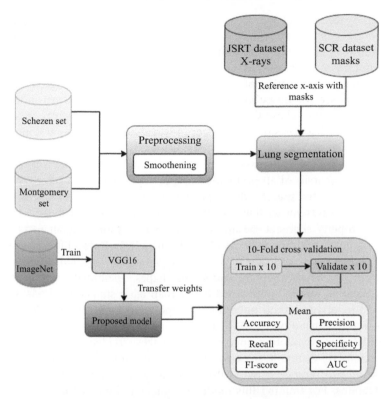

Figure 3.1   Structure of the proposed work

X-rays, and in the second step, the feature extraction and classification are per-formed. For lung segmentation, we have employed the method presented in Ref. [18] and for efficient feature extraction, a transfer learning model with a bidirec-tional long-term short-memory (Bi-LSTM) model is used. Classification is per-formed using a fully connected layer activated with softmax function. The remainder of this chapter is organized as follows. Section 3.2 describes the existing literature, Section 3.3 describes the proposed methodology, Section 3.4 discusses the results reported by the proposed model, followed by the conclusion in Section 3.5.

3.2   Related works

The introduction of digital chest X-rays and the development of digital image processing have increased the scope for computer-aided diagnosis (CAD) and screening. Although there is omnipresence of chest X-rays across various special-ties of medicine, they remain a complex imaging tool. For the past decade several papers have been proposed on using computerized methods to diagnose diseases from chest X-rays. However, there is a need for more research to be make these systems deployable in real life. According to a survey presented in Ref. [16], Van Ginneken *et al.* stated that even after 45 years of research in computerized methods in chest radiology there were no systems that could accurately read chest radiograms. Automated diagnosis of lung nodules using computerized methods is becoming a mature application of decision support for chest x-rays. Several studies have been proposed for investigating the capability of CAD systems in the diagnosis of lung nodules. These CAD systems can be used successfully in assisting radiologists in the diagnosis of lung cancer [15]. However, nodules are only one of the manifestations of TB.

In recent years, by understanding the complexity in designing a single CAD system for the diagnosis of all problems using X-rays, researchers have focused on developing systems for specific diseases such as pneumonia, tuberculosis, cancer, etc. For designing systems to diagnose lung-related diseases from chest X-rays, it is essential to properly segment the lungs. Even segmentation of other parts such as the clavicles, heart, and ribs may also be helpful [17]. In Refs. [17,22] the authors performed a comparative study of various segmentation methods such as pixel classification, rule-based methods, and active shapes. Their study reported that the pixel classification method performed better than other studied methods. Dawoud [23] used an iterative method to combine shape priors with intensity information. This work was evaluated on the JSRT dataset. In one study [24], the authors used a patch-based feature extraction approach where they divided the lungs into overlapping regions of different sizes for feature extraction. In the latter study, the authors used the difference between the corresponding regions of the right and left lungs as features. For training this model a separate training set is constructed for each region and the classification is performed using the weighted voting classifier.

Several CAD systems have been proposed for diagnosing lung abnormalities from chest X-ray rather than focusing on a specific disease. Among them, there were very few CAD systems specializing in TB diagnosis. Hongeweg *et al.* [25] designed a system by combining the stages of clavicle detection with texture-based abnormal detection to reduce false-positive predictions. The same group of researchers in Ref. [25] proposed a clavicle segmentation model built using active shape models and pixel classifiers. The diagnosis of TB from clavicle regions is very difficult because these regions can conceal the TB manifestations in the apex of the lung. In a study performed by Freedman *et al.* [26], it was reported that the suppression of clavicles and ribs can enhance the performance of radiologists in TB diagnosis. The upper lung regions with cavities containing high air–fluid levels indicate that TB has progressed into a highly infectious state. In their study [27], Shen *et al.* proposed a Bayesian approach to detect these cavities in chest X-rays. Xu *et al.* [28] proposed another method that uses the model-based template-matching technique for the same problem. In this work, the Hessian matrix was used for image enhancement. Santosh *et al.* [29] used the pyramid-HOG (histogram of oriented gradients) method for encoding thoracic edge map features and used a MLP (multilayer perceptron) classifier for TB diagnosis. In one study [30], the authors extracted the texture, edge, shape, and symmetrical features of the lung and performed classification using a voting ensemble of MLP, random forest (RF), and

Bayesian network (BN). Vajde *et al.* [31] considered three feature sets and used wrapper-based feature selection techniques to select the best feature set to train an artificial neural network algorithm for diagnosis. In another study [31], the authors used gray-level cooccurrence matrix features, first-order statistical features, and shape-based features to train the support vector machine (SVM) algorithm for diagnosis. Jaeger *et al.* [32] used Frangi, HOG, local binary patterns (LBPs), and GIST methods for extracting features and used SVM for classification.

Transfer learning is a learning approach used to enhance the performance of a model while using small datasets. The transfer learning approach works by applying the knowledge that is gained while solving one specific task to be used to solve another similar task. This learning approach is widely used across various domains in medical imaging [33]. Tawsifur *et al.* [34] performed a study using the transfer learning of pretrained models, namely MobileNet, SqueezeNet, DenseNet201, VGG19, InceptionV3, ChexNet, ResNet101, ResNet50, and ResNet18, for the diagnosis of TB.

3.3 Methods

3.3.1 Data preprocessing

In this phase, the quantum noise from the chest X-rays is removed. This noise is due to the random dispersal of photons on the receptor plate during the process of X-ray imaging [35]. Several algorithms were proposed for noise removal [36]. However, in this work, a guided filter with a kernel mask (k_m) of 3×3 is used. A guided filter preserves the edges during the process of noise removal. The denoised image is represented in the following equation (3.1).

$$D_j = x_k I_j + y_k, \forall j \in k_m \tag{3.1}$$

In (3.1), x_k and y_k are the coefficients of input image, I_j is the pixel intensity, k_m represents the kernel mask, and D_j is the denoised image.

3.3.2 Proposed methodology

The proposed methodology consists of two modules, namely the segmentation module and the diagnostic module. In the segmentation module, a three-step approach learned from Ref. [18] was used to segment the lung regions from the chest X-rays, and in the diagnostic module, a novel CNN-Bi-LSTM transfer learning method was proposed for feature extraction and classification. The lung segmentation module and the diagnostic modules are explained in Sections 3.3.2.1 and 3.3.2.2.

3.3.2.1 Lung segmentation module

Chest X-rays contain many anatomical structures such as the ribs, soft tissues, heart apex, mediastinum, and various organs. These structures show ambiguous appearance in the radiographic responses and make the diagnosis of disease manifestation

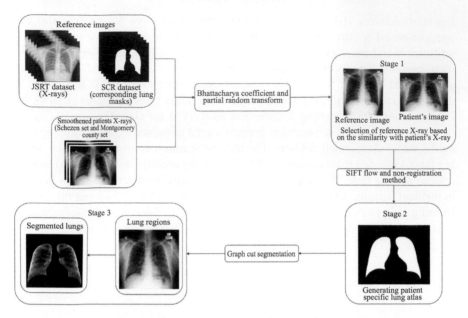

Figure 3.2   Segmentation of a sample X-ray

more complex. Segmentation of lung regions from chest X-rays can resolve these issues. Several segmentation methods have been proposed [18,37–39]. In this work, we used a segmentation approach learned from Ref. [18]. This is a three-step approach, in which the first step involves selecting the reference image (with masks) for each input image. The selection of reference images is based on the similarity between the training image (with mask) and the input image. The similarity is computed using the Bhattacharya coefficient and partial random transform. In the second step, scale-invariant feature transform (SIFT) flow and nonrigid registration method are used for creating a lung atlas for the input X-ray. And in the last step, the graph-cut approach is used for marking and segmenting the lung regions. Figure 3.2 shows this segmentation approach on a sample image.

For training, chest X-rays from the JSRT dataset are used. The ground truth masks for the images in the JSRT dataset are available in Ref. [36]. Note that the lung masks do not contain the posterior inferior regions behind the diaphragm. In this work, we excluded these regions because TB manifestation in these regions is less likely to occur.

3.3.2.2   TB diagnostic module

CNN-based feature extraction

Learning important and highly discriminative features from the input medical images is a complex task in the field of medical imaging. With the rapid improvements in deep learning methodologies, the transfer learning of pretrained CNNs is extensively used for the extraction of efficient and highly discriminative features. There have been several studies [7,40] across various image classification

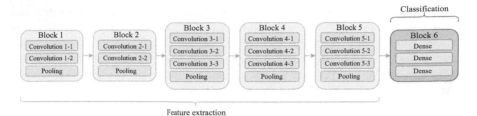

Figure 3.3   Structure of VGG16

applications that have reported excellent results while using this method. With this motivation, we employ a pretrained CNN named VGG16 developed by Visual Geometry Group (VGG) of Oxford University trained on ImageNet database for extracting high-level discriminative features.

The VGG16 CNN consists of five convolutional blocks, with each block consisting of two or three convolutional layers, as shown in Figure 3.3, for feature extraction. In each block, the convolutional layers have the same number of filters and the number of filters is doubled after each max-pooling layer. All the convolutional layers have the same receptive fields of 3×3, which results in an increase in the non-linearity in the feature extraction module. The max-pooling layers are used in this network to reduce the size of feature maps produced by the convolutional layers by maintaining a pool size of 2×2, thus these pool layers reduce the size of the feature map by half its width and height. The main reason behind such a design is to use minimum computational resources for extracting highly diverse features. Following the feature extraction module, there is one classification module with three fully connected layers consisting of 512, 256, and 1000 neurons. The last fully connected layer is activated with the softmax function and is used for classification. Except for the last fully connected layer, the remaining convolutional and dense layers are activated with the ReLU function. Since, in this work, the VGG16 is used as a feature extractor, the classification module of the network is removed and the parameters of the original network are preserved.

Bi-LSTM-based class dependency learning

Recurrent neural networks (RNNs) are a subset of deep learning mainly used for dealing with sequential data such as temporal series and textual data. These RNNs are capable of exploiting implicit dependencies among inputs. RNNs contain recurrent neurons, and their activations are dependent on previously hidden states and current input. However, these RNNs suffer from the problem of vanishing gradients and they find it difficult to learn long-term dependencies. In this work, we use the RNN-based LSTM approach proposed in Ref. [43] to model class dependencies these have shown excellent performance in Refs. [44–49] for processing long sequences.

LSTM does not sum up the inputs like convolutional RNNs, instead, these networks have hidden units known as LSTM units, where the information regarding the class dependencies between different categories is memorized, transmitted, and updated with a memory cell and various gates. However, a single LSTM is not sufficient to obtain a complete view of interclass relevance, so a comprehensive bidirectional-LSTM (Bi-LSTM) approach is proposed in this chapter. This Bi-LSTM consists of two LSTMs placed in opposite directions to each other and the units in this network are not only updated with previous states but also with subsequent ones.

As can be seen in Figure 3.4, two Bi-LSTMs are used in this work. The output from the CNN feature extractor cannot be given as an input to the Bi-LSTM layers due to shape constraints. Therefore, a Reshape layer is used to connect the CNN module with the Bi-LSTM layers. After feature extraction, the extracted features are flattened using a flatten layer and are fed into a dense layer with two neurons activated with a softmax activation function for classification. A summary of the proposed model is presented in Table 3.1.

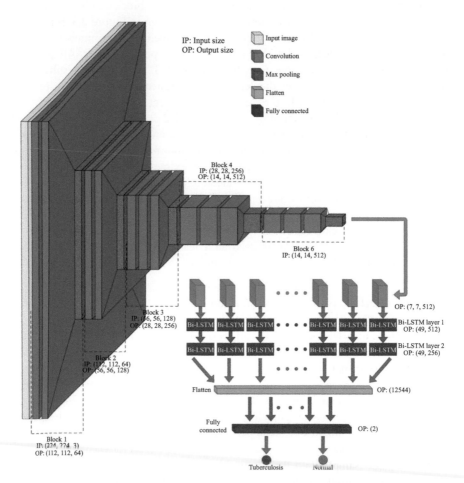

Figure 3.4   Structure of the proposed work

Table 3.1   Summary of the proposed model

Block	Layer	Output shape
Input	Input layer	(224, 224, 3)
Block 1	Convolution	(224, 224, 64)
	Convolution	(224, 224, 64)
	Max pooling	(112, 112, 64)
Block 2	Convolution	(112, 112, 128)
	Convolution	(112, 112, 128)
	Max pooling	(56, 56, 128)
Block 3	Convolution	(56, 56, 256)
	Convolution	(56, 56, 256)
	Convolution	(56, 56, 256)
	Max pooling	(28, 28, 256)
Block 4	Convolution	(28, 28, 512)
	Convolution	(28, 28, 512)
	Convolution	(28, 28, 512)
	Max pooling	(14, 14, 512)
Block 5	Convolution	(14, 14, 512)
	Convolution	(14, 14, 512)
	Convolution	(14, 14, 512)
	Max pooling	(7, 7, 512)
Reshape	Reshape	(49, 512)
Bi-LSTM block	Bi-LSTM	(49, 512)
	Bi-LSTM	(49, 256)
Classification	Flatten	(12544)
	Dense	(2)

3.4   Results and discussion

3.4.1   Databases

For our work, three chest X-ray datasets are used. The first dataset is used for training our lung segmentation model and the second and third datasets are used for training and testing our classifier.

Our first dataset is from the Japanese Society of Radiological Technology (JSRT). The data in this dataset are the result of a study performed for understanding the performance of radiologists in identifying pulmonary modules [52]. This dataset contains 247 chest X-rays, each of size 2048 x 2048 pixels in a 12-bit grayscale color coding scheme extracted from 14 medical centers. Out of these 247 chest X-rays, 154 are abnormal and 93 are normal. Each abnormal chest X-ray has one pulmonary nodule, and these nodules are categorized into five classes ranging from obvious to extremely subtle. These lung nodules do not affect the shape of the lung. Therefore we can use the entire dataset for training our segmentation model. In order to do so, we used segmentation masks provided by Ginneken *et al.* [17] in their SCR dataset (Segmentation in Chest Radiographs). This dataset contains manually segmented masks for each chest X-ray in the JSRT dataset. Samples from both datasets are shown in Figure 3.5.

Our second dataset, the Shenzhen dataset (Shenzhen set) [53], was developed by one of the best hospitals for treating infectious diseases in China, Shenzhen

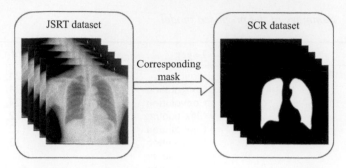

Figure 3.5   *Sample X-rays and corresponding masks from the JSRT and SCR datasets*

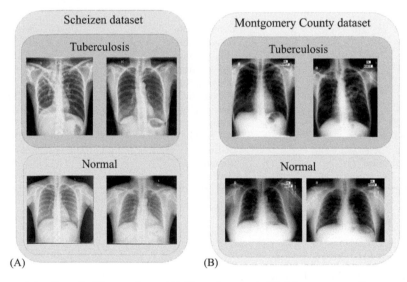

Figure 3.6   *Sample X-rays from (A) Shenzhen and (B) Montgomery County datasets*

hospital located in Guangdong province. All the images were collected in September 2012 by the hospital radiology department. This dataset contains a total of 662 chest X-rays, of which 336 show TB infection and 326 are normal. These X-rays were extracted using a Philips DR digital diagnostic system.

Our third dataset, the Montgomery County (Montgomery set) dataset is a subset of the large chest X-ray database collected during the tuberculosis control program organized by the Department of Health and Human Services of Montgomery County in Maryland [54]. This dataset contains a total of 138 posteroanterior chest x-rays, of which 58 contain lungs with tuberculosis manifestations and 80 are normal. All the images in this dataset are 12-bit grayscale color coding schemes and were taken using Eureka stationary X-ray devices. Samples of X-rays from the Shenzhen and Montgomery datasets are shown in Figure 3.6.

3.4.2 Performance metrics

The robustness of the proposed model in diagnosing TB from chest X-rays is evaluated using six performance metrics, namely accuracy, sensitivity, specificity, precision, negative predicted value (NPV), and F1-measure. These performance metrics were calculated using true positive (TP), true negative (TN), false positive (FP), and false negative (FN) values. These performance metrics are represented in Equations (3.2)–(3.6).

$$Accuracy = \frac{(TP + TN)}{(TP + TN + FP + FN)} \tag{3.2}$$

$$Precision = \frac{TP}{(TP + FP)} \tag{3.3}$$

$$Recall = \frac{TP}{(TP + FN)} \tag{3.4}$$

$$Specificity = \frac{TN}{(TN + FP)} \tag{3.5}$$

$$F1 - score = \frac{(2 \times precision \times recall)}{(precision + recall)} \tag{3.6}$$

In the above equations, *TP* represents the number of samples that were correctly predicted as TB, *TN* represents the number of samples that were correctly predicted as normal, and *FP* and *FN* represent the number of samples that were wrongly predicted as TB and normal, respectively. In addition to these metrics, the area under the curve (AUC) is also considered for understanding the efficacy of the proposed model [55,56].

3.4.3 Results reported

In this work, the tenfold cross-validation protocol is employed for validating the performance of the model. The tenfold cross-validation results reported by the proposed model on Shenzhen and Montgomery datasets are shown in Table 3.2.

Table 3.2 Tenfold cross-validation results reported by the proposed model on the Shenzhen and Montgomery datasets

Dataset	Accuracy	Precision	Recall	Specificity	F1-score	AUC
Shenzhen set	97.76	98.48	97.01	98.50	97.74	0.9786
Montgomery set	96.42	100	94.11	100	96.96	0.9589

3.4.4   Comparison

3.4.4.1   Comparison with pretrained models

In this work, the tenfold cross-validation results reported by the proposed model are compared with the performance of well-known transfer learning models, namely InceptionV3, VGG16, VGG19, ResNet50, Xception, DenseNet201, MobileNet, MobileNetV2, and InceptionResNetV2. To make these models suitable for our task, the last fully connected layer is modified by changing the number of units to two. Then these models were trained with data from both datasets, and their performance is shown in Tables 3.3 and 3.4.

In medical imaging, accuracy and recall are the two performance metrics used to determine the robustness and efficiency of a model. On the Shenzhen dataset, InceptionResNetV2 and MobileNet are the models with the highest accuracy and recall among the considered networks. On the Montgomery dataset, ResNet50 is the model with the highest accuracy and recall among the other networks. The proposed model reported an enhanced performance in diagnosing TB from both datasets. Table 3.5 shows the percentage increase in accuracy and recall reported by

Table 3.3   Performance comparison on the Shenzhen dataset

Models	Accuracy	Precision	Recall	Specificity	F1-score	AUC
InceptionV3	85.07	77.27	91.07	80.76	83.6	0.8495
VGG16	85.07	83.33	85.93	84.28	84.61	0.8504
VGG19	86.56	93.93	81.57	93.1	87.32	0.8667
ResNet50	85.82	96.96	79.01	96.22	87.07	0.8598
Xception	79.1	98.48	70.65	97.61	82.27	0.7938
DenseNet201	84.32	96.96	77.1	96.07	85.9	0.8451
MobileNet	84.32	71.21	95.91	77.64	81.73	0.8413
MobileNetV2	76.11	53.03	96.22	68.36	68.62	0.7577
InceptionResNetV2	88.8	83.33	93.22	85.33	88	0.8872
Proposed model	**97.76**	**98.48**	**97.01**	**98.50**	**97.74**	**0.9786**

Table 3.4   Performance comparison on the Montgomery dataset

Models	Accuracy	Precision	Recall	Specificity	F1-score	AUC
InceptionV3	80	88.88	72.72	88.88	79.99	0.8333
VGG16	70	87.5	58.33	87.5	70	0.7291
VGG19	85	75	85.71	84.61	79.99	0.8334
ResNet50	90	87.5	87.5	91.66	87.5	0.8958
Xception	80	62.5	83.33	78.57	71.42	0.8125
DenseNet201	70	87.5	58.33	87.5	70	0.7291
MobileNet	80	87.5	70	90	77.77	0.8125
MobileNetV2	80	77.77	77.77	81.81	77.77	0.8129
InceptionResNetV2	80	62.5	83.33	78.57	71.42	0.7708
Proposed model	**96.42**	**100**	**94.11**	**100**	**96.96**	**0.9589**

Table 3.5   Percentage increase in accuracy and recall while using the proposed model compared with other pretrained networks

Datasets	High-performing models			Proposed model		Percentage increase	
	Models	Accuracy	Recall	Accuracy	Recall	Accuracy	Recall
Shenzhen set	InceptionRes NetV2	88.8	93.22	97.76	97.01	8.96	3.79
	MobileNet	76.11	96.22			21.65	0.79
Montgomery set	ResNet50	90	87.5	96.42	94.11	6.42	6.61

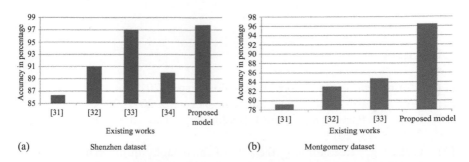

Figure 3.7   Performance comparison of the Shenzhen and Montgomery datasets

the proposed model compared with the high-performing models on both datasets shown in Tables 3.3 and 3.4.

3.4.4.2   Comparison with the existing literature

In this work, the performance of the proposed model is compared with other existing works discussed in the literature review section of the chapter. The cross-validation accuracy of the proposed model is higher than the accuracy reported by the other works. This comparison of accuracy of the Montgomery and Shenzhen datasets is shown in Figure 3.7.

From Figure 3.5, the methods proposed in Ref. [31] reported a high accuracy of 97.03% and 84.75% on the Shenzhen and Montgomery datasets, respectively, compared with the proposed model. This clearly illustrates that while using the proposed model the accuracy in diagnosing TB is increased by 0.7% and 11.68% on the Shenzhen and Montgomery datasets. This percentage increase from Table 3.5 and Figure 3.7 shows that the proposed model is more efficient and effective than other pretrained models and existing works.

3.5   Conclusion

In this chapter, an automatic approach for the diagnosis of tuberculosis from chest X-rays is presented. This approach focuses on diagnosing TB from segmented lung regions. Since the work focuses more on diagnosis than segmentation, we used the graph cut-based segmentation method presented in Ref. [18] for extracting the lung regions from chest X-rays. For the diagnosis, we present an efficient feature extraction module built by combining a transfer learning model with a recurrent neural network. In this feature extraction module, the VGG16 pretrained network is used for extracting deep features and two bidirectional LSTMs are used for extracting the class-dependent features. The proposed model is evaluated on the Shenzhen and Montgomery County datasets. The proposed model reported a higher performance than other pretrained networks and existing works by achieving a sensitivity of 97.01% and 94.11% on the Shenzhen and Montgomery County datasets.

References

[1]   World Health Org., Global tuberculosis report 2012.
[2]   World Health Org., Global tuberculosis control 2011, 2011.
[3]   Stop TB Partnership, World Health Org., The Global Plan to Stop TB 2011–2015, 2011.
[4]   C. Leung, "Reexamining the role of radiography in tuberculosis case finding," *International Journal of Tuberculosis Lung Disease*, 2011;15 (10):1279–1279.
[5]   P. Rajpurkar, J. Irvin, K. Zhu, *et al.* (2017). Chexnet: Radiologist-level pneumonia detection on chest x-rays with deep learning. *arXiv preprint arXiv:1711.05225*.
[6]   O. Stephen, M. Sain, U.J. Maduh, and D.U. Jeong. An efficient deep learning approach to pneumonia classification in healthcare. *Journal of Healthcare Engineering*, 2019.
[7]   G.J. Chowdary. Impact of machine learning models in pneumonia diagnosis with features extracted from chest X-rays using VGG16. *Turkish Journal of Computer and Mathematics Education (TURCOMAT)*, 2021;12(5):1521–1530.
[8]   G.J. Chowdary. Effective prediction of cardiovascular disease using cluster of machine learning algorithms. *Journal of Critical Reviews*, 2020;7 (18):2192–2201. https://doi.org/10.31838/jcr.07.18.273.
[9]   G. Litjens, C.I. Sánchez, N. Timofeeva, *et al.* Deep learning as a tool for increased accuracy and efficiency of histopathological diagnosis. *Scientific Reports*, 2016;6(1):1–11.
[10]   W. Sun, B. Zheng, and W. Qian. Automatic feature learning using multi-channel ROI based on deep structured algorithms for computerized lung cancer diagnosis. *Computers in Biology and Medicine*, 2017;89:530–539.

[11] J. Premaladha and K.S. Ravichandran. Novel approaches for diagnosing melanoma skin lesions through supervised and deep learning algorithms. *Journal of Medical Systems*, 2016;40(4):1–12.

[12] M. Talo, O. Yildirim, U.B. Baloglu, G. Aydin, and U.R. Acharya. Convolutional neural networks for multi-class brain disease detection using MRI images. *Computerized Medical Imaging and Graphics*, 2019;78:01673.

[13] M. Havaei, A. Davy, D. Warde-Farley, *et al.* Brain tumor segmentation with deep neural networks. *Medical Image Analysis* 2017;35:18–31.

[14] S. Kakeda, J. Moriya, H. Sato, *et al.* Improved detection of lung nodules on chest radiographs using a commercial computer-aided diagnosis system. *American Journal of Roentgenology*, 2004;182(2):505–510.

[15] K. Doi. Current status and future potential of computer-aided diagnosis in medical imaging. *British Journal of Radiology*, 2005;78(1):3–19.

[16] B. Van Ginneken, B. ter Haar Romeny, and M. Viergever. Computer aided diagnosis in chest radiography: a survey. *IEEE Transactions on Medical Imaging*, 2001;20(12):1228–1241.

[17] B. Van Ginneken, M. Stegmann, and M. Loog. Segmentation of anatomical structures in chest radiographs using supervised methods: a comparative study on a public database. *Medical Image Analysis*, 2006;10(1):19–40.

[18] S. Candemir, S. Jaeger, K. Palaniappan, *et al.* Lung segmentation in chest radiographs using anatomical atlases with nonrigid registration. *IEEE Transactions on Medical Imaging*, 2013;33(2):577–590.

[19] B. van Ginneken, L. Hogeweg, and M. Prokop. Computer-aided diagnosis in chest radiography: beyond nodules. *European Journal of Radiolog*, 2009; 72(2):226–230.

[20] S. Sakai, H. Soeda, N. Takahashi, *et al.* Computer aided nodule detection on digital chest radiography: validation test on consecutive T1 cases of resectable lung cancer. *Journal of Digital Imaging*, 2006;19(4):376–382.

[21] J. Shiraishi, H. Abe, F. Li, R. Engelmann, H. MacMahon, and K. Doi. Computer-aided diagnosis for the detection and classification of lung cancers on chest radiographs: ROC analysis of radiologists' performance. *Academic Radiology*, 2006;13(8):995–1003.

[22] B. van Ginneken and B. ter Haar Romeny. Automatic segmentation of lung fields in chest radiographs. *Medical Physics*, 2000;27(10):2445–2455.

[23] A. Dawoud. Fusing shape information in lung segmentation in chest radiographs. *Image Analysis and Recognition*, 2010:70–78.

[24] B. van Ginneken, S. Katsuragawa, B. ter Haar Romeny, K. Doi, and M. Viergever. Automatic detection of abnormalities in chest radiographs using local texture analysis. *IEEE Transactions on Medical Imaging*, 2002;21(2):139–149.

[25] L. Hogeweg, C. Mol, P. de Jong, R. Dawson, H. Ayles, and B. van Ginneken. Fusion of local and global detection systems to detect tuberculosis in chest radiographs. In Proceedings of the MICCAI, 2010, pp. 650–657.

[26] M. Freedman, S. Lo, J. Seibel, and C. Bromley. Lung nodules: Improved detection with software that suppresses the rib and clavicle on chest radiographs. *Radiology*, 2011;260(1):265–273.

[27] R. Shen, I. Cheng, and A. Basu. A hybrid knowledge-guided detection technique for screening of infectious pulmonary tuberculosis from chest radiographs. *IEEE Transactions on Biomedical Engineering*, 2010;57(11): 2646–2656.

[28] T. Xu, I. Cheng, and M. Mandal. Automated cavity detection of infectious pulmonary tuberculosis in chest radiographs. In Proc. Int. IEEE Eng. Med. Biol. Soc., 2011, pp. 5178–5181.

[29] K.C. Santosh, S. Vajda, S. Antani, and G.R. Thoma. Edge map analysis in chest X-rays for automatic pulmonary abnormality screening. *International Journal of Computer Assisted Radiology and Surgery*, 2016; 11(9):1637–1646.

[30] K.C. Santosh and S. Antani. Automated chest X-ray screening: Can lung region symmetry help detect pulmonary abnormalities? *IEEE Transactions on Medical Imaging*, 2017;37(5):1168–1177.

[31] S. Vajda, A. Karargyris, S. Jaeger, *et al.* Feature selection for automatic tuberculosis screening in frontal chest radiographs. *Journal of Medical Systems*, 2018;42(8):1–11.

[32] M. Ding, S. Antani, S. Jaeger, *et al.* Local-global classifier fusion for screening chest radiographs. In *Medical Imaging 2017: Imaging Informatics for Healthcare, Research, and Applications* (Vol. 10138, p. 101380A). International Society for Optics and Photonics, 2017.

[33] M.A. Morid, A. Borjali, and G. Del Fiol. A scoping review of transfer learning research on medical image analysis using ImageNet. *Computers in Biology and Medicine*, 2020:104115.

[34] T. Rahman *et al.*, Reliable tuberculosis detection using chest X-ray with deep learning, segmentation and visualization. *IEEE Access*, 2020; 8.191586–191601, doi: 10.1109/ACCESS.2020.3031384.

[35] T. Kirti, K. Jitendra, and S. Ashok Poisson noise reduction from X-ray images by region classification and response median filtering. *Sādhanā*, 2017;42(6):855–863.

[36] S. Lee, M.S. Lee, and M.G. Kang. Poisson–Gaussian noise analysis and estimation for low-dose X-ray images in the NSCT domain. *Sensors*, 2018;18(4):1019.

[37] W. Yang, Y. Liu, L. Lin, *et al.* Lung field segmentation in chest radiographs from boundary maps by a structured edge detector. *IEEE Journal of Biomedical and Health Informatics*, 2017;22(3):842–851.

[38] W. Dai, J. Doyle, X. Liang, *et al.* SCAN: Structure correcting adversarial network for organ segmentation in chest X-rays, 2017. *arXiv preprint arXiv*:1703.08770.

[39] S. Candemir, S. Antani, S. Jaeger, R. Browning, and G.R. Thoma. Lung boundary detection in pediatric chest X-rays. In Medical Imaging 2015: PACS and Imaging Informatics: Next Generation and Innovations (Vol. 9418, p. 94180Q). International Society for Optics and Photonics, 2015.

[40] T.B. Chandra and K. Verma. Pneumonia detection on chest X-Ray using machine learning paradigm. In *Proceedings of 3rd International Conference on Computer Vision and Image Processing*, pp. 21–33. Springer, Singapore, 2020.

[41] G.J. Chowdary, N.S. Punn, S.K. Sonbhadra, and S. Agarwal. Face mask detection using transfer learning of inceptionv3. In *International Conference on Big Data Analytics*, pp. 81–90. Springer, Cham, 2020.

[42] S. Jaeger, A. Karargyris, S. Antani, and G. Thoma. Detecting tuberculosis in radiographs using combined lung masks. In *Proc. Int. Conf. IEEE Eng. Med. Biol. Soc.*, 2012, pp. 4978–4981.

[43] S. Hochreiter and J. Schmidhuber. Long short-term memory. *Neural Computation* 1997;9(8):1735–1780.

[44] L. Mou, L. Bruzzone, and X.X. Zhu. Learning spectral-spatial-temporal features via a recurrent convolutional neural network for change detection in multispectral imagery. *IEEE Transactions on Geoscience and Remote Sensing*, 2018;57(2):924–935.

[45] L. Mou, P. Ghamisi, and X.X. Zhu. Deep recurrent neural networks for hyperspectral image classification. *IEEE Transactions on Geoscience and Remote Sensing*, 2017;55(7):3639–3655.

[46] K. Xu, J. Ba, R. Kiros, *et al.* Show, attend and tell: Neural image caption generation with visual attention. In *International Conference on Machine Learning*, pp. 2048–2057. PMLR, 2015.

[47] F.A. Gers, J. Schmidhuber, and F. Cummins. Learning to forget: Continual prediction with LSTM. *Neural Computation*, 2000;12(10):2451–2471.

[48] A. Graves. Generating Sequences with Recurrent Neural Networks, 2013. arXiv preprint arXiv:1308.0850.

[49] G. Nagasubramanian, M. Sankayya, F. Al-Turjman, and G. Tsaramirsis. Parkinson data analysis and prediction system using multi-variant stacked auto encoder. *IEEE Access*, 2020;8:127004–127013, 10.1109/ACCESS.2020.3007140.

[50] J. Shiraishi, S. Katsuragawa, J. Ikezoe, *et al.* Development of a digital image database for chest radiographs with and without a lung nodule. *American Journal of Roentgenology*, 2000;174(1):71–74.

[51] G. Nagasubramanian, R.K. Sakthivel, R. Patan, A.H. Gandomi, M. Sankayya, and B. Balusamy. Securing e-health records using keyless signature infra-structure blockchain technology in the cloud. *Neural Computing and Applications*, 2020;32(3):639–647. https://doi.org/10.1007/s00521-018-3915-1.

[52] S.R. Kumar, N. Gayathri, S. Muthuramalingam, B. Balamurugan, C. Ramesh, and M.K. Nallakaruppan. Medical big data mining and processing in e-Healthcare. In *Internet of Things in Biomedical Engineering*, pp. 323–339. Academic Press, 2019. https://doi.org/10.1016/B978-0-12-817356-5.00016-4.

[53] S. Candemir, S. Jaeger, K. Palaniappan, *et al.* Lung segmentation in chest radiographs using anatomical atlases with nonrigid registration. *IEEE Transactions on Medical Imaging*, 2014;33(2):577–590. doi:10.1109/TMI.2013.2290491. PMID: 24239990.

[54]   P. Dhingra, N. Gayathri, S.R. Kumar, V. Singanamalla, C. Ramesh, and B. Balamurugan. Internet of Things–based pharmaceutics data analysis. In *Emergence of Pharmaceutical Industry Growth with Industrial IoT Approach*, pp. 85–131. Academic Press, 2020.

[55]   S.K. Sharma, N. Gayathri, R.K. Modanval, and S. Muthuramalingam. Artificial intelligence-based systems for combating COVID-19. In *Applications of Artificial Intelligence in COVID-19*, pp. 19–34. Springer, Singapore, 2021.

[56]   V. Kavidha, N. Gayathri, and S.R. Kumar. AI, IoT and robotics in the medical and healthcare field. *AI and IoT-Based Intelligent Automation in Robotics* 2021;165–187.

[57]   L. Hogeweg, C.I. Sánchez, P.A. de Jong, P. Maduskar, and B. van Ginneken, Clavicle segmentation in chest radiographs. *Medical Image Analysis*, 2012;16(8):1490–1502.

[58]   G. Nagasubramanian and M. Sankayya. Multi-variate vocal data analysis for detection of Parkinson's disease using deep learning. *Neural Computing and Applications*, 2021;33(10):4849–4864. https://link.springer.com/article/10.1007/s00521-020-05233-7.

Chapter 4

Drug discovery clinical trial exploratory process and bioactivity analysis optimizer using deep convolutional neural network for E-prosperity

K. Jaisharma[1], K. Logu[1], S. Rakesh Kumar[2] and N. Gayathri[2]

Abstract

Drug discovery is a complex and a time-consuming process as its success depends on various factors. An optimum and precise combination of drug compounds is key to treating individual health conditions. The current coronavirus pandemic witnessed an increase in adoption of the E-Prosperity system. E-Prosperity helps doctors perform various kinds of research and drug discovery operations by continuous monitoring of quarantined patients as well as frontline workers to keep them safe. According to WHO, around 82 million COVID-19 cases were reported worldwide at end of 2020. This created high demand for E-Prosperity system for disease diagnosis and monitoring. Another challenge is the discovery of drug; various researches are being carried out to find the effective drug for coronavirus infection. But most of the researchers face difficulties such as lack of physical apparatus or system to handle large number of patients remotely, short time to perform four-phases of drug clinical trials, and to find the optimal drug composition to cure the disease without causing any side effects to the patients. The major challenge we face here is to handle huge amounts of data generated during the clinical trial process, considering the correct parameters required for efficient discovery. Machine learning provides some advanced solutions, such as reinforcement learning, generative learning, and more. Deep learning is an emerging technology that helps overcome the drawbacks like dimensionality reduction and feature extraction. In the proposed model, we used a novel model called Optimized Deep Convolution Neural Network Outer-Loop, which is based on data to improve the clinical trial results and to suggest effective decisions in the field of drug discovery using the information collected over the electronic devices.

[1]Department of Computer Science & Engineering, Saveetha School of Engineering, Saveetha Institute of Medical and Technical Sciences, Chennai, India
[2]School of Computing Science and Engineering, Galgotias University, Uttar Pradesh, India

Keywords: Bioactivity analysis; Clinical trial; Deep convolutional neural network; Drug discovery; Deep learning; E-Healthcare; Outer-loop

4.1 Introduction

India is developing cutting-edge technologies. For this purpose, the MoHFW initiated diverse e-Gov exercises in health care in several regions across the country. One such division is the e-Health. e-Health is broadly portrayed as the usage of Information and Communication Technology (ICT) in prosperity. This would improve things fundamentally around the country, where large-scale developments are being implemented. The IT sector in India is quite sensational, they organize prosperity information structure and serve the prerequisites, everything being equal, by contributing generally up to 8% to the GDP. Advancements in organization frameworks can contribute unimaginably to the health care sector. The choice of such development for clinical benefits is somewhat due to the decentralized nature of clinical sector. This is also because clinical research professionals often face imbalances with PCs and associated systems, and feel that such advancements are not central to their clinical objective. Therefore, precise record keeping and correspondence are imperative for efficient clinical considerations.

The e-clinical consideration structure can be viewed as an emerging field that uses information and correspondence containing information about a patient's clinical records, including their clinical history and medical reports from different specialists. The electronic health record (EHR) stores all the necessary information eliminates the need to carry or pass genuine health reports in physical form. This system is vital in patient health care as it aids direct exchange of data between different health care providers. It, moreover, benefits patients by allowing them to share test reports with a care provider of choice who may be in a different country.

The fundamental objective of this electronic clinical consideration system is the basic organization and sharing of information across different prosperity affiliations. The data set aside in cutting-edge arrangement can be successfully recuperated and changed, which simplifies it for prosperity affiliations and customers to streamline their work cycle. There has been a significant increase in the number of electronic record systems over the years. This is a consequence of the awareness about the benefits of these systems among patients and clinical benefits affiliations. In most of the cases, government affiliations are expected to provide customers with adequate workplaces to make use of these advanced systems. With the assistance of these IT overhauls, it is favorable to deal with customers and prosperity specialists in a simple manner. One of the advantages of the clinical consideration system is that they are being adopted by organizations that offer online services. Moreover, the e-clinical consideration structure allows patients as well as experts to obtain and view the information remotely. There are various benefits of e-clinical structure for customers. Furthermore, the workplace of My Health Record is one more factor, which helps patients save and send their data.

This article portrays these headways in an incredibly detailed manner and allows its perusers to grasp the thoughts, from start to end.

E-prosperity comprises many advancements. The Internet, for example, licenses e-prosperity customers to connect with clinical benefits specialists through email, to view clinical records, to investigate prosperity information, as well as to offer data in the form of text, audio, video, and any other type of data. Instinctive TV, also called polycom, allows communication through both audio and video to any two individuals at any rate located in different regions seamlessly. Stands, which are unattached contraptions (for the most part PCs), are used in e-prosperity to give instinctive information to the customer. Most of the information is given through visuals of natural prompts on a touch screen. Corners can moreover be used to assemble data and information from customers. DVDs, USB streak drives, and other media are used to store data cautiously. Various smart phones are arranged for individualized figuring and Internet limits and are reasonable with down-loadable application (or applications) that enable customers to get prosperity information. A number of advanced features are accessible to all customers, especially those with some form of disability like loss of vision or hearing. On the other hand, use of e-prosperity by clinical benefits providers is associated with shortfalls like unavailability of financial stimuli and reimbursement for users, which could boost its adoption in and across affiliations. Moreover, the fundamental combination of new e-prosperity features required set up measures (on account of the assumption to retain data expected to be executed by new instruments and devices) before more-streamlined structures are set up. There are various limitations to e-prosperity advancement, such as consolidation costs, for instance, those related with hardware and programming purchases and backups and updates, and the shortfalls of standards concerning the setup and safety of e-prosperity information, particularly private patient prosperity related information, which has legal and monetary implications for providers. The high-level partition can be described as a uniqueness in induction to modernized developments, particularly the Internet. Despite the fact that people on one side of the partition approach those developments and use them, people on the contrary side typically do not. On the contrary, its use requires several permissions, which differs in each country, and its adoption is not uniform that lead to irregularities in openness and capacity level. Issues like cost, training level, social acceptance, and maintenance consistency with regard to standards hinder the use of e-prosperity. Various issues are associated with the security insurance, confidentiality, and need for consent, similarly as those related to the straightforwardness of e-prosperity developments.

4.2 Related works

Wearable wireless body area networks is an important segment of advance e-medical services framework (e.g., remote medicine). The significance of such frameworks is that they are proved to be very supportive in the current pandemic situation (COVID-19). Notwithstanding the requirement for a protected assortment of clinical information, there is likewise a need to handle information progressively. In this article, we enhance a symmetric homomorphic cryptosystem along with MIST-based correspondence design to help postponement or time-based observation and other allied applications. In particular, clinical information can be broken down by MIST workers in a safe way. This will work with dynamic, for instance, permitting pertinent partners to recognize and react to crisis circumstances, in light of ongoing information investigation.

We represent two assault games to prove that our methodology is safe (i.e., picked plaintext assault versatility under the computational Diffie–Hellman presumption), and assess the intricacy of its calculations. A similar outline of its presentation and three other related methodologies recommends that our methodology empowers protection guaranteed clinical information conglomeration, and the recreation tests utilizing Microsoft Azure further exhibit our plan [1,2]. With rapid improvements in e-medical care frameworks, patients that use e-medical care gadgets (Internet of Things) generate vast amount of health information. These information have huge clinical worth when totalled from these circulated gadgets. Notwithstanding, proficient health information total represents a few security and protection issues like privacy revelation and differential assaults, just as patients might be hesitant to share their information for collection. In this paper, we adduce a protection safeguarding health information conglomeration that safely gathers information from numerous sources for various purposes from patients. In particular, we utilize signature procedures to save reasonable motivations for patients. In the mean time, we incorporate noise with the wellbeing information for differential protection. Moreover, we integrate Boneh-Goh-Nissim cryptosystem and Shamir's secret sharing to keep information secure and adapt to any internal failures.

Security and protection conversations show that our plan can oppose differential assaults, endure medical care settings disappointments, and save reasonable motivations for patients. Execution assessments exhibit cost-productive calculation, correspondence, and capacity overhead [3]. With the assistance of patients' wellbeing information, e-medical services providers can offer solid information administrations for better clinical outcomes. For instance, the clinical pathway gives ideal and detailed direction for clinical medication. Notwithstanding with the e-medical services, suppliers are inept with vast volumes of e-medical care information, and a well-known arrangement is thus utilized to re-appropriate the clinical information to amazing cloud workers (CSs). Since the clinical information is personal yet the rethought workers are not completely trusted, the direct execution of clinical pathway inquiry administration will unavoidably bring tremendous security issues to patients' information. In addition to the security issues, the productivity issues likewise should be considered, like the correspondence overhead and computational expense among workers and suppliers. Thinking about the above issues, this article proposes a privacy protecting optimization for a clinical pathway query (PPO-CPQ) to ensure safe clinical pathway with regard to e-medical services CSs without uncovering the private data of patients, like name, sexual orientation, age, and actual record, nor the personal health data from clinics, like therapy, prescription, and cost.

In our proposed plot, we first plan on security and protection saving a few subprotocols, for example, security saving correlation, protection safeguarding clinical examination, protection saving stage determination, and security saving stage update convention, to ensure protection in the e-medical care framework. The output shows that our plan is reasonable as well as productive as far as computational expense and correspondence overhead are concerned [4]. Remote clinical sensor networks are gaining popularity in improving the nature of the medical care frameworks. Since the information to be taken care of are exceptionally personal, the trading of data over uncertain remote channels can cause genuine openings. The confirmation plans to be utilized with sensor organizations ought to be maneuvered carefully on account of the restricted assets and energy accessible with the sensor hubs. Accordingly, this examination targets improving existing validation conspires by giving insurance to medical care foundations against potential, notable assaults while limiting the overhead. An unknown client verification conspire is introduced for upgrading the security highlights, calculation, and correspondence overhead of the remote sensor organizations.

The proposed conspire uses an improvised elliptic bend cryptography and it is safe against password speculating assaults and keen card lost/taken verifier assaults, and furthermore protects client anonymity. Through ritualistic and casual security investigations, it is shown that the proposed conspire is secure against conceivable known assaults, including the password speculating assaults and keen card lost/taken verifier assaults, and that it likewise safeguards the client obscurity property. What's more, for the conventional security check, the proposed plot is reenacted utilizing the broadly acknowledged robotized approval of web security conventions and applications (AVISPA) instrument. The proposed plot gives high preservation with low computational and correspondence price [5].

4.3 Neural network

AI calculations that utilize neural organizations by and large should not be customized with explicit principles that characterize what's in store from the info. The neural network undertakes calculations rather than gains from handling many marked models (for example information with "answers") that are provided during preparing and utilizing this answer key to realize what qualities of the information are expected to build the right yield. When an adequate number of models have been prepared, the neural organization can start to deal with new, inconspicuous sources of info and effectively return exact outcomes [6,7]. The more models and assortment of data sources the program sees, the more exact the outcomes regularly become on the grounds that the program learns with experience.

4.3.1 Artificial neuron

This is perhaps the easiest type of counterfeit neural organization. In a feedforward neural organization, the information travels through the diverse information hubs until it arrives at the yield hub. As such, information moves in a single direction

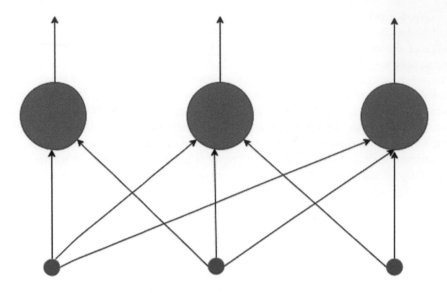

Figure 4.1   Feed forward neural network – artificial neuron

from the main level onward until it arrives at the yield hub. This is otherwise called a front engendered wave, which is normally accomplished by utilizing a grouping actuation work. Different to other perplexing types of neural organizations, there is no backpropagation and information moves in a single direction in particular. A feedforward neural organization could have a solitary layer, if not it might have covered up layers.

In a feedforward neural organization, the amount of results at the information sources and their loads are determined (Figure 4.12). Here is a representation of a single layer feedforward neural association. Feedforward neural organizations are utilized in applications like face acknowledgment and PC vision. This is on the grounds that the objective classes in these applications are difficult to arrange. A basic feedforward neural organization is furnished to manage information that contains a ton of noise. Feedforward neural organizations are likewise moderately easy to keep up with (Figure 4.1).

4.3.2   Spiral basis function neural network

A spiral premise work considers the interval of any direct relative toward the center. These neural organizations have two levels. In the internal level, the highlights are joined with the spiral premise work. At that point the yield of these highlights is considered while computing a similar yield in the following time-step. To work a neural organization (Figure 4.2).

The outspread premise work neural organization are being implemented broadly in energy rebuilding frameworks. In recent years, power frameworks have expanded and have become more unpredictable. This leads to the danger of power

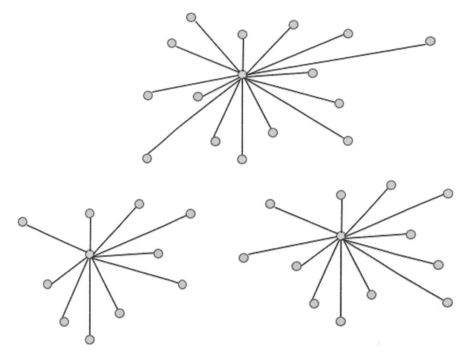

Figure 4.2   Radial basis function neural network

outage. This neural organization is utilized in force reclamation frameworks to re-establish power in the most limited conceivable time.

4.3.3   Multilayer perceptron

A multi-layer perceptron has at least three layers. It is utilized for ordering the information that cannot be isolated straightly. It is a sort of fake neural organization that is completely associated. This is on the grounds that each and every hub in a layer is associated with every hub in the accompanying layer (Figure 4.3). A multi-layer perceptron utilizes a nonlinear actuation work (fundamentally exaggerated digression or strategic capacity). This is what a multi-facet perceptron resembles (Figure 4.3).

4.3.4   Long- and short-term memory

A recurrent neural network is a sort of counterfeit neural organization wherein the yield of a specific layer is preserved and taken care in the previous information. By this way, layers are predicted. The essential layer is outlined comparatively wherein everything is equal in the feedforward network, i.e., with the result of the amount loads and highlights. Notwithstanding, in ensuing layers, the repetitive neural organization measure starts. From each time-step to the following, every hub will recall some data that had a past time-step (Figure 4.10). Finally, every hub acts like a memory cell while registering and doing activities. These neural organization

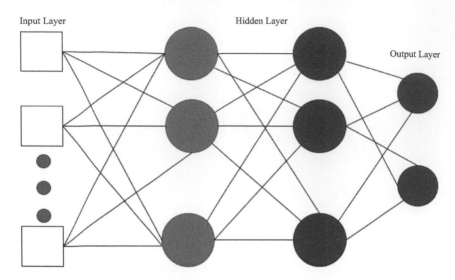

*Figure 4.3   Multi-layer perceptron. This type of neural network is applied
extensively in speech recognition and machine translation
technologies*

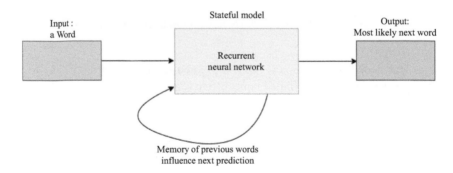

Figure 4.4   Recurrent neural network (RNN) – long short-term memory

starts with the front engendering as normal, yet recalls the data it might have to
utilize later (Figure 4.4).

If the assumption is not correct, the circumstance undergoes self-learning and
seeks after making the right estimate during the backpropagation (Figure 4.9). This
type of neural organization is extremely powerful in text-to-discourse transformation innovation. This is what a repetitive neural organization resembles.

4.3.5   Modular neural network

A modular neural organization has various organizations that work autonomously
and perform sub-undertakings. The various organizations do not actually communicate with or signal one other during the calculation interaction. They are allowed

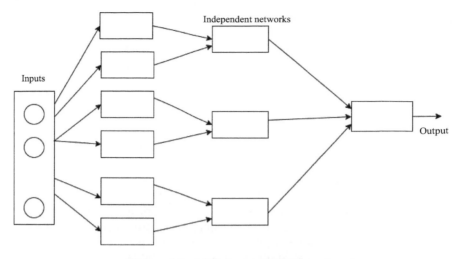

Figure 4.5   Modular neural network

to work freely for accomplishing their yield. Subsequently, a huge and intricate computational interaction should be possible fundamentally quicker by separating it into autonomous parts (Figure 4.5). The calculation speed increments on the grounds that the organizations are not cooperating with or even associated with one another. Figure 4.5 depicts a modular neural network.

4.3.6   Sequence-to-sequence models

The method of grouping to arrangement replica comprises two repetitive neural organizations. There is an encoder that actions the data and a decoder that actions the yield. Both encoder and decoder can utilize something very similar or various boundaries. This model is especially relevant in those situations where the length of the information is not equivalent to the range of the yield information. Grouping to arrangement models were applied chiefly in chatbots, machine interpretation, and question noting frameworks (Figure 4.6).

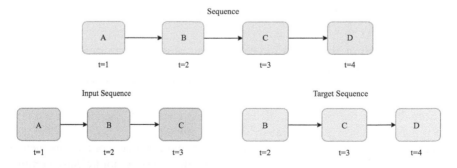

Figure 4.6   Sequence modeling with neural networks

4.4   Convolutional neural network

A convolutional neural network, or CNN, is a profound neural organization intended for preparing organized varieties of information like pictures. CNN is broadly utilized in PC vision and have become the cutting edge for some visual applications, for example, picture order, and have additionally discovered accomplishments in normal language handling for text characterization. CNN is truly adept at getting on designs in the info picture, like lines, angles, circles, or even eyes and faces (Figure 4.7). It is this property that makes CNN so amazing for PC vision [8,9]. Dissimilar to prior PC vision calculations, CNN can work straightforwardly on a crude picture and does not require any preprocessing.

A CNN is a feed-forward neural organization, which consists of up to 20 or 30 layers. The force of a convolutional neural comes from an extraordinary sort of layer called the convolutional layer. CNN contains numerous convolutional layers stacked on top of one another; each one equipped for perceiving more modern shapes. With three or four convolutional layers it is feasible to perceive transcribed digits and with 25 layers it is feasible to recognize human countenances (Figure 4.8). The utilization of convolutional layers in neural organization reflects the construction of the human visual cortex, where a progression of layers measures an approaching picture and recognizes dynamically more intricate highlights [10,11].

1. Input layers: It is the layer wherein we offer contribution to our model. The quantity of neurons in this layer is similar to adding up number of highlights in our information (number of pixels in case of a picture).
2. Hidden layer: The contribution from input layer is then fed into the secret layer. There can be numerous mysterious layers depending on our model and data size. Each secret layers can have different variety of neurons that are by and large more important than the quantity of highlights. The supply from each layer is figured by framework duplication of yield of the past layer with learnable heaps of that layer and thereafter by extension of learnable inclinations followed by commencement work that makes the association nonlinear.
3. Yield layer: The yield from the secret layer is taken care of into a calculated capacity like sigmoid or softmax, which changes over the yield of each class into likelihood into probability score of each class.

Algorithm 1:
The calculation related to the preparation stage is presented below.

Step 1. Dispatch the calculation comparing to the preparation stage. Aggregate the quantity of tests comparing to each labelled word and decide the low-recurrence comment word set.

Step 2. From the program, all the low-recurrence tests, this preparation tests were separated to frame a low-recurrence preparing set.

Step 3. Develop a DCNN model with other two channels: DCNN0 as well as DCNN1. DCNN0 identifies with the channel with a little convolutional partition and its gigantic development, and DCNN1 compares to the channel with an

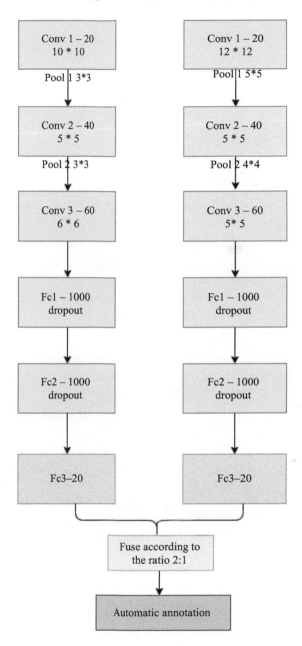

Figure 4.7   Two channel convolutional neural network

enormous convolutional piece and a little advance. The principal layer of the DCNN1 channel is completely associated with the second layer of the completely associated layer for highlight combination.

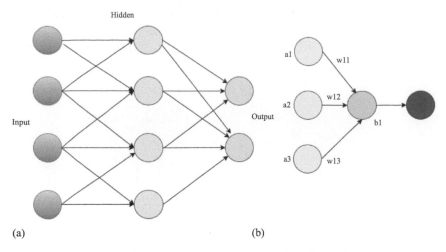

Figure 4.8   Deep neural network. A straightforward outline of neural organizations (NNs). (a) ANN is made out of info, covered up and yield layers. (b) The yield of a secret unit is determined from input esteems by means of an enactment work

Step 4. Combine information of all the arrangement sets into the DCNN0 channel along with the data simply by low-repeat planning tests inside the DCNN1 channel. Lead model is then ready until the model gets consistent.

Algorithm 2:

The labeling phase algorithm is as follows.

Stage 1. Send the information of the test picture toward the two channels (DCNN0 and DCNN1) of the prepared two-channel CNN for highlight uprooting.

Stage 2. Wire the yield vectors of the two directs in a 2:1 ratio (the particular proportion is tentatively decided).

Stage 3. Consolidate the choice after effects of both the channels and perform picture explanation.

The first CNN was proposed by Hubel and Wiesel [9] during the 1960s through investigations of neurons in monkey cortexes identified with nearby affectability and course choice. CNNs utilize weighted sharing, downsampling, and neighborhood association methods that extraordinarily reduce the quantity of essential boundaries and the intricacy of the neural organization. CNNs have been contrasted with conventional strategies for pictures that include extraction like the Histogram of Oriented Gradient (HOG) and Scale-Invariant Feature Transform (SIFT) techniques; be that as it may, CNNs can commonly separate more unique and extensive highlights. Furthermore, CNNs keep away from the requirement for complex picture preprocessing on the grounds that they can utilize the first pictures straightforwardly as info

CNNs principally made out of a convolution is a pooled layer, which is a completely associated layer. The convolutional layer is a vital piece of the CNN.

This layers' capacity is neither extricate highlights from input pictures nor highlight maps. Each convolutional layer has numerous convolution bits, which can be utilized to obtain different element maps. The convolution layer is determined as follows [12]:

$$x_j^1 = f\left(\sum_{i \in M_j} x_i^{t-1} * k_{ij}^l + b_j^t\right) \tag{4.1}$$

where i is the trademark guide of the yield of the past layer, which is yield of the ith channel of the jth convolution layer, and is known as the enactment work. Here, which is an subset for the information highlight maps used to figure, is a convolution part, and is the relating counter balanced to obtain a different element maps.

A pooling layer is, by and large, sandwiched between two convolutional layers. The principle capacity of these layers is to diminish the components of the element plan and keep up the scale invariance of the highlights somewhat. The pooling cycle is like the convolution interaction in that it includes a sliding window like a channel, yet the computation can be more straightforward. Mean pooling utilizes the normal worth in a picture territory as the pooled estimation of the space. By this methodology, the foundation of the picture is saved. Max pooling takes up most extreme estimation of the picture region as the pooled estimation of the space and jam the surface of the picture well. The capacity of the completely associated layer is to coordinate the different picture maps received after the picture has gone through various convolution layers and pooling layers for acquiring the high-layer semantic highlights of the picture for resulting picture order.

Figure 4.7 depicts the construction of a two-channel convolutional neural organization. Conv = convolutional layer; Pool = pooling layer; Fc = fully associated layer. The x in conv-x signifies the quantity of convolution parts in the layer; the size of the convolution portion or pooling window in the layer is $y \times y$; the z in Fc-z means the quantity of neurons in the completely associated layer; and dropout shows the expansion of a dropout layer to the first layer.

4.4.1 Deep convolutional neural network

A convolution is the straightforward use of a channel to an info that outcomes in an enactment. Rehashed utilization of similar channel to an info brings about a guide of enactments called an element map, showing the areas and strength of a distinguished component in an information, like a picture. The advancement of convolutional neural organizations is the capacity to naturally get familiar with an enormous number of channels in equal explicit to a preparation dataset under the requirements of a particular prescient demonstrating issue, for example, picture order. The outcome is exceptionally explicit highlights that can be distinguished any place on input pictures.

1. Convolutional neural organizations apply a channel to a contribution to make a component map that sums up the presence of identified highlights in the information.

2. Filters can be high quality, for example, line identifiers, yet the advancement of convolutional neural organizations is to get familiar with the channels during preparation with regard to a particular expectation issue.
3. How to figure the element map for one- and two-dimensional convolutional layers in a convolutional neural organization?

The convolutional neural organization, or CNN for short, is a specific sort of neural organization model intended for working with two-dimensional picture information, in spite of the fact that they can be utilized with one-dimensional and three-dimensional information. Vital to the convolutional neural organization is the convolutional layer that gives the organization its name. This layer plays out an activity called a "convolution". With regard to a convolutional neural organization, a convolution is a direct activity that includes the increase of a bunch of loads with the information, similar to a conventional neural organization. Given that the method was intended for two-dimensional info, the increase is performed between a variety of information and a two-dimensional cluster of loads, called a channel or a piece.

The channel is more modest than the info information and the kind of augmentation applied between a channel estimated fix of the information and the channel is a speck item. A spot item is the component insightful increase between the channel estimated fix of the information and channel, which is then added, continually bringing about a solitary worth. Since it brings about a solitary worth, the activity is frequently alluded to as the "scalar item". Utilizing a channel more modest than the information is deliberate as it permits a similar channel (set of loads) to be increased by the info exhibit on various occasions at various focuses on the info. In particular, the channel is applied deliberately to each covering part or channel measured fix of the info information, left to right, through and through [22]. The yield from duplicating the channel with the info exhibit one time is a solitary worth. As the channel is applied on numerous occasions to the info exhibit, the outcome is a two-dimensional cluster of yield esteems that address a separating of the information. In that capacity, the two-dimensional yield cluster from this activity is known as a "include map":

$$\omega := \omega - \alpha * \sigma L / \sigma W \tag{4.2}$$

where W represents each learnable boundary, α represents a learning rate, and L represents a misfortune work. It is of note that, by and by, a learning rate is quite possibly the main hyperparameters to be set before the preparation begins.

DL is a class of AI calculations that utilizes fake neural organizations (ANNs) with numerous layers of nonlinear handling units for learning information portrayals. The earliest ANN can be followed back to 1943 [13,14], when Warren McCulloch and Walter Pitts built up a computational model for NNs dependent on both arithmetic as well as calculations known as edge rationale. The essential construction of an advanced ANN is addressed and motivated from the design of human's mind [23]. In an ANN, there are three fundamental layers – the info layer, covered up layer, and yield layer. Contingent upon the kind of ANN, the hubs, additionally called neurons, in adjoining layers are either completely associated or mostly associated. Info factors are taken by input hubs and the factors are changed through secret hubs, and at the end yield esteems are determined at yield hubs:

$$Y_i = g\left(\sum_j Wij * aj\right) \qquad (4.3)$$

where aj are the information factors, Wij is the heaviness of info hub j on hub I and capacity g is the initiation work, which is regularly a nonlinear capacity (e.g., sigmoid or Gaussian capacity) to change the straight mix of information signal from input hubs to a yield (Figure 4.8).

4.4.2 Convolutional layer

The convolutional layer is the center structure square of a convolutional network that does a large portion of the computational truly difficult work.

Nearby connectivity is managing high-dimensional sources of info like pictures, as we saw above it is unreasonable to associate neurons to all neurons in the past volume. All things considered, we associate every neuron to just a nearby district of the info volume. The spatial degree of this network is a hyperparameter called the responsive field of the neuron (comparably this is the channel size). The degree of the availability along the profundity hub is consistently equivalent to the profundity of the information volume [15]. It is essential to underline again this unevenness by they way we treat the spatial measurements (width and tallness) and the profundity measurement: the associations are nearby in space (along width and stature), yet in every case full along the whole profundity of the info volume.

Spatial course of action are network of every neuron in the convolutional layer to the information volume; however, we have not yet talked about the number of neurons there are in the yield volume or how they are masterminded [24]. Three hyperparameters control the size of the yield volume: the profundity, step, and zero-cushioning.

In the first place, the depth of the yield volume is a hyperparameter: it compares to the quantity of channels we might want to utilize, each figuring out how to search for something else in the info. For instance, on the off chance that the primary convolutional layer takes as info the crude picture, various neurons along the profundity measurement may initiate in presence of different arranged edges, or masses of shading [16]. We allude to a bunch of neurons that are on the whole viewing at a similar area of the contribution as a depth column (some individuals likewise favor the term fiber).

Second, we should indicate the stride with which we slide the channel. At the point in step 1 we move the channels toward each pixel in turn [21]. In this step 2 (or remarkably at least 3, however this is uncommon by and by) at that point the channels hop 2 pixels all at once as we slide them around. This creates more modest yield volumes spatially.

As we will before long see, at times it will be helpful to cushion the information volume with zeros around the line. The size of this zero-padding is a hyperparameter. The decent element of zero cushioning is that it will permit us to control the spatial size of the yield volumes (most normally as we will see soon and utilize it to precisely protect the spatial size of the info volume so the information and yield width and tallness are something very similar).

We can register the spatial size of the yield volume as an element of the info volume size (W), the responsive field size of the convolutional layer neurons (F), the step with which they are applied (S), and the measure of zero cushioning utilized (P) on the boundary. You can persuade yourself that the right equation for figuring the number of neurons "fit" is given by (W − F + 2P)/S + 1. For instance, for a 7 × 7 info and a 3 × 3 channel with step 1 and cushion 0 we would get a 5 × 5 yield. With step 2 we would get a 3 × 3 yield.

4.4.2.1   Standardization layer

Numerous kinds of standardization layers have been proposed for use in ConvNet designs now and then with the aim of carrying out hindrance plans seen in the organic cerebrum.

4.4.2.2   Completely associated layer

Neurons in a completely associated layer have full associations with all actuations in the past layer, as found in customary neural networks. Their initiations can consequently be enrolled with a lattice augmentation, which come after by a pre-disposition balance. See the Neural Network section of the notes for more data.

4.5   Simulation and analysis

The solid adsorption of BOR on graphene surface principally begins from the hydrophobic π–π stacking connections, which are resolved dependent on two mathematical rules: the distance between two adjoining sweet-smelling planes ($d < 0.53$ nm) and the points between tomahawks typical to the two neighboring planes ($\alpha < 20°$) of the sweet-smelling structures [17,18]. It is determined that a couple of fragrant rings on BOR adhere to the PG/GO surface in the previously adsorbed layer (Figures 4.9 and 4.10). The average designs of π–π stacking are introduced in Figure 4.11, in which the two sweet-smelling rings are near the PG/GO surface with practically equal directions. As to GO, it ought to be brought up that π–π associations are set up between fragrant rings and unoxided areas of GO. Two boundaries, to be specific, the vertical distance and included point between two fragrant rings and PG/GO are utilized to portray these collaborations. The most likely vertical distance between sweet-smelling rings and PG/GO surface is situated at $z = 0.42$ nm, which is reliable with the vdW range of carbon molecules. In the interim, the most likely included points among BOR and PG/GO are roughly 12° and 24°, demonstrating that the sweet-smelling rings of BOR are practically corresponding to the PG surface [20]. These outcomes further affirm that the stacking of BOR on PG/GO is exceptionally steady and π–π stacking is the primary power in such adsorption. Other than π–π associations, there are some arrived at the midpoint of 1.4 hydrogen bonds shaped among BOR and GO in view of the

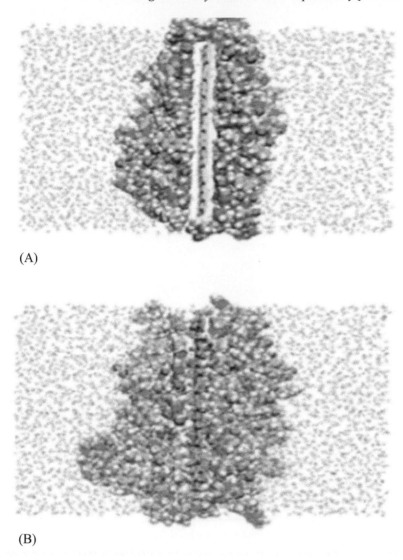

Figure 4.9 PG/GO surface. The adsorption of BORs on PG and GO nanosheets. (A and B) The designs of BOR atoms on PG/GO surface

oxygen-containing gatherings, which can clarify the higher adsorption energy (∼10 kJ mol^{-1}) of BOR on GO than that on PG surface.

Essentially, in light of the hydrophobic π–π stacking communications, BOR particles are inclined to frame bunch in the water arrangement [19]. We subsequently figure the firm energy of BOR at fluid stage, which is portrayed by the PMF of BOR at the distinctive situation, as demonstrated in Figure 4.10. The strong energy of BOR bunch is roughly -37.5 ± 0.7 kJ mol^{-1}, somewhat more vulnerable

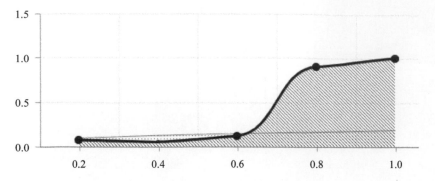

Figure 4.10   Distance (nm). The designs of BOR on PG and GO the likelihood of the vertical distance and included point between two fragrant ring

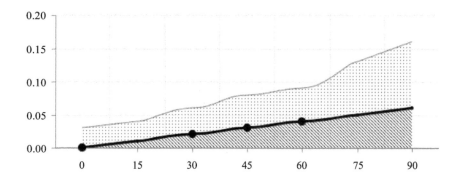

Figure 4.11   Angle (θ). The likelihood of the vertical distance and included point between two sweet-smelling rings and PG/GO, the quantity of bonds framed among BOR and GO

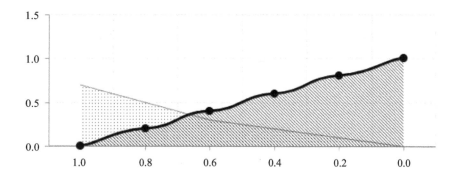

Figure 4.12   Specificity/sensitivity. Recipient working trademark bends of (a) model triphasic, (b) model workmanship/del, (c) model unenhanced, (d) model blood vessel, and (e) model deferred

than the adsorption energy of BOR on P, demonstrating that BOR can be ideally adsorbed on PG/GO surface. Then again, this solid durable energy makes BOR particles stacked firmly (Figure 4.12).

4.6   Conclusion

This paper introduced the disclosure of a medication for illnesses, different discovery methods are being employed to find efficient medications for COVID-19. The challenge for actual mechanical assembly is to deal with colossal patients remotely, short duration to plan out four-phase clinical trial for discovery of ideal treatment for conditions without any side effects to patients. In Optimized Deep Convolution Neural Network Outer-Loop, it depends on the information collected to improve the clinical preliminary attempt to achieve optimum results for different studies pertaining to medications, utilizing the data gathered with regard to specificity, point, and distance.

References

[1]   C. Guo, P. Tian, and K. -K. R. Choo, "Enabling privacy-assured fog-based data aggregation in E-healthcare systems," in *IEEE Transactions on Industrial Informatics*, vol. 17, no. 3, pp. 1948–1957, 2021, doi: 10.1109/TII.2020.2995228.

[2]   P. Dhingra, N. Gayathri, S. R. Kumar, V. Singanamalla, C. Ramesh, and B. Balamurugan, Internet of Things-based pharmaceutics data analysis. In *Emergence of Pharmaceutical Industry Growth with Industrial IoT Approach*. Academic Press, London, 2020, pp. 85–131.

[3]   W. Tang, J. Ren, K. Deng, and Y. Zhang, "Secure data aggregation of lightweight E-healthcare IoT devices with fair incentives," *IEEE Internet of Things Journal*, vol. 6, no. 5, pp. 8714–8726, 2019, doi:10.1109/JIOT.2019.2923261.

[4]   M. Zhang, Y. Chen, and W. Susilo, "PPO-CPQ: a privacy-preserving optimization of clinical pathway query for E-healthcare systems," *IEEE Internet of Things Journal*, vol. 7, no. 10, pp. 10660–10672, 2020, doi: 10.1109/JIOT.2020.3007518.

[5]   Y. Kirsal Ever, "Secure-anonymous user authentication scheme for e-healthcare application using wireless medical sensor networks" *IEEE Systems Journal*, vol. 13, no. 1, pp. 456–467, 2019, doi: 10.1109/JSYST.2018.2866067.

[6]   G. Nagasubramanian, M. Sankayya, F. Al-Turjman, and G. Tsaramirsis, "Parkinson data analysis and prediction system using multi-variant stacked auto encoder," *IEEE Access*, vol. 8, pp. 127004–127013, 2020, 10.1109/ACCESS.2020.3007140.

[7]   G. Nagasubramanian, R. K. Sakthivel, R. Patan, A. H. Gandomi, M. Sankayya, and B. Balusamy, Securing e-health records using keyless

signature infrastructure blockchain technology in the cloud. *Neural Computing and Applications*, vol. 32, no. 3, pp. 639–647, 2020. https://doi.org/10.1007/s00521-018-3915-1

[8]   N. Deepa and S. P. Chokkalingam, "Deep convolutional neural networks (CNN) for medical image analysis," *International Journal of Engineering and Advanced Technology*, vol. 8, no. 3, pp. 607–610, 2019.

[9]   S. R. Kumar, N. Gayathri, S. Muthuramalingam, B. Balamurugan, C. Ramesh, and M. K. Nallakaruppan, Medical big data mining and processing in e-Healthcare. In *Internet of Things in Biomedical Engineering*. Academic Press, London, 2019, pp. 323–339. https://doi.org/10.1016/B978-0-12-817356-5.00016-4.

[10]   S. K. Sharma, N. Gayathri, R. K. Modanval, and S. Muthuramalingam, *Artificial Intelligence-Based Systems for Combating COVID-19. In Applications of Artificial Intelligence in COVID-19*, Springer, Singapore, 2021, pp. 19–34.

[11]   V. Kavidha, N. Gayathri, and S. R. Kumar, AI, IoT and robotics in the medical and healthcare field. In *AI and IoT-Based Intelligent Automation in Robotics*, 2021, 165–187.

[12]   B. D. Deebak, F. Al-Turjman, M. Aloqaily, and O. Alfandi, "An authentic-based privacy preservation protocol for smart e-healthcare systems in IoT," *IEEE Access*, vol. 7, pp. 135632–135649, 2019, doi: 10.1109/ACCESS.2019.2941575.

[13]   M. Niharika, N. Deepa, and T. Devi, "Image segmentation and detection for health care datas in deep learning," *Test Engineering and Management*, vol. 81, no. 11–12, pp. 5402–5407, 2019.

[14]   G. Nagasubramanian and M. Sankayya, "Multi-variate vocal data analysis for detection of Parkinson's disease using deep learning," *Neural Computing and Applications*, vol. 33, no. 10, 4849–4864, 2021. https://link.springer.com/article/10.1007/s00521-020-05233-7.

[15]   N. Deepa and S. P. Chokkalingam, "A deep learning method on medical image dataset predicting early dementia in patients Alzheimer's disease using convolution neural network (CNN)," *International Journal of Recent Technology and Engineering*, vol. 8, 3 Special Issue, pp. 604–609, 2019.

[16]   T. Devi, K. Padmapriya, N. Deepa, and S. Kumar, "Towards secure storage of electronic health information (EHI) in cloud environment," *Journal of Advanced Research in Dynamical and Control Systems*, vol. 9, Special Issue 17, pp. 520–531, 2017.

[17]   M. Ahmed Sahi, H. Abbas, K. Saleem, *et al.*, "Privacy preservation in e-healthcare environments: state of the art and future directions," *IEEE Access*, vol. 6, pp. 464–478, 2018, doi: 10.1109/ACCESS.2017.2767561.

[18]   H. Park and S. Hahm, "Changes in stress mindset and EEG through E-healthcare based education," *IEEE Access*, vol. 7, pp. 20163–20171, 2019, doi: 10.1109/ACCESS.2019.2895655.

[19]   P. P. Ray, N. Kumar, and D. Dash, "BLWN: blockchain-based lightweight simplified payment verification in IoT-assisted e-healthcare," *IEEE Systems*

Journal, vol. 15, no. 1, pp. 134–145, 2021, doi: 10.1109/JSYST. 2020.2968614.

[20] X. Yang, R. Lu, J. Shao, X. Tang, and H. Yang, "An efficient and privacy-preserving disease risk prediction scheme for E-healthcare," *IEEE Internet of Things Journal*, vol. 6, no. 2, pp. 3284–3297, 2019, doi:10.1109/ JIOT.2018.2882224.

[21] W. Zhang, Y. Lin, J. Wu, and T. Zhou, "Inference attack-resistant e-healthcare cloud system with fine-grained access control," *IEEE Transactions on Services Computing*, vol. 14, no. 1, pp. 167–178, 2021, doi: 10.1109/TSC.2018.2790943.

[22] G. K. Verma, B. B. Singh, N. Kumar, O. Kaiwartya, and M. S. Obaidat, "PFCBAS: pairing free and provable certificate-based aggregate signature scheme for the e-healthcare monitoring system," *IEEE Systems Journal*, vol. 14, no. 2, pp. 1704–1715, 2020, doi: 10.1109/JSYST.2019.2921788.

[23] C. Xu, N. Wang, L. Zhu, K. Sharif, and C. Zhang, "Achieving searchable and privacy-preserving data sharing for cloud-assisted E-healthcare system," *IEEE Internet of Things Journal*, vol. 6, no. 5, pp. 8345–8356, 2019, doi:10.1109/JIOT.2019.2917186.

[24] G. Farooq, Z. Iqbal, K. Saleem, *et al.*, "A dynamic three-bit image stega-nography algorithm for medical and e-Healthcare systems," *IEEE Access*, vol. 8, pp. 181893–181903, 2020, doi: 10.1109/ACCESS.2020.3028315.

Chapter 5

An automated NLP methodology to predict ICU mortality CLINICAL dataset using multiclass grouping with LSTM RNN approach

N. Deepa[1], T. Devi[1], N. Gayathri[2] and S. Rakesh Kumar[2]

Abstract

A large amount of data is generated in the fields of medicine, as healthcare is a major component of a tech-oriented lifestyle. Even now, the pandemic situation in 2020 led to a huge burden as well as medical emergencies. A need for a detailed understanding of various healthcare electronic clinical data (HECD) using Natural Language Processing (NLP) techniques has been recognized. High protection for clinical data that are being analyzed, the patient processed information generated from diagnosis using various methods, such as in ICU (intensive care unit), mortality levels, and resource allocation are performed instantly. Experts from the medical field use a patient's information from the laboratory results, such as X-ray, MRI, CTC scan, etc., to diagnose the disease using various inputs. The known vital parameters from clinical results, such as blood pressure (BP) and heart rate, always fluctuate and are inconsistent as well as the mismatch of information based on age, name, etc., are to be focused on to resolve the major challenges. Here we used the ICU clinical data as a sample to consider the features based on multiclass word phrase classification from unstructured data using a long short-term approach (LSTM). We categorize the data according to classes and group them into valid information wherein records can be minimal and help reduce the text. Also, valuable information can be protected and sensitive data can be kept confidential by phenomenal support, which is automated using NLP approaches. There are typical steps for treatment based on the critical level of the patients, in such stage time-series is mostly handled as development variables for mortality extraction from ICU data. A supervised structured data from clinical processing involve a bi-directional LSTM approach for processing the samples and brings efficient results from the records to make a reliable model from multiclass prediction.

Keywords: ICU; HECD; BP; LSTM; Supervised; Healthcare; NLP; Multiclass; MRI

[1]Department of Computer Science & Engineering, Saveetha School of Engineering, Saveetha Institute of Medical and Technical Sciences, Chennai, India
[2]School of Computing Science and Engineering, Galgotias University, Noida, India

5.1   Introduction to natural language processing

The paper presents information that can relate to the medical dataset [29–31] that can be combined with NLP. In general, the data which are applied with many classification techniques using the latest tools can produce accurate results based on features that are considered for prediction. This classification is purely based on text classification that implies a healthcare ICU mortality clinical dataset. The resources are from various weblogs, standard papers, and Kaggle, which provides raw data as input to process based on classification (Horecki and Mazurkiewicz 2015). Similar to the importance of databases in mining, Big Data analysis and analytics is a huge part of data observation and processing NLP that help obtain promising results when compared to the other techniques. When the resources are increasing in numbers and their use from Internet has also increased, users are in need of integrity assurance as well as correct data. NLP can also play a role in differentiating the data as supervised, unsupervised, semi-supervised, and reinforcement learning and can provide the optimum framework to deal with.

Figure 5.1 shows the data types, such as supervised, unsupervised, and reinforcement learning that find various applications. Supervised learning, which has

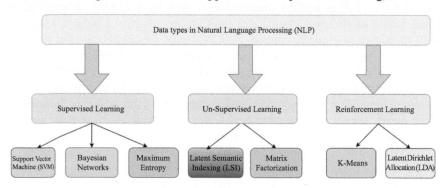

Figure 5.1   Data types in Natural Language Processing (NLP)

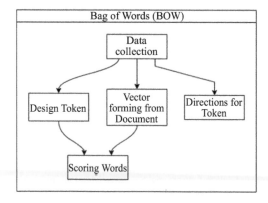

Figure 5.2   Bag of Words (BOW)

applications in support vector machines (SVM), Bayesian Networks, Maximum Entropy, are some of the algorithms. Second, unsupervised learning has applications in latent semantic indexing and matrix factorization. Third, reinforcement learning has major applications in K-means and Latent Dirichlet (LDI).

5.1.1 Text representation

NLP concentrates on the most important text representation as follows:

(a) Bag of Words (BOW)
(b) Concept Modeling

These two models focus on the NLP discovering the different features during healthcare data analysis. The first model illustrates the documents to classify the text and extract the required parameters. In general, modeling in NLP works based on linguistic direct access to each and every word from the vector formation. These kinds of feature mapping techniques with their properties are described as feature encoding. BOW is the special structure progress to find the words from the documents that are repeatedly occurring in the entire text. Based on the tokens, the vocabulary of the given text is initiated to find the complexity of words, based on which the occurrence scoring is performed. The example below shows in detail the working model of BOW.

Steps to be followed for generating BOW are

(a) Data preparation
(b) Token designing
(c) Vector formation from the document
(d) Direction for tokens
(e) Frequency score for unique words

Each step of the working model can be divided into the following steps and examples for knowing feature encoding or extraction. For example, we consider a corpus from the dataset.

5.1.1.1 Process 1: data are collected as below snippets

- It was the severe disease
- It was the mild symptoms
- It was the stage of features
- It was the stage of prediction

5.1.1.2 Process 2: token designing

Tokens are designed based on the above snippets, by ignoring the NA and punctuation and all unique words are represented here:

- "It"
- "Was"
- "The"
- "Severe"
- "Disease"

- "Mild"
- "Symptoms"
- "Stage"
- "of"
- "Features"
- "Prediction"

Based on the token design, vocabulary has been framed on the basis of uniqueness such that from the entire corpus 11 words were identified from 22 words.

5.1.1.3   Process 3: vector forming from the document

The third process is to score the words from a unique document. Based on the NLP model the data is converted into text for referring to the input and produced as output. As the vocabulary count has been created as 11 words, fixed-length is determined from the document. Based on the individual position after token designing, the vector is mapped to each word. This kind of mapping is a scoring technique to map the current words as a Boolean number "0" for incorrect and "1" for correct words.

From random choice of words to understand the correct words from the list (it was the severe disease) and then convert those Booleans to binary vectors. Now token based score is listed as below:

"It" = 1
"Was" = 1
"The" = 1
"Severe" = 1
"Disease" = 1
"Mild" = 0
"Symptoms" = 0
"Stage" = 0
"of" = 0
"Features" = 0
"Prediction" = 0

Now the binary vector formation shows in order [1,1,1,1,1,0,0,0,0,0,0]
Similar statement also mentioned for document as:
"It was the mild symptoms" = [1, 1, 1, 0, 0, 1, 1, 0, 0, 0]
"It was the stage of features" = [1, 1, 1, 0, 1, 0, 0, 1, 1, 0]
"It was the stage of Prediction" = [1, 1, 1, 0, 1, 0, 0, 1, 0, 1]

Frequent words are extracted for features from the document in the available corpus; only the nominal words are encoded and score given whereas new occurred words are discarded.

5.1.1.4   Process 4: directions for tokens

When the token value is maximized vector mapping is also increased. For the incorrect score the spare generation makes computation for memory as well as resource allocation. To minimize the value of a token when those words are accessed from the bad-of-words model following ways are used. Deleting the upper and lower case, not available data, punctuation, repeated words, and wrong spelling are also avoided. A model is defined as N-Gram for multi-class feature prediction and direction for both access terms as a sequence of words.

5.1.1.5   Process 5: scoring words

From token, scores are assigned based on the correct words by frequency, counts from the document. In such cases, hashing tables are generated to refer to the lookup for each correct word. These can be applied to a large corpus also by encoding the feature hash function. With reference to the frequency, the scores are rescaled and checked for rare matching across the entire corpus, which helps inverse the search. This kind of method is called term-frequency inverse document frequency.

5.1.2   Medical field impacted using NLP

Advancements in medical fields bring drastic changes in experimenting the diseases and medicines. Using clinical data, the stages and the effects of various diseases can be categorized to enhance the methods and analyze accordingly (Hesse, Ahern, and Beckjord 2016). There are two important terms in NLP – word formation and linguistic format, which can be organized from any form of speech, sentence, or any other development that can take place for research purposes. If the models are designed for any word identification or frequency of its occurrence, the main strategies to know are the distribution patterns. Based on the approach, the probability statistics are gathered. Based on various measures the correlations and estimations take place for clinical observation and optimal results (Funes *et al.* 2021).

5.1.3   NLP – a driven resource for healthcare to improve outcomes

Let us consider the below terms:

Recurrent neural network (RNN) that repeatedly Accept new input a
count the hidden state – h
produce the output b∧, RNN which moves right side in unfolded duration
Individual RNN with the time duration it takes to accept the input (a_t)
last visited hidden state as ht-1 produced output c_t
Label Prediction – z^t
memory cell – m_t
input gate – in_t
output gate – ou_t
forget gate - fo_t

5.1.4   LSTM–RNN a novel approach in prediction

The main approach for prediction is LSTM abbreviated as Long Short-Term Memory. The benefit obtained while utilizing LSTM is that it can handle the long-term dependency problem of RNN. Predicting the word that is stored in LSTM cannot be done using RNN. At the same time, based on the recent information predictions can be made accurately. RNN does not provide performance effectively when the length of the gap increases. LSTM on the other hand retains this information for a long duration. Data processing, prediction, as well as classification based on the time series information is the major application of the LSTM technique.

The structure of the chain is followed by LSTM and the cells retain this information along with the manipulations done by memory using gates, such as Forget gate as well as the Input gate including the Output gate. Another problem is the vanishing gradient, which gets completely removed in LSTM compared with RNN where the problem occurs during the process of training. LSTM applications include captioning using images [27,32], translation using machines, and language modeling.

5.1.5   RNN

Another significant type in neural networks is Recurrent Neural Network (RNN) where the output from the preceding stage is used as input for the present stage. Traditionally, both the inputs as well as outputs are independent in neural networks. For example, the previous words should be remembered for the prediction of succeeding words in the sentence. This problem was solved by the introduction of RNN where the hidden layer tackled this issue. Data regarding the sequence in RNN is remembered by Hidden state, which is a significant feature. The memory in RNN helps in remembrance of all the information regarding the calculations made. The parameters being used are also the same as the similar tasks being performed for every input to produce the output, thereby reducing the complexity of the parameters. The present state is calculated using the below formula where h_t (5.1) is the present state, h_{t-1} is the preceding state, and x_t is the state of the input

$$h_t = f(h_{t-1}, X_t) \tag{5.1}$$

To apply activation function

$$h_t = \tanh(W_{hh}h_{t-1} + W_{xh}X_t) \tag{5.2}$$

where w_{hh} is the recurrent neuron weight and w_{xh} is the input neuron weight. The activation function depicted in (5.2) defines the order that is applied in the dataset.

The output is computed using the below formula,

$$y_t = W_{hy}h_t \tag{5.3}$$

where y_t is the output and W_{hy} is the output layer weight shown in (5.3).

5.1.5.1   Algorithm 1 LSTM-RNN forward move
Step 1: INPUT:
    ICU MORTALITY as sequences of correct Patient Id,
    Num Diagnosis, Intervention Hospitalized Origin and time delayed

Table 5.1 Dataset/corpus to predict the ICU mortality

	Data as of	Start date	End date	Group	Year	MMWR week	Week ending date	State	COVID-19 deaths	Total deaths	Percent of expected deaths	Pneumonia deaths	Pneumonia and COVID-19 deaths	Influenza deaths	Pneumonia, influenza, or COVID-19 deaths
0	4/9/2021	12/29/2019	1/4/2020	By Week	2019/2020	1.0	1/4/2020	United States	0.0	60163.0	98.0	4105.0	0.0	434.0	4539.0
1	4/9/2021	1/5/2020	1/11/2020	By Week	2020	2.0	1/11/2020	United States	0.0	60720.0	97.0	4153.0	0.0	474.0	4627.0
2	4/9/2021	1/12/2020	1/18/2020	By Week	2020	3.0	1/18/2020	United States	2.0	59350.0	97.0	4064.0	2.0	467.0	4531.0
3	4/9/2021	1/19/2020	1/25/2020	By Week	2020	4.0	1/25/2020	United States	1.0	59150.0	99.0	3917.0	0.0	499.0	4417.0
4	4/9/2021	1/26/2020	2/1/2020	By Week	2020	5.0	2/1/2020	United States	0.0	58821.0	99.0	3817.0	0.0	481.0	4298.0

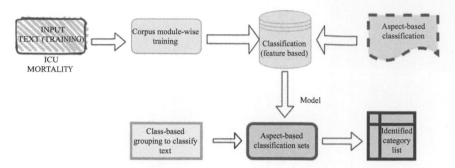

Figure 5.3   Multiclass feature aspect-based classification

Step 2: for each step time
    *[at,qt] = embedding(z_1 to x_h,m_1 to m_h)
    Compute input, forget and output gates : iteration$_t$
    Computer c_t and h_t
Step 3: if the spot is analyzed affected
    *perform the probability for finding
    *perform the log-loss
Step 4: if the spot is ICU mortality suggestion
    compute to find the predicted disease
    *perform the log-loss
    endif

Table 5.1 represents the various features of COVID-19 to predict mortality. Using the sample data set, input for training text classification is determined for feature extraction. Based on the aspect-based classification shown in Figure 5.3, classes are categorized. The text classification from the set of trained data can be preprocessed according to the LSTM approach.

The chapter organization is as follows: Section 5.1 deals with the introduction on Natural Language Processing (NLP), Section 5.2 deals with the data collection, Section 5.3 explains the novel approach, results are presented in Section 5.4, and Conclusion is presented in Section 5.5.

5.2   Data collection

Dataset based on COVID-19 was officially collected from the Centers for Disease Control and Prevention website, which provides COVID-19 death rates and monthly mortality information. During the pandemic situation from March 2020 to date (April 2021), according to NCHS, the death rate is highly increased. The origin of statistical views differs based on the severity and health [28,33,34] condition by applying the important features like age as a factor for updating the rate from the available resources. Table 5.1 shows the sample dataset that contains the date of death rate, such as start date, end date, grouped by mortality based on the

Table 5.2 Sample ICU mortality dataset

Data as of	Start date	End date	Group	Year	MMWR week	Week ending date	State	COVID-19 deaths	Total deaths	Percent of expected deaths	Pneumonia deaths	Pneumonia and COVID-19 deaths	Influenza deaths	Pneumonia, influenza, or COVID-19 deaths
4/9/2021	12/29/2019	1/4/2020	By Week	2019/2020	1	1/4/2020	United States	0	60163	98	4105	0	434	453
4/9/2021	1/5/2020	1/11/2020	By Week	2020	2	1/11/2020	United States	0	60720	97	4153	0	474	462
4/9/2021	1/12/2020	1/18/2020	By Week	2020	3	1/18/2020	United States	2	59350	97	4064	2	467	453
4/9/2021	1/19/2020	1/25/2020	By Week	2020	4	1/25/2020	United States	1	59150	99	3917	0	499	441
4/9/2021	1/26/2020	2/1/2020	By Week	2020	5	2/1/2020	United States	0	58821	99	3817	0	481	429
4/9/2021	2/2/2020	2/8/2020	By Week	2020	6	2/8/2020	United States	2	59455	100	3820	1	521	434
4/9/2021	2/9/2020	2/15/2020	By Week	2020	7	2/15/2020	United States	0	58799	100	3843	0	561	440
4/9/2021	2/16/2020	2/22/2020	By Week	2020	8	2/22/2020	United States	5	58885	101	3713	2	566	428
4/9/2021	2/23/2020	2/29/2020	By Week	2020	9	2/29/2020	United States	9	59311	103	3838	5	655	449
4/9/2021	3/1/2020	3/7/2020	By Week	2020	10	3/7/2020	United States	37	59680	103	3976	18	636	463
4/9/2021	3/8/2020	3/14/2020	By Week	2020	11	3/14/2020	United States	57	58662	103	3973	29	627	462
4/9/2021	3/15/2020	3/21/2020	By Week	2020	12	3/21/2020	United States	575	59202	104	4551	251	559	542
4/9/2021	3/22/2020	3/28/2020	By Week	2020	13	3/28/2020	United States	3183	62998	113	6188	1438	445	832
4/9/2021	3/29/2020	4/4/2020	By Week	2020	14	4/4/2020	United States	10082	72277	130	9932	4773	478	1548
4/9/2021	4/5/2020	4/11/2020	By Week	2020	15	4/11/2020	United States	16254	79085	143	12008	7236	474	2116
4/9/2021	4/12/2020	4/18/2020	By Week	2020	16	4/18/2020	United States	17120	76784	142	11412	7319	265	2128
4/9/2021	4/19/2020	4/25/2020	By Week	2020	17	4/25/2020	United States	15499	73895	138	10388	6616	144	1931
4/9/2021	4/26/2020	5/2/2020	By Week	2020	18	5/2/2020	United States	13191	69285	129	8948	5520	65	1666
4/9/2021	5/3/2020	5/9/2020	By Week	2020	19	5/9/2020	United States	11216	66795	127	7836	4716	48	1437
4/9/2021	5/10/2020	5/16/2020	By Week	2020	20	5/16/2020	United States	9201	64455	123	6784	3786	22	1221
4/9/2021	5/17/2020	5/23/2020	By Week	2020	21	5/23/2020	United States	7217	61605	118	5899	2979	24	1015
4/9/2021	5/24/2020	5/30/2020	By Week	2020	22	5/30/2020	United States	6154	59653	115	5282	2488	12	896
4/9/2021	5/31/2020	6/6/2020	By Week	2020	23	6/6/2020	United States	5026	58865	113	4901	2149	11	778
4/9/2021	6/7/2020	6/13/2020	By Week	2020	24	6/13/2020	United States	4222	58008	112	4545	1863	11	691
4/9/2021	6/14/2020	6/20/2020	By Week	2020	25	6/20/2020	United States	3830	57969	112	4369	1607	8	659
4/9/2021	6/21/2020	6/27/2020	By Week	2020	26	6/27/2020	United States	3815	58474	114	4269	1555	12	654
4/9/2021	6/28/2020	7/4/2020	By Week	2020	27	7/4/2020	United States	4523	59788	115	4564	2002	5	708

(Continues)

Table 5.2 (*Continued*)

Data as of	Start date	End date	Group	Year	MMWR week	Week ending date	State	COVID-19 deaths	Total deaths	Percent of expected deaths	Pneumonia deaths	Pneumonia and COVID-19 deaths	Influenza deaths	Pneumonia, influenza, or COVID-19 deaths
4/9/2021	7/5/2020	7/11/2020	By Week	2020	28	7/11/2020	United States	5758	61903	121	5541	2711	10	859
4/9/2021	7/12/2020	7/18/2020	By Week	2020	29	7/18/2020	United States	7164	63128	124	6190	3450	13	991
4/9/2021	7/19/2020	7/25/2020	By Week	2020	30	7/25/2020	Unted States	8206	64206	127	6760	3959	11	1101
4/9/2021	7/26/2020	8/1/2020	By Week	2020	31	8/1/2020	United States	8280	64180	126	6843	4074	13	1105

Table 5.3   Cumulative mortality

S. no	Country	Age	Age (count)	Gender	Count (gender)	Confidential interval	Cumulative mortality (as of April 2021)
1	Alaska	<65	6388	Women	3242	20,498(52)	664(100)
2	India	>=65	681	Men	3752	17,995(46)	71(66–77)
Cumulative mortality							
Total					208(100)		

period of occurring, Morbidity and Mortality Weekly Report (MMWR week), weekend date, COVID-19 death, total death rate, percentage of expectation of death.

In Table 5.2, the death rate due to pneumonia, influenza, and COVID-19 from 2019 to 2021 (till date) is given in percentage. Both the mortality and hospitalized ratio are identified where variance can be referred from the input data. Based on aspect-based features, such as by week, by month, etc., are grouping features with the MMWR week that are mostly over increased. Age factor is also a dependent variable for classification that is anticipated to help understand the reported people and influenza based on testing specimens, which are also categorized.

Table 5.3 shows the cumulative mortality death rate based on gender and age. From the incidence and mortality ratio, the death cases are drastically increased and differentiated by features such as age, gender, and combination of Hispanic and non-Hispanic people. From the ethnic data, the patients were not correctly updated with the exact gender categories, and groups are also not mentioned [35,36].

5.2.1   Multiclass feature analysis

Data on ICU mortality death rates are based on many countries from all over the world. Based on a few factors like race, gender, and others, combination classes are created. Behind the feature selection and extraction, the initial features are in need of analysis with the help of learning algorithms, such as supervised learning. Initially, data have been collected followed by text pre-processing for understanding the corpus text that is relevant to avoid the complexity of the repeated cleaning process. By eliminating the repeated words, stop words, the second step is over. Along with stop words, punctuation, and NA, poor characters and small case words are also eliminated. After removing the repeated words ICU data are still in millions due to a large number of patients [37]. Third, the splitting form of data takes place for selecting the features. Based on the country, patient influence by COVID-19, the transformation IDs have been generated. Once the ID has been identified the matrix for the count is represented such that normalization for the batch is continued. With the trained features, the classification of each group is also performed.

5.3   Proposed system

A predictive model is proposed using the model to classify and predict the ICU mortality or death rate based on COVID-19, pneumonia, or influenza, which is being performed by LSTM–RNN neural network model. Based on the category list, initial data are formed as multiclass features such that unsupervised data due to high death rates are not stable. By large volume of analysis also labels are unpredictable. However, the LSTM approach can analyze the part of data based on the type of deaths and control the independent variables to single class sequence vectors. Also, the RNN network provides the platform to learn classification based on total deaths that can feed-forward with the number of multiple weights. Not only the output depends on the weights, but also bias is included to find the last visited sequence since the new state is already combined with the weight of the previous state. The tanh activation function can pass the forwarded state to get multiples for preference of the new state. The objective of the work using ICU mortality data is to

(i)   Build a predictive model using the LSTM–RNN approach for making new state predictions without losing the connectivity of previous sequences.
(ii) To generate the multiclass feature analysis without using the word2vector model in such a way that multiple sequences discover the new state.
(iii) Corpus can be utilized to frame the aspect-based model to form advanced selection to predict the exact cause for death due to COVID-19.

5.4   Results and discussion

The COVID-19 dataset can be imported directly as data using a Jupyter Notebook along with the library packages, such as Keras for building the proposed model. Using the ICU mortality data the embedded keywords are analyzed from the total death rates and type of death rates for data preprocessing. Also, the model that needs to perform the training and testing steps, using the sklearn model those features for extracting according to class and label are created, The repeated words, stop words, and count vectorizer from the text can also be processed to find the tokenizer. Based on the tokenized format the multi-sequence, such as origin, is generated using padding and categorical analysis. From the updated dataset the present structured data are accounted as column basis for forming the aspect-based results.

Figure 5.4 illustrates the LSTM approach and model built for the provided dataset.

When the influence of diseases gets very high in number and multiple times the same phrases were interpreted based on the terms used for information, those repeated words create confusion for online and reading persons. In NLP, there is a technique used for dealing this problem, such as LSTM that uses RNN. In this technique, embedding a token from a word can be a neural network where the previous state is always dependent on the context. In such a way, hidden layers behave as persist for interconnected loops.

Model: "sequential_10"

Layer (type)	Output Shape	Param #
Istam_10 (LSTM)	(None, 100)	40800
dense_10 (Dense)	(None, 1)	101

Total params: 40,901
Trainable params: 40,901
Non–trainable params: 0

Figure 5.4   LSTM sequential model

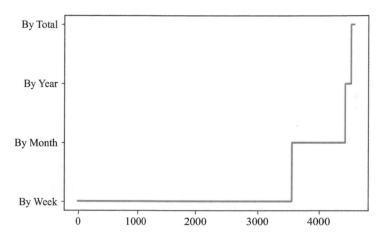

Figure 5.5   MMWR week strategies from ICU mortality dataset

Among the many issues arising in healthcare data analysis, we have extracted the features based on the death rate due to COVID-19 on various disease issues. Aspect-based rates have been identified, such as pneumonia, COVID-19, and influenza from various countries and MMWR week has also been analyzed from various states using the Keras package. The processing of text from the two columns required is tokenized. Based on the LSTM–RNN selection of parameters, the cross-validation is done by calculating the f1 score as well as optimization based on the neural network. Using the strategic aspect-based column the MMWR analysis is executed and shown in Figure 5.5.

To create a layer from the size of the token that is from input trained and test for vocabulary size, the padding along with the unique index are also indicated. When the embedded matrix is across the word length, those words can have three states – initial state as input, hidden state, and last state as cell state. Based on the batch size and initial element entry the shape is accessed with its dimension.

According to the expected accuracy and actual metric, the prediction of disease through the rate of tokenized and other tokens are used in preprocessing shown in Figure 5.6.

Multiclass feature extraction that can map the entries and fix the model layer for finding the structure. As hidden states are in the neural network and framed for knowing the activation function so that the linear layer among the two different columns can avoid the overfitting problem. Due to repeated epochs, the optimizer also gives the best accuracy along with the root mean square value of 0.84 and accuracy of 72% that are identified. Figure 5.7 shows the combination of COVID-19 death rate vs influenza deaths.

Out{194} : <matplotlib.legend.Legend at 0x13a22b9e820>

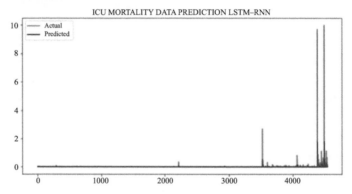

Figure 5.6   Actual vs prediction rate using LSTM–RNN

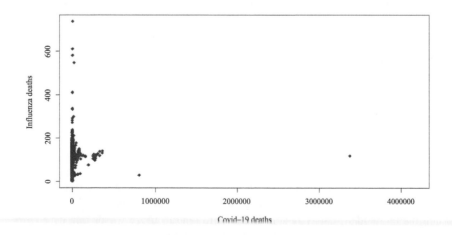

Figure 5.7   Correlation between COVID-19 deaths and influenza deaths

The training time for accepting the previously visited state with its length of the variable as input differs from the call of sequence through the function and its batch size padding. The three steps are to train the model based on the parameters, epoch size, and linear regression for understanding the huge data as much as the pre-trained vector size that is analyzed. The analysis is shown in Figure 5.8.

Supervised classification using all columns from the ICU mortality dataset, the correlation matrix was generated along with the LSTM model that can predict the accurate death rates based on the affected diseases on aspect-based learning.

ICU DATA COVID-19 DATA ANALYSIS

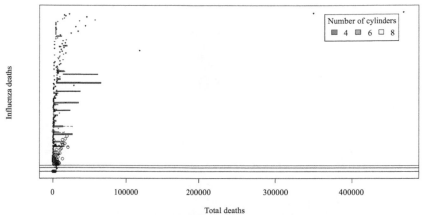

Figure 5.8   Analysis between total deaths and influenza deaths

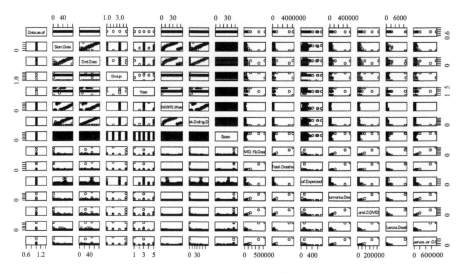

Figure 5.9   Correlation matrix of ICU mortality dataset

Based on the training and testing model the average rate of total death year-wise is shown in Figure 5.9, which are embedded features that can be used with necessary filters.

LSTM–RNN model that was implemented using COVID-19 dataset along with the rate of the affected disease as well ICU data mortality death rates was shown in Figures 5.10 and 5.11.

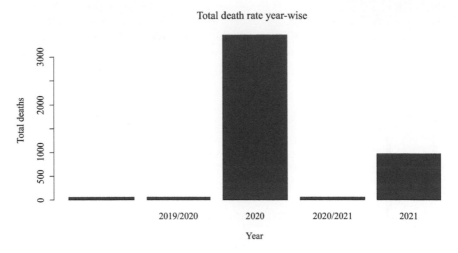

Figure 5.10   Total death rate year wise

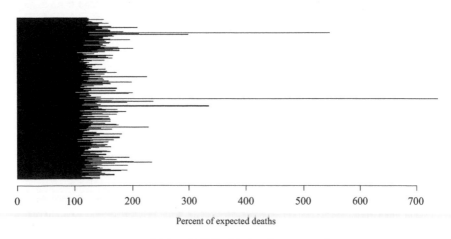

Figure 5.11   COVID-19 death rate analysis

5.5   Conclusion

This proposed work focuses on the ICU mortality COVID-19 dataset that was obtained identified from a website that provides the death rate from 2019 to 2021 till date. The LSTM–RNN model was proposed as sequential analysis for the data that are used for implementation. According to the results, they intervened using a different column to find the total deaths with the rate of death due to influenza, COVID-19, and pneumonia. The accuracy and performance shown is higher as compared to the existing systems. The activation function tanh also gives the optimized results from the various states of the structured list. Sequences of data are being analyzed and treated using NLP techniques such that in the future multiclass feature extraction can be utilized for reducing the rate of death. Overall accuracy was found to be optimum in comparison to the other structures that built models for the same data in neural networks.

References

[1] R. Catelli, F. Gargiulo, V. Casola, G. De Pietro, H. Fujita, and M. Esposito. 2020. "Crosslingual named entity recognition for clinical de-identification applied to a COVID-19 Italian data set." *Applied Soft Computing* 97(Part A): 1067792.

[2] K. Horecki and J. Mazurkiewicz. 2015. "Natural language processing methods used for automatic prediction mechanism of related phenomenon." In: L. Rutkowski, M. Korytkowski, R. Scherer, R. Tadeusiewicz, L. Zadeh, and J. Zurada (eds), *Artificial Intelligence and Soft Computing. ICAISC 2015. Lecture Notes in Computer Science*, vol. 9120. Cham: Springer.

[3] S. Bird, E. Klein, and E. Loper. 2009. Natural language processing with python: analyzing text with the natural language toolkit. O'Reilly Media, Inc., Newton, MA.

[4] J. Brownlee. 2017. Deep Learning for Natural Language Processing: Develop Deep Learning Models for Your Natural Language Problems. Machine Learning Mastery.

[5] G. Chetty and M. Chetty. 2010. "Multiclass microarray gene expression classification based on fusion of correlation features." 2010 13th International Conference on Information Fusion. https://doi.org/10.1109/icif.2010.5711915.

[6] M. Fernandes, H. Sun, A. Jain, *et al.* 2021. "Classification of the disposition of patients hospitalized with COVID-19: reading discharge summaries using natural language processing." *JMIR Medical Informatics* 9(2): e25457.

[7] Q. Chen, L. Zhang, S. Ge, W. He, and M. Zeng. 2019. Prognosis predictive value of the Oxford Acute Severity of Illness Score for sepsis: a retrospective cohort study. *PeerJ* 7: e7083.

[8] S.A. Funes, C. Flores, A.L. Davidow, S. Friedman, P. Korenblit, and P. Thomas. 2021. "Adaptation of the flu-FIT program for patient-aligned care teams: a quality improvement project." *Journal of Public Health Management and Practice: JPHMP* 27 (Suppl 3): S159–63.

[9]   J. Gao, H. Zhang, P. Lu, and Z. Wang. 2019. "An effective LSTM recurrent network to detect arrhythmia on imbalanced ECG dataset." *Journal of Healthcare Engineering.* https://doi.org/10.1155/2019/6320651.

[10]   W. Ge, J.-W. Huh, Y.R. Park, J.-H. Lee, Y.-H. Kim, and A. Turchin. 2018. "An Interpretable ICU Mortality Prediction Model Based on Logistic Regression and Recurrent Neural Networks with LSTM Units." AMIA ... Annual Symposium Proceedings / AMIA Symposium. AMIA Symposium 2018 (December), pp. 460–469.

[11]   B.W. Hesse, D. Ahern, and E. Beckjord. 2016. *Oncology Informatics: Using Health Information Technology to Improve Processes and Outcomes in Cancer.* Academic Press, London.

[12]   K. Horecki and J. Mazurkiewicz. 2015. "Natural language processing methods used for automatic prediction mechanism of related phenomenon." *Artificial Intelligence and Soft Computing.* https://doi.org/10.1007/978-3-319-19369-4_2.

[13]   M.G. Huddar, S.S. Sannakki, and V.S. Rajpurohit. 2020. "Attention-based multi-modal sentiment analysis and emotion detection in conversation using RNN." *International Journal of Interactive Multimedia and Artificial Intelligence.* https://doi.org/10.9781/ijimai.2020.07.004.

[14]   S. Kim, W. Kim, R.W. Park. 2011. "A comparison of intensive care unit mortality prediction models through the use of data mining techniques." *Healthcare Informatics Research* 17(4): 232–243.

[15]   M.D.S. Islam, H.M. Umran, S.M. Umran, and M. Karim. 2019. "Intelligent healthcare platform: cardiovascular disease risk factors prediction using attention module based LSTM." 2019 2nd International Conference on Artificial Intelligence and Big Data (ICAIBD). https://doi.org/10.1109/icaibd.2019.8836998.

[16]   M. Jenckel, S.S. Parkala, S.S. Bukhari, and A. Dengel. 2018. "Impact of training LSTM-RNN with fuzzy ground truth." Proceedings of the 7th International Conference on Pattern Recognition Applications and Methods. https://doi.org/10.5220/0006592703880393.

[17]   M. Lindholm and L. Palmborg. n.d. "Efficient use of data for LSTM mortality forecasting." *SSRN Electronic Journal.* https://doi.org/10.2139/ssrn.3805843.

[18]   R. Messina and J. Louradour. 2015. "Segmentation-free handwritten Chinese text recognition with LSTM-RNN." 2015 13th International Conference on Document Analysis and Recognition (ICDAR). https://doi.org/10.1109/icdar.2015.7333746.

[19]   K. Vani, S. Vani, and T.D. Sravani. 2014. "Multiclass unbalanced protein data classification using sequence features." 2014 IEEE Conference on Computational Intelligence in Bioinformatics and Computational Biology. https://doi.org/10.1109/cibcb.2014.6845517.

[20]   J. Parreco, A. Hidalgo, and R. Kozol. 2018. "Predicting mortality in the surgical intensive care unit using artificial intelligence and natural language processing of physician documentation." *The American Surgeon* 84(7): 1190–1194.

[21] M.G. Huddar, S.S. Sannakki, and V.S. Rajpurohit. 2020. "Multi-level context extraction and attention-based contextual inter-modal fusion for multimodal sentiment analysis and emotion classification." *International Journal of Multimedia Information Retrieval* 9: 103–112.

[22] W. Ge, J.W. Huh, Y.R. Park, J.H. Lee, Y.H. Kim, and A. Turchin. 2018. "An interpretable ICU mortality prediction model based on logistic regression and recurrent neural networks with LSTM units." *AMIA Annual Symposium Proceedings* 2018: 460–469.

[23] L.S.S. Wong and J.D. Young. 1999. "A comparison of ICU mortality prediction using the APACHE II scoring system and artificial neural networks." *Anaesthesia*, 54(11): 1048–1054.

[24] X. Zhang, M.H. Chen, and Y. Qin. 2018. "NLP-QA framework based on LSTM-RNN." 2018 2nd International Conference on Data Science and Business Analytics (ICDSBA). https://doi.org/10.1109/icdsba.2018.00065.

[25] D.-Q. Sun, C.-F. Zheng, F.-B. Lu, *et al.* 2018. "Serum lactate level accurately predicts mortality in critically ill patients with cirrhosis with acute kidney injury." *European Journal of Gastroenterology & Hepatology* 30(11): 1361–1367.

[26] S. Brownlee, K. Chalkidou, J. Doust, *et al.* 2017. "Evidence for overuse of medical services around the world." *The Lancet* 390(10090): 156–168.

[27] M. Niharika, N. Deepa, and T. Devi. 2019. "Image segmentation and detection for health care datas in deep learning." *Test Engineering and Management*, 81(11–12), pp. 5402–5407.

[28] T. Devi, K. Padmapriya, N. Deepa, and S. Kumar. 2017. "Towards secure storage of electronic health information (EHI) in cloud environment." *Journal of Advanced Research in Dynamical and Control Systems*, 9(Special Issue 17), pp. 520–531.

[29] N. Deepa and S.P. Chokkalingam. 2019. "A deep learning method on medical image dataset predicting early dementia in patients Alzheimer's disease using convolution neural network (CNN)." *International Journal of Recent Technology and Engineering*, 8(3 Special Issue), pp. 604–609.

[30] N. Deepa and S.P. Chokkalingam. 2019. "Deep convolutional neural networks (CNN) for medical image analysis." *International Journal of Engineering and Advanced Technology*, 8(3), pp. 607–610.

[31] R. Jaya Prakash and T. Devi. 2019. "Resolving presentation attack using CNN (convolutional neural network)." *Test Engineering and Management*, 81(11–12), pp. 5454–5458.

[32] G. Nagasubramanian and M. Sankayya. 2021. "Multi-variate vocal data analysis for detection of Parkinson disease using deep learning." *Neural Computing and Applications*, 33(10), 4849–4864. https://link.springer.com/article/10.1007/s00521-020-05233-7.

[33] G. Nagasubramanian, M. Sankayya, F. Al-Turjman, and G. Tsaramirsis. 2020. "Parkinson data analysis and prediction system using multi-variant stacked auto encoder." *IEEE Access*, 8, 127004–127013, doi:10.1109/ACCESS.2020.3007140.

[34]   G. Nagasubramanian, R.K. Sakthivel, R. Patan, A.H. Gandomi, M. Sankayya, and B. Balusamy. 2020. "Securing e-health records using keyless signature infrastructure blockchain technology in the cloud." *Neural Computing and Applications*, 32(3), 6392020647. https://doi.org/10.1007/s00521-018-3915-1.

[35]   S.R. Kumar, N. Gayathri, S. Muthuramalingam, B. Balamurugan, C. Ramesh, and M.K. Nallakaruppan. 2019. "Medical big data mining and processing in e-healthcare." In *Internet of Things in Biomedical Engineering*, Academic Press, London, pp. 323–339. https://doi.org/10.1016/B978-0-12-817356-5.00016-4.

[36]   P. Dhingra, N. Gayathri, S.R. Kumar, V. Singanamalla, C. Ramesh, and B. Balamurugan. 2020. "Internet of Things-based pharmaceutics data analysis." In *Emergence of Pharmaceutical Industry Growth with Industrial IoT Approach*, Academic Press, London, pp. 85–131.

[37]   S.K. Sharma, N. Gayathri, R.K. Modanval, and S. Muthuramalingam. 2021. "Artificial intelligence-based systems for combating COVID-19." In *Applications of Artificial Intelligence in COVID-19*, Springer, Singapore, pp. 19–34.

[38]   V. Kavidha, N. Gayathri, and S.R. Kumar. 2021. "AI, IoT and robotics in the medical and healthcare field." In *AI and IoT-Based Intelligent Automation in Robotics*, pp. 165–187.

Chapter 6

Applying machine learning techniques to build a hybrid machine learning model for cancer prediction

A. Anandh[1], K. Muthulakshmi[1], R. Ramya[1], A. Meenakshi[1], N. Gayathri[2] and S. Rakesh Kumar[2]

Abstract

With the arrival of the latest advancements in the area of medicine, massive amounts of information related to cancer are being collected and available on the market to the medical analysis community. However, forecasting disease is one of the foremost, fascinating, and difficult responsibilities of physicians. Machine learning methods are becoming a preferred tool for medical researchers. In our proposed method, a hybrid machine learning model (HMLM) is built using ensemble learning techniques, using stacking of models such as multilayer perceptron (MLP), decision tree (DT), support vector machine (SVM), and logistic regression (LR). Initially, preprocessing is done and then the output is passed to the feature selection method, where each feature is ranked in accordance with the dependent attribute. Once the features are selected, HMLM is used for classification. The output is then validated using a confusion matrix and also by calculating the score of the model. The proposed model performs well with the reduced number of features and gives higher accuracy than existing models.

Keywords: Feature extraction; machine learning; ensemble learning

6.1 Introduction

In recent decades, an endless evolution associated with cancer analysis has been instigated. Scientists have used a variety of approaches, such as early-stage screening, to identify cancer types before they cause symptoms. Furthermore, they

[1]Department of Computer Science and Engineering, Kamaraj College of Engineering and Technology, Madurai, Tamil Nadu, India
[2]School of Computing Science and Engineering, Galgotias University, Uttar Pradesh, India

need to develop novel methods for the prediction of cancer treatment outcomes. Significant quantities of knowledge about cancer have been gathered and made accessible to the medical analysis community with the advent of new technology in the field. However, one of the most interesting and daunting tasks for physicians is correctly predicting the disease outcome. For medical researchers, machine learning approaches have become a preferred tool. From advanced datasets, these techniques can discover and establish trends and associations between them, allowing them to accurately predict potential cancer outcomes.

Given the importance of personalized drugs and the growing trend of applying machine learning techniques to cancer prediction and prognosis, a framework of studies enabled the use of a variety of methods for cancer prediction and prognosis. Prognostic and prophetic choices are taken into account for the development of a specific treatment and direct medical care for cancer patients [1].

The three most common ailments are malignant thyroid growth, melanoma, and cancer. Family ancestry is one of the risk variables. Surveys have been conducted to find the most common cancers by Medical Council. As per this study, breast cancer was selected as the second most common cancer in women. As per the statistics issued by the Medical Council, around 1.1 million cases were recorded in 2004. Women in the age group between 30 and 40 years were most severely affected by breast cancer in some countries. From social contemplations, it is observed that breast cancer is the foremost and typically possible cancer in women. The women having the lowest breast malignancy survival rate was in the age group between 20 and 29 years.

Cancer staging is a method for determining the degree to which a cancer has spread, and is based on the following four characteristics: (1) the size of the tumor; (2) whether or not the cancer is invasive or noninvasive; (3) the neoplasm's spread through bodily fluids and nodes; and (4) the neoplasm's spread through various body components (i.e., metastasis). Stage I cancer describes a solitary cancer and stage IV cancer describes a metastatic cancer. Most cancers spread from the primary organ to other organs [2].

It is also difficult to analyze heart conditions as a result of many risk issues such as polygenic disorder, high pressure level, high sterol, irregular pulse, etc. Various methods of data processing and neural networks are used to reveal the severity of heart conditions. The severity of the disease is assessed using varied ways such as k-nearest neighbor (kNN), DT, genetic algorithm (GA), and naive Bayes (NB). The characteristics of the heart are complicated and thus any diseases should be handled cautiously. If not, it can have an effect on the heart or cause premature death. Data processing and classification plays a major part in the prediction of heart conditions and knowledge exploration.

Decision trees are often employed in predicting the accuracy of methods associated with the prediction of the progress of cardiopathy. Various strategies are available for data abstraction and information mining to predict cardiopathy progression. Diverse practices are disbursed for prediction model exploitation by involving two or more additional techniques. These integrated novel techniques are normally called hybrid strategies. A new tendency is to introduce neural networks for exploitation. This technique uses varied clinical records for making predictions such as left bundle branch block (LBBB), right bundle branch block (RBBB), normal sinus rhythm (NSR), and premature ventricular contraction (PVC) to uncover the precise illness of the patient in regard to cardiopathy. The radial basis function network (RBFN) is employed for classification, where 70% of the information is employed for training and remaining 30% is employed for classification. Within the field of drugs and analysis, a computer-aided decision support system (CADSS) was additionally introduced. A noticeable trend in many works comprises of the combination of varied knowledge, such as clinical and genomic. However, a standard downside in such works is the absence of external justification or testing related to the prognostic performance of the models.

It is obvious that the use of machine learning (ML) methods could increase the accuracy of cancer prediction, recurrence, and survival prediction. It is vital to identify this life-threatening illness at an early stage. The prediction of the type of breast cancer saves valuable time that may facilitate in dominant morbidity to an outsized extent. Prediction of breast cancer with precision can greatly aid oncologists. This could facilitate a reduction in the high cost of treatment for patients, while helping oncologists to make the correct diagnosis and treatment of the patient's disease.

As the amount of relevant knowledge is growing at a rapid rate, there is a need for techniques to analyze the data and generate critical results that can be used to diagnose diseases. Data analysis is extremely useful for analyzing and estimating medical information at the same time, which is critical in the higher cognitive phase of diagnosing. The science of having computers learn without being specifically programmed is known as machine learning. Self-driving vehicles, functional speech recognition, successful web search, and a greatly enhanced understanding of the human genome have all been made possible by machine learning in the last decade. Machine learning is now so popular that it is probably used hundreds of times a day by each of us without us even realizing it. Many scientists claim that it is the most efficient method for approaching human-level artificial intelligence.

Machine learning is a branch of artificial intelligence that involves systems that can mechanically learn and develop from experience without being explicitly programmed. The first goal is to enable computers to learn mechanically without human interference or assistance, and to control their behavior as a result.

Much of the data processing and machine learning techniques for breast cancer detection and classification have been established in recent decades [3–5], with three main stages: preprocessing, feature extraction, and classification. Preprocessing helps to increase the visibility of peripheral areas and intensity distribution, and a variety of other techniques are used to aid perception and analysis throughout this phase. Feature extraction is an important step in the identification of breast cancer because it aids in the differentiation of benign and malignant tumors.

Segmentation extracts image properties such as smoothness, coarseness, depth, and regularity [6]. With the aid of ML algorithms, several studies have attempted to identify the breast cancer class. For example, Zheng *et al.* [7] used K-means rule and SVM to classify breast cancers. Artificial intelligence (AI) enables computers to make predictions based on massive amounts of data [8] and so eliminates the need for people to routinely code and analyze data in order to find a solution.

6.2   Literature review

For the clinical management of patients, early analysis and prediction of cancer type is mandatory in cancer investigation. Cancer is a heterogeneous illness that has many different categories. Artificial neural networks (ANNs), SVMs, Bayesian networks (BNs) and DTs are the different methods that are extensively used in cancer investigations in order to build predictive models, resulting in an effective investigation. Konstantina Kourou *et al.* gave an analysis of topical ML methods in the modeling of cancer advancement [9]. The predictive models were developed on diverse input features and data samples using supervised ML techniques.

Women's physical and emotional well-being is affected by breast cancer. The manual elucidation of the disease using computed tomography (CT) images is tedious. Santhosh Kumar *et al.* utilized an arrangement calculation which would order the malignant growth images quickly and viably [10]. The information pre-handling stage was concentrated more to enhance the unpolished information and the last informational index was set up. This final information was given as input to the kNN classification algorithm to predict the cancer progression in the early phases.

A huge volume of data is generated by the healthcare domain daily. ML has been found to be effective in supporting decision-making processes and predictions from that data. By using ML techniques, Mohan *et al.* proposed an innovative technique that aids in learning noteworthy features, resulting in refining of the accuracy for the prediction of cardiovascular illness [11]. Different combinations of features have been introduced by the prediction model and several known classification techniques have been used. A model for predicting heart disease using Hybrid Random Forest with a Linear Model (HRFLM) was introduced and achieved a performance level of 88.7%.

Abdeldjouad *et al.* proposed a novel hybrid approach for the prediction of cardiovascular illness using various ML techniques such as LR, Adaptive Boosting (AdaBoostM1), Multi-Objective Evolutionary Fuzzy Classifier (MOEFC), Fuzzy Unordered Rule Induction (FURIA), Genetic Fuzzy System-LogitBoost (GFS-LB) and Fuzzy Hybrid Genetic Based Machine Learning (FH-GBML) [12]. A comparison study was given for each classifier in order to select the best classifier for accurate prediction of the cardiovascular illness. Weka and Keel tools were used to carry out the performance evaluations of the ML techniques.

Liu *et al.* introduced a hybrid approach based on ML techniques to choose a reduced number of genes that are informative to improve the accuracy of classification [13]. The highest ranked genes were identified by feature filtering algorithms and core cancer genes were selected by hierarchical clustering and collapsing dense clustering. This method was proficient in choosing a relatively lower number of core cancer genes. It was used in an empirical study while making high-accuracy predictions. Using systems biology analysis, the biological impor-tance of these genes was assessed [14,15].

Megha Rathi *et al.* proposed a hybrid methodology for developing a tool that can be used for the prediction of breast cancer with the support of ML techniques [16]. The existence of bioinformatics tools for predicting a target is very scarce and rare. The performances of ML algorithms were analyzed to predict the target based on certain key attributes. In order to discover the best classifier that could be used in the breast cancer domain, the Minimum Redundancy Maximum Relevance (MRMR) feature selection procedure along with four diverse classifiers were used. SVM, FT (Function Tree), End Meta, and NB were used to carry out the assessment of different parameters such as accuracy, root mean square error, mean absolute error, kappa statistics, sensi-tivity, and specificity. This aids oncologists in diagnosing the breast cancer type and improves the chances of identifying those at risk of breast cancer.

A rule-based classification with ML methods was proposed by Montazeri *et al.* to predict the survival rate for different types of breast cancer [17]. A dataset with eight features was used, which included the archives of 900 patients where 876 patients (97.3%) were females and 24 (2.7%) were males. For breast cancer pre-diction, NB, Trees Random Forest (TRF), 1-Nearest Neighbor (1NN), AdaBoost (AD), SVM, Radial Basis Function Network (RBFN), and MLP methods with a 10-fold cross-validation technique were used in building the model.

In radiation oncology, convolutional neural networks (CNNs) were used for lung cancer recognition and segmentation using CT images. CNNs were chosen as the primary tool for cancer prediction in digital pathology. A computer-assisted prediction methodology to stratify stage III colon cancer was proposed by Dan Jiang *et al.* using CNNs and ML classifiers [18]. Survival was predicted based on the hematoxylin and eosin (H&E)-stained whole tissue slides. The ML classifier selected for prediction was validated by means of histological images from the Cancer Genome Atlas (TCGA) database.

Shikha Agrawal *et al.* showed the effectiveness of neural network-based technologies for cancer detection [19]. Most neural network architectures such as Perceptron, MLP, Adaptive Resonance Theory (ART1), and Probabilistic Neural Network (PNN) showed remarkable results for the classification of tumor cells in their survey. The results of the different neural network architectures can be increased by properly setting the parameters in the network. Even though these neural network architectures provide good classification results, the time taken for training is extremely high. Most of the neural network techniques were hybridized with optimization algorithms such as Particle Swarm Optimization (PSO) for the improvement of accuracy. The optimization algorithms achieved dimensionality reduction and reduced search space, decreasing the training time. They also improved the accuracy of the results by increasing the number of neurons present in the hidden layer. Moreover, various learning rules were used in training to enhance the accuracy of the results.

Mohammad R. Mohebian proposed a method for predicting the 5-year recur-rence rate of breast cancer [20]. Clinicopathologic features were analyzed and significant features were chosen by means of statistical methods for 579 cancer patients. They were additionally refined by PSO. With the correctly chosen categorical features and proper weight interval measurement scale, features were chosen by PSO algorithm. The result of Hybrid Predictor of Breast Cancer Recurrence (HPBCR) was evaluated based on holdout and four-fold cross-validation. For comparison, three different classifiers such as SVM, decision trees, and multilayer perceptron neural network were used.

Bandyopadhyay *et al.* proposed an automatic tool that uses potent causes of cancer as input and finds patients with higher chances of being affected by this illness [21]. A neural network classifier with k-fold cross-validation technique was recommended as a tool for prediction. Later, this was compared with an alternative standard classifier called Gradient Boosting for improving the performance prediction. By analyzing the potent causes of lung cancer, they accomplished a classification model for disease prediction with an accuracy rate of 95%.

Habib Dhahri *et al.* carried out a study to build a system using genetic programming and ML that distinguishes between breast tumors that are benign and those that are malignant [22]. They aimed to optimize the learning algorithm. Genetic programming was applied to choose the significant features and classifier parameter values. The performance was analyzed based on various parameters such as sensitivity, specificity, precision, accuracy, and ROC curves. They proved that genetic programming can be used to recommend a model that combines preprocessing and classification.

Fatima *et al.* presented a comparative analysis of various techniques such as ML, deep learning, and data mining to predict breast cancer [23]. Different techniques were used for different situations depending on the tools and datasets used. They started with the types, indications, and causes of breast cancer. They provided an analysis of various techniques such as ML, ensembles, and deep learning. They also discussed issues such as dataset availability, and unbalanced positive and negative data [24,25].

Cruz *et al.* identified various learning methods with respect to the different kinds of ML methods that were used, training data that were integrated, end-point predictions that were made, and types of cancers that were studied [4]. These learning methods were used to predict susceptibility to cancer. They showed that the evolving group of ML classifiers outweighs the ANN.

For predicting breast cancer, Javed Mehedi Shamrat *et al.* used different ML classifiers [26–28]. They evaluated six different supervised classification algorithms, SVM, NB, kNN, Random Forest (RF), DT, and LR, to predict breast cancer early. They evaluated the performance based on various parameters such as sensitivity, specificity, accuracy, and f1 measure, and indicated that SVM attained the maximum performance with an accuracy of 97.07%, whereas NB and RF achieved the second best performance. They reduced the occurrence of breast cancer by developing an ML-based predictive system for early diagnosis.

David *et al.* proposed a hybrid approach for the diagnosis of breast cancer that reduced the dimension of features using Linear Discriminant Analysis (LDA), and then SVM was used for prediction using the reduced set of features [29]. They applied the machine learning classification algorithms such as SVM with radial basis kernel, ANN and NB to Wisconsin Diagnostic Breast Cancer (WDBC) dataset. They integrated the ML methods with feature selection methods to find the suitable approach. Jensen *et al.* conducted a review of techniques to select features based on rough set theory. Moreover, they highlighted a feature grouping technique based on rough sets [30,31]. This is useful in applications involving vast feature sets, which are difficult to process further.

Patra *et al.* studied different ML classifiers to predict lung cancer using the dataset available in the UCI Machine Learning repository as benign and malignant [32]. They showed that the RBF classifier provided an accuracy of 81.25% for the prediction of lung cancer.

An intelligent predictive system was proposed by Muhammad *et al.* to identify and diagnose cardiac disease [33]. Four feature selection algorithms were applied to remove the data that were irrelevant and noisy. The output of various feature selection algorithms together with different classifiers were analyzed using different performance evaluation metrics such as sensitivity, specificity, accuracy, area under the ROC curve (AUC), F1 score, Matthews Correlation Coefficient (MCC), and receiver operating characteristic (ROC) curve. Both the full and optimal features spaces were evaluated. In the feature space that was highly varied, there was a boost in performance. For the Extra Trees (ET) classifier, the p-value and chi-square were also calculated together with the feature selection technique.

Ensemble methods can be either homogeneous or heterogeneous. Homogeneous ensemble methods [34] use the same type of classifiers that are built using different data; whereas heterogeneous ensemble methods use two or more types of classifiers that are built using the same data. Ensemble techniques rely on supervised learning that provide good assessments of the ideas behind certain hypothesis [1]. The collective model works accurately when the results are combined from each of the models. Because of these advantages, our proposed system uses a hybrid machine learning model.

Combined global and local semantic feature–based image retrieval analysis with interactive feedback was suggested by Anandh *et al.* to identify the various diseases with the help of medical image related data sets [35]. The combination of more features was used in this system to retrieve more accurate results. Two similar images that are semantically different are identified using this approach.

Classification problem was focused by Begum *et al.* with k Nearest Neighbour (kNN) algorithm is recommended to classify the dataset [36]. For clustering and classification, the kNN is one of the best algorithms. This algorithm performed very well for different kinds of dataset. In this system, three different feature selection algorithm such as Consistency Based Feature Selection (CBFS), Fuzzy Preference Based Rough Set (FPRS) and Kernelized Fuzzy Rough Set (KFRS) were used for better classification.

In machine learning, the input feature set must be analyzed to select the best features [37] whereas in deep learning, the features are automatically selected by using the combination of CNN and transfer learning [38].

6.3   Dataset description

The cancer patient dataset has dimension of 1000×25 (the details of 1000 persons, each having 25 attributes) based on which a person can be predicted as high,

Table 6.1   Dataset description

S. no	Attribute name	Description	Range of values
1	Patient Id	Unique id assigned to each patient	P1 to P1000
2	Age	Patient's age	14 to 73
3	Gender	Gender of each person	Male, 1; female, 2
4	Air pollution	Amount of air quality	1 to 8
5	Alcohol use	Usage of alcohol by the patient	1 to 8
6	Dust allergy	Patients that are allergic to dust	1 to 8
7	Occupational hazards	Hazards that are present in occupational areas	1 to 8
8	Genetic risk	Rate of causing cancer due to genetic risk	1 to 7
9	Chronic lung disease	Long-term breathing problems in premature babies	1 to 7
10	Balanced diet	Supplies of nutrients your body needs to work effectively	1 to 7
11	Obesity	A condition characterized by irregular or extreme gathering of fat	1 to 7
12	Smoking	Practice in which a material is burnt and the subsequent smoke is inhaled in to be tasted and immersed into the bloodstream	1 to 8
13	Passive smoker	Involuntary inhalation of smoke from cigarettes or other tobacco products smoked by other people	1 to 8
14	Chest pain	Discomfort that one feels between the neck and upper abdomen	1 to 9
15	Coughing of blood	Release of blood while coughing	1 to 9
16	Fatigue	Described as an overall feeling of tiredness or lack of energy	1 to 9
17	Weight loss	A sudden loss in weight	1 to 8
18	Shortness of breath	A prickly condition that makes it difficult to get air completely into the lungs	1 to 9
19	Wheezing	Difficulty in breathing	1 to 8
20	Swallowing difficulty	A condition in which a person's ability to eat and drink is disrupted	1 to 8
21	Clubbing of fingernails	The fingernails appear broader and rounder	1 to 9
22	Frequent cold	Cold occurs frequently in regular intervals	1 to 7
23	Dry cough	A cough not accompanied by phlegm production	1 to 7
24	Snoring	Sound of a person's breathing while they are asleep	1 to 7
25	Level	Level of patient, whether cancer will occur or not	High, medium, and low

medium, or low risk of developing cancer. Each attribute indicates the lifestyle of the person in a row such as age, diet, obesity, active smoker, passive smoker, etc. These attributes are ranked on a scale of 1–9. The database is taken from https://www.kaggle.com/rishidamarla/cancer-patients-data. A full explanation of the dataset is given in Table 6.1.

6.4 System methodology

The cancer dataset is analyzed to check if it has any null value, missing value, or outliers. The preprocessed dataset is then passed to a feature selection method, where each feature is ranked in accordance with the dependent attribute, Level. Once the features are selected for classification, it is divided into two chunks for training and testing in the ratio 1:4. The training part of the data is used in creating the model. The Hybrid Machine Learning Model (HMLM) is used for classification. The output is then validated using a confusion matrix and also by calculating the score of the model. The overall system architecture is shown in Figure 6.1.

HMLM is basically a combination of different ML models, which are used to increase the performance of the model. It combines the characteristics of two or more ML models and hence the overall performance is increased and the prediction is more accurate.

6.4.1 Dataset analysis

The dataset is analyzed; the bar graph as shown in Figure 6.2 illustrates the number of patients in the dataset who have low, medium, or high risk of having cancer.

As indicated, the data are fairly balanced; the dataset can be broken down further by gender as shown in Figure 6.3.

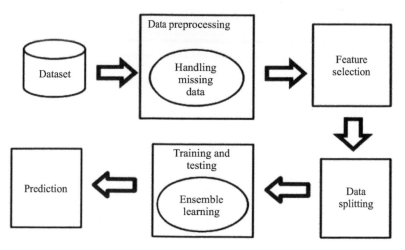

Figure 6.1 System architecture

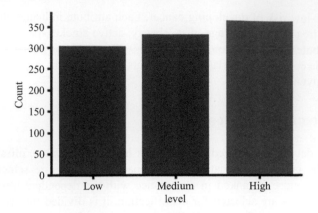

Figure 6.2   Analysis of dataset by level

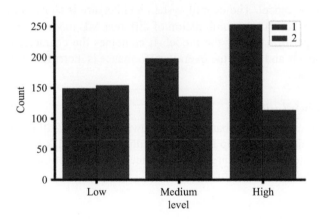

Figure 6.3   Analysis of dataset by gender

It can be observed that there is a higher representation for gender 1 than gender 2. Further, the dataset is analyzed to check if there is a correlation between some of the data, as shown in Figure 6.4. It is observed that alcohol usage and fatigue are related to the level of cancer risk.

There are two different clusters for low and high levels by alcohol use and fatigue while a medium level is a combination of both, as shown in Figure 6.5.

Finally, to select features, the F-ratio score of features is generated as shown in Figure 6.6 to determine which to use for machine learning.

All the features that scored over 200 are selected as they show the least redundancy. Finally, 13 features are selected and a new data frame is created for further processing. The dataset is then divided into the training and test sets; and preprocessing of the dataset is also carried out.

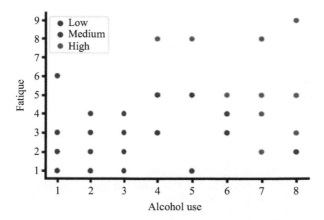

Figure 6.4   Correlation between alcohol use and fatigue

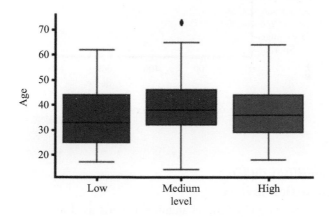

Figure 6.5   Clusters for level by alcohol use and fatigue

6.4.2   Splitting of the dataset and preprocessing

The dataset is split so that the scalar model is trained and tested with an unknown (test) dataset. A total of 25% of the data are saved for testing. Next, the data are scaled to reduce the effect of outliers when modeling later using formula (6.1):

$$X' = X - \mu * \sigma \tag{6.1}$$

where X' is scaled output of X, μ indicates mean, and σ indicates standard deviation of the data.

6.4.3   Training and testing the dataset using HMLM

A hybrid machine model is built using ensemble learning technique, using stacking of models such as MLP, decision tree, SVM, and logistic regression. The trained model is tested with the remaining 25% of the test dataset.

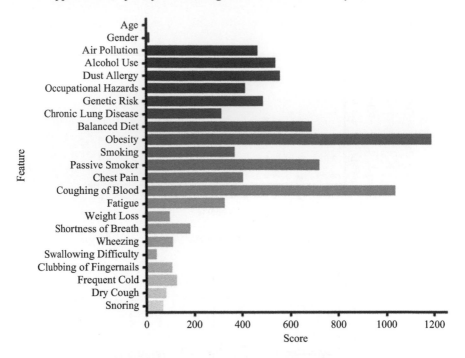

Figure 6.6   F-ratio score of features

6.4.4   Evaluation metrics

6.4.4.1   Confusion matrix

A confusion matrix is one of the evaluation metrics used to describe the classification accuracy of the trained model using the test dataset. Each row in the confusion matrix shows the actual true labels in the test set. The columns in the matrix give the prediction labels from the classifier.

- **True positives (TP):** The numbers of true values correctly predicted as true (true) by the classifier.
- **True negatives (TN):** The classifier correctly predicted as "no disease," if no disease is found.
- **False positives (FP):** The classifier predicted as "disease is true," but the actual value is false (actually the disease is not present) ("type I error").
- **False negatives (FN):** The classifier predicted as "no disease," but the actual value is true (actually the disease is true) ("type II error").

6.4.4.2   Precision

The precision is the proportion of correct number of predictions in the list of all returned results by the search engine of the trained model. It can be easily calculated using the values present in the confusion matrix with the help of formula (6.2):

$$\text{Precision} = (\text{True Positive})/(\text{True Positive} + \text{False Positive}) \tag{6.2}$$

6.4.4.3   Recall or sensitivity

The recall is the proportion of the correct number of predictions returned by the search engine of the trained model out of the total number of correct predictions that could have been returned. It can be easily calculated using the values present in the confusion matrix with the help of formula (6.3):

$$\text{Recall} = (\text{True Positive})/(\text{True Positive} + \text{False Negative}) \tag{6.3}$$

6.4.4.4   F1 score

The F1 score is the classification accuracy score, which ranges from 0.0 to 1.0. The higher the score, the greater is the prediction accuracy. It is calculated using the weighted average of precision and recall. The formula for calculating f1 score is given in formula (6.4)

$$\text{F1} = 2 * (\text{Precision} * \text{Recall})/(\text{Precision} + \text{Recall}) \tag{6.4}$$

6.4.5   Output interpretation

Figure 6.7 shows the confusion matrix that is obtained for our proposed model. From the figure, the different values are inferred as follows.

- TP = 91
- TN = (85 + 0 + 74 + 0) = 159

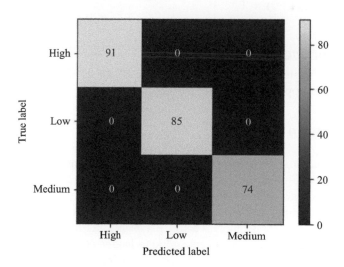

Figure 6.7   Confusion matrix

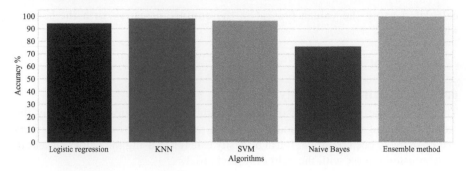

Figure 6.8   Comparison with existing ML models

Table 6.2   Comparison with existing ML models

S. no.	Model	Accuracy
1	Logistic regression	94.00%
2	k-Nearest neighbors	98.00%
3	Support vector machine	96.00%
4	Naive Bayes	76.00%
5	Proposed model (HMLM)	100.00%

- FP = (0+0) = 0
- FN = (0+0) = 0
- Precision = 91/(91+0) = 1
- Recall = 91/(91+0) = 1
- F1-score = 1

6.4.6   Result analysis

Figure 6.8 and Table 6.2 present a comparison of the existing machine learning models with the proposed model.

6.5   Conclusion

The accurate diagnosis of cancer is of paramount importance since cancer deaths represent about one-third of all deaths globally. The accurate classification helps the patient to undergo the most appropriate treatment. The hybrid machine model is built using an ensemble learning technique, using stacking of models such as MLP classifier, decision tree, support vector machine, and logistic regression. The development of the model using an ensemble technique paved the way to the design of a new model. The proposed model helps in reducing the mortality due to cancer. This model will help in predicting cancer diseases more accurately. The model performs better with a reduced number of features and gives higher accuracy than existing models. The model has been evaluated and an accuracy of 100% was achieved in the dataset used. This system is capable of predicting whether a patient has cancer or not, using hybrid machine learning methods (HMLMs). This system improves accuracy; predicting patients with cancer at earlier stages and better enabling control of the disease.

6.6   Future work

The prediction of cancer could be further enhanced and expanded by the implementation of real-time collection of required datasets using light-weight wearable devices that monitor cancer cells. An early alert system should be set up to notify the relevant healthcare personnel if any abnormality occurs. Additionally, different feature selection methods can be combined to provide a wider perception of the important features to increase the performance of cancer disease prediction.

References

[1] Abdar M and Makarenkov V, "CWV-BANN-SVM ensemble learning classifier for an accurate diagnosis of breast cancer", *Measurement*, vol. 146, pp. 557–570, 2019.

[2] de Martel A, Ferlay J, Franceschi S, *et al.*, "Global burden of cancers attributable to infections in 2018: a review and synthetic analysis", *The Lancet Oncology*, vol. 13, no. 6, pp. 607–615, 2019.

[3] Akay MF, "Support vector machines combined with feature selection for breast cancer diagnosis", *Expert Systems with Applications*, vol. 36, no. 2, pp. 3240–3247, 2009.

[4] Cruz AJ and Wishart DS, "Applications of machine learning in cancer prediction and prognosis", *Cancer Informatics*, vol. 2, pp. 59–77, 2006.

[5] Valvano G, Santini G, and Martini N, "Convolutional neural networks for the segmentation of microcalcification in mammography imaging," *Journal of Healthcare Engineering*, vol. 2019, pp. 1–9, 2019.

[6] Salembier P and Garrido L, "Binary partition tree as an efficient representation for image processing, segmentation, and information retrieval," *IEEE Transactions on Image Processing*, vol. 9, no. 4, pp. 561–576, 2000.

[7] Zheng B, Yoon SW and Lam SS, "Breast cancer diagnosis based on feature extraction using a hybrid of K-means and support vector machine algorithms", *Expert Systems with Applications*, vol. 41, no. 4, pp. 1476–1482, 2014.

[8] Polley M-YC, Freidlin B, Korn EL, Conley BA, Abrams JS, and McShane LM, "Statistical and practical considerations for clinical evaluation of predictive biomarkers", *JNCI: Journal of the National Cancer Institute*, vol. 105, no. 22, pp. 1677–1683, 2013.

[9]   Kourou K, Exarchos TP, Exarchos KP, Karamouzis MV, and Fotiadis DI, "Machine learning applications in cancer prognosis and prediction", *Computational and Structural Biotechnology Journal*, vol. 13, pp. 8–17, 2015.

[10]   Santhosh Kumar B, Daniya T, and Ajayan J, *"Breast Cancer Prediction Using Machine Learning Algorithms"*, vol. 29, pp. 7819–7828, 2020.

[11]   Mohan S, Thirumalai CS, and Srivastava G, "Effective heart disease prediction using hybrid machine learning techniques", *IEEE Access*, vol. 7, pp. 81542–81554, 2019.

[12]   Abdeldjouad FZ, Brahami M, and Matta N, "A hybrid approach for heart disease diagnosis and prediction using machine learning techniques", In: Jmaiel M, Mokhtari M, Abdulrazak B, Aloulou H, Kallel S (eds), *The Impact of Digital Technologies on Public Health in Developed and Developing Countries, ICOST* 2020, Lecture Notes in Computer Science, vol. 12157, Springer, Cham, 2020.

[13]   Liu YX, Zhang NN, He Y, and Lun LJ, "Prediction of core cancer genes using a hybrid of feature selection and machine learning methods", *Genetics and Molecular Research Journal*, vol. 14, no. 3, pp. 8871–8882, 2015.

[14]   Sharma SK, Gayathri N, Modanval RK, and Muthuramalingam S. *Artificial Intelligence-Based Systems for Combating COVID-19. In Applications of Artificial Intelligence in COVID-19*. Springer, Singapore, 2021, pp. 19–34.

[15]   Kavidha V, Gayathri N, and Kumar SR, AI, IoT and robotics in the medical and healthcare field. In *AI and IoT-Based Intelligent Automation in Robotics*, 2021, pp. 165–187.

[16]   Rathi M, and Pareek V, "Hybrid approach to predict breast cancer using machine learning techniques", *International Journal of Computer Science Engineering (IJCSE)*, vol. 5, no. 3, pp. 125–136, 2016.

[17]   Montazeri M, and Beigzadeh A, "Machine learning models in breast cancer survival prediction", *Technol Health Care*, vol. 24, no. 1, pp. 31–42, 2016.

[18]   Jiang D, Liao J, and Duan H, "A machine learning-based prognostic predictor for stage III colon cancer", *Science Reports* 10, p. 10333, 2020.

[19]   Agrawal S, and Agrawal J, "Neural network techniques for cancer prediction: a survey", *Procedia Computer Science*, vol. 60, pp. 769–774, 2015.

[20]   Mohebian MR, Marateb HR, Mansourian M, Mañanas MA, and Mokarian F, "A hybrid computer-aided-diagnosis system for prediction of breast cancer recurrence (HPBCR) using optimized ensemble learning", *Computational and Structural Biotechnology Journal*, vol. 15, pp. 75–85, 2017.

[21]   Bandyopadhyay S, and Dutta S, "Early lung cancer prediction using neural network with cross-validation", *Asian Journal of Research in Infectious Diseases*, vol. 4, no. 4, pp. 15–22, 2020.

[22]   Dhahri H, Al Maghayreh E, Mahmood A, Elkilani W, and Nagi MF, "Automated breast cancer diagnosis based on machine learning algorithms", *Journal of Healthcare Engineering*, vol. 2019, no. 4253641, 2019.

[23] Fatima N, Liu L, Hong S, and Ahmed H, "Prediction of breast cancer, comparative review of machine learning techniques, and their analysis," *IEEE Access*, vol. 8, pp. 150360–150376, 2020.

[24] Kumar SR, Gayathri N, Muthuramalingam S, Balamurugan B, Ramesh C, and Nallakaruppan MK. Medical big data mining and processing in e-healthcare. In *Internet of Things in Biomedical Engineering*. Academic Press, London, 2019, pp. 323–339. https://doi.org/10.1016/B978-0-12-817356-5.00016-4

[25] Dhingra, P, Gayathri, N, Kumar, SR, Singanamalla, V, Ramesh, C, and Balamurugan, B, Internet of Things-based pharmaceutics data analysis. In *Emergence of Pharmaceutical Industry Growth with Industrial IoT Approach*. Academic Press, London, 2020, pp. 85–131.

[26] Javed Mehedi Shamrat FM, Raihan A, Sazzadur Rahman AKM, Mahmud I, and Akter R, "An analysis on breast disease prediction using machine learning approaches", *International Journal of Scientific & Technology Research*, vol. 9, no. 2, pp. 2450–2455, 2020.

[27] Nagasubramanian G and Sankayya M. "Multi-variate vocal data analysis for detection of Parkinson's disease using deep learning", *Neural Computing and Applications*, vol. 33, no. 10, pp. 4849–4864, 2021. https://link.springer.com/article/10.1007/s00521-020-05233-7.

[28] Nagasubramanian G, Sankayya M, Al-Turjman F and Tsaramirsis G, "Parkinson data analysis and prediction system using multi-variant stacked auto encoder", *IEEE Access*, vol. 8, pp. 127004–127013, 2020, 10.1109/ACCESS.2020.3007140.

[29] Omondiagbe DA, Veeramani S, and Amandeep S, "Machine learning classification techniques for breast cancer diagnosis", IOP Conference Series: Materials Science and Engineering, 2019.

[30] Jensen Rand Shen Q, "Semantics preserving dimensionality reduction. Rough and fuzzy rough-based approaches", *IEEE Transaction of Knowledge and Data Engineering*, vol. 16, pp. 1457, 2004.

[31] Nagasubramanian G, Sakthivel RK, Patan R, Gandomi AH, Sankayya M, and Balusamy B, "Securing e-health records using keyless signature infrastructure blockchain technology in the cloud", *Neural Computing and Applications*, vol. 32, no. 3, pp. 639–647, 2020. https://doi.org/10.1007/s00521-018-3915-1.

[32] Patra R, "Prediction of lung cancer using machine learning classifier", In: Chaubey N, Parikh S, Amin K. (eds) *Computing Science, Communication and Security*. COMS2 2020, Communications in Computer and Information Science, vol. 1235, Springer, Singapore, 2020.

[33] Muhammad Y, Tahir M, and Hayat M, "Early and accurate detection and diagnosis of heart disease using intelligent computational model", *Science Report*, vol. 10, p. 19747, 2020.

[34] Hosni M, Abnane I, Idri A, De Gea JMC, and Fernández Alemán JL, "Reviewing ensemble classification methods in breast cancer", *Computer Methods and Programs in Biomedicine*, vol. 177, pp. 89–112, 2019.

[35] Anandh A, Mala K, and Suresh Babu, R, "Combined global and local semantic feature–based image retrieval analysis with interactive feedback", *Measurement and Control*, vol. 53, no. 1–2, pp. 3–17, 2020.

[36] Begum S, Chakraborty D, and Sarkar R, "Data classification using feature selection and K-nearest neighbour machine learning approach", IEEE International Conference on Computational Intelligence and Communication Networks (CICN), 2015.

[37] Ramya R, Mala K, and Sindhuja C, "Student engagement identification based on facial expression analysis using 3D video/image of students", *Taga Journal*, vol. 14, pp. 2446–2454, 2018.

[38] Ramya R, Mala K, and Selva Nidhyananthan S, "3D facial expression recognition using multi-channel deep learning framework", *Circuits Syst Signal Process*, vol. 39, pp. 789–804, 2020.

Chapter 7

AI in healthcare: challenges and opportunities

C. Deepanjali[1], P. Bhuvanashree[1], D. Kavitha[1] and Mithileysh Sathiyanarayanan[2]

Abstract

Artificial intelligence (AI) is the part of computer science which focuses on developing automated advanced technologies that can execute specific tasks that would normally require human knowledge. AI is a particular concept of science with many unique methods and advanced machine learning techniques which has effected fundamental changes in nearly almost all fields of the technology sector. AI can be classified into two parts, the first is narrow AI, which is always based on executing tasks in the correct way, and although certain systems appear smart, there are some constraints and limitations. The second is artificial general intelligence (AGI) which describes a device that has intellectual ability and which can use that ability to make improvements, in much the same was as a human. Healthcare 4.0 is about collecting massive quantities of data and bringing them to use in apps, aiming for better health business decisions as well as huge cost reductions and control of those costs. Virtual assistants can respond to questions, track patients, and have fast responses because they are available 24/7. Today, many personal assistant apps allow for more contact among patients and healthcare providers during doctors' visits, reducing the risk of readmission to the clinic or repeated medical visits. The world has been struggling greatly with the COVID-19 pandemic, although each step of advanced technical knowledge and creative problem solving is bringing us closer to ending this global situation. Both machine learning and artificial intelligence are helping to solve the problems caused by COVID-19 and to rid society of this pandemic. Machine learning allows advanced technologies to imitate humans, and consumes vast amounts of data in order to recognize technical patterns and perceptions rapidly. Institutions were fast to implement machine learning abilities in the battle against COVID-19 in many ways, including scaling consumer interactions, identifying how COVID-19 grows, and speeding up testing and diagnosis.

Many of these trends are converging, including data collection, increased AI usage, and the implementation of web apps. As a result of the emphasis on

[1]SRM Institute of Science and Technology, Ramapuram Campus, Chennai, India
[2]Innovation & Research, MIT Square, London, UK

implementation and transformation, health services are becoming much more reliable. Such programs will be capable of transforming multiple stages of medication, as well as smart devices and the change to personalized medicine (PM). We address herein a number of AI challenges and opportunities in healthcare, which could help experts and stakeholders in taking the best possible decisions.

Keywords: Healthcare; artificial intelligence; Industry 4.0; Healthcare 4.0; cyberphysical system

7.1   Introduction

Healthcare 4.0 is the processing of massive quantities of data as well as the transmission of that information to machines that can help clinical administrators meet their obligations to provide improved results. This enables exceptional efficiency and budget management. Computer systems, communication, data, protocols, biosensing, and bioactuators are all part of Healthcare 4.0 in the cyberphysical system (HCPS). The HCPS model allows for the observation of working mechanisms and the use of biosensors to track clinicians before, during, and after surgeries. Furthermore, HCPSs include bioactuators that carry out the planned treatments, as well as many other innovative personalized medicine treatments. A biosensor detects some vital external and internal patient conditions and transmits the information to a decision-making unit (DMU). Biosensors can be used in a variety of products, including mobile phones and wearable technology. When signals are transmitted by the DMU, they are linked to the patient's clinical background, allowing a series of actions to be taken to enable treatment of a given scenario.

Content-based image retrieval (CBIR) devices can integrate and provide access to data through digital and sentiment analysis images, that can help in medical reviews and personal decision-making. Military devices that use CBIR makes use of measurable knowledge and experiences in image data. This requires only images that look similar to the provided original image. It was created to aid in the management of increasingly large biomedical image collections and to fund research, learning, and healthcare. We are currently confronted with numerous problems in healthcare-related projects and services for monitoring doctors and healthcare teams in order to improve medications without disrupting treatment. The healthcare industry will be pushed further into the new era as technology advances. Clinical decision support systems (CDSSs) are among the first interesting technological implementations, concentrating in determining the condition of the patient based on their symptoms [1].

7.1.1   *Progressive way of life: Healthcare 4.0*

The advent of Healthcare 4.0 is currently on-going. These innovations, combined with real-time data processing, have increased the use of AI and an overlay of obscure user interfaces, are coming together. Healthcare can be more predictive and personalized by relying on teamwork, coherence, and integration. Healthcare 4.0 is a hospital operational implementation and management paradigm influenced by Industry 4.0. To facilitate the personalized experience of healthcare for patients, staff, and explicit and implicit caregivers, Healthcare 4.0 requires incremental virtual machines. Figure 7.1 shows how a robotic arms are used in surgery. There are some distinct technologies which contain advanced robotic arms for handling cameras and surgical tools. Surgery using a robots is more accurate for some complicated procedures compared with manual techniques [2].

Technology suitable for multiple systems and big data, algorithms, and artifacts can be digitized using a temporal framework with the support of the CPS paradigm. Processing requires real-time monitoring of space constraints windows of the actual life and therefore facilitates customized and effective medication therapy. This customization of healthcare involves the extensive use of CPSs, cloud technology, expanded advanced Internet of Things (IoT) and Internet of Everything (IoE) technology, covering equipment, utilities, individuals, and 5G connectivity networks.

The following sections elaborate on the evolution and developments of Industry 4.0 in AI in healthcare. They also discuss the challenges and opportunities of using AI in healthcare. During the early days, doctors became experts in some particular challenges of various human body parts. Some damaged body parts would be removed and replaced with artificial implants. Figure 7.2 shows how Healthcare 4.0 demonstrates the concept of innovative surgical sciences (ISS) [3]. The advancement of healthcare is entering its fifth stage, known as Healthcare 5.0. This is a transition to digital systems in healthcare with more advanced artificial

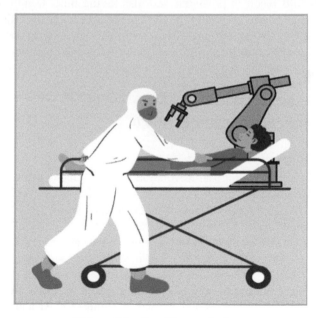

Figure 7.1 Intelligent devices

Figure 7.2   Surgery 4.0

intelligence, IoT, and fifth-generation technologies. The advancement of automated technologies would result is precision and also saving time. Healthcare 5.0 considers customers as having a dominant role and shifts business operating models to respond to customer-based systems, from customer relationship management to customer-managed relationships, focusing on the individual mind set. The fifth step in healthcare services is moving away from patient-centered care and toward customer-centric care.

7.2   Development of Healthcare 4.0

7.2.1   Evolution of Industry 4.0

In the mid-1700s, the first Industrial Revolution occurred. During that time, production was developed by concentrating on menial work undertaken by workers and supported by domestic animals to a more automated mode of employment carried out by individuals with the use of water and heat engines as well as other forms of manufacturing equipment. The Second Revolution took place during the early part of the 20th century when a number of changes that transformed civilization were triggered by advancements in heavy industry, electronics, and fuel. Railways increased greatly with the manufacture of cost-effective steel and much more industrial equipment was developed [4–7].

The evolution of Industry 4.0 is shown in Figure 7.3. The third technology breakthrough began in the 1950s and introduced semiconductor materials,

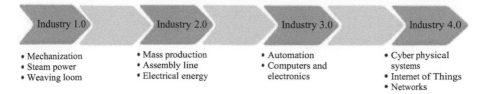

Industry 1.0	Industry 2.0	Industry 3.0	Industry 4.0

• Mechanization
• Steam power
• Weaving loom
	• Mass production
	• Assembly line
	• Electrical energy
		• Automation
		• Computers and
		  electronics
			• Cyber physical
			  systems
			• Internet of Things
			• Networks

Figure 7.3   Applications of Industry 4.0

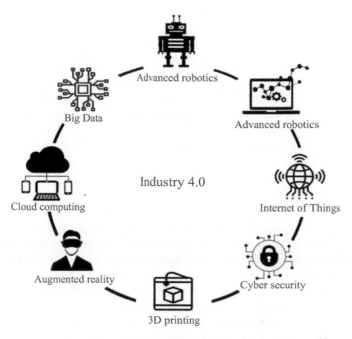

Figure 7.4   Application areas for Industry 4.0

mainframe computing, desktop computers, as well as digital technology. Producers started to undergo a change that placed less focus on analog and mechanical technologies, and more about applications for electronic technological advances. Industry 4.0 includes fields such as smart cities and smart buildings that are not generally listed as technology implementations. Industry 4.0 applies to a new generation of industrialization, focused extensively on interactivity, robotics, artificial intelligence, and actual information. Industry 5.0 is now being addressed and includes robotics and smart devices that allow people to function efficiently and easier. The various applications of Industry 4.0 have been included in Figure 7.4.

7.2.2   Evolution of Healthcare 4.0

Healthcare is evolving from conventional hospital treatment to more automated, interactive treatment that utilizes artificial intelligence, pattern recognition, big

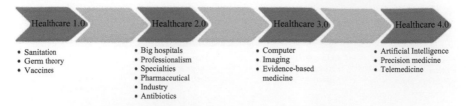

Figure 7.5   Developments in Healthcare 4.0

data, biotechnology, deep learning, home-based treatment, robots, and three-dimensional tissue and implant-printing technologies. AI offers connectivity using the Internet for billions of items worldwide. The medical sector has evolved from an era of 1.0 to 4.0 in the AI era. Healthcare 1.0 was an era in which paper documents, nonexperimental, standardized procedures and therapies regulated the sector. This period was based on the human side of healthcare relative to the technical one.

Healthcare 2.0 was developed at the start of the 21st century to reflect a time when, as opposed to human activity, it was technologically advanced. The original concept added for Healthcare 2.0 was the use of innovation as purely an enterprise agent for change. The building block in Healthcare 3.0 was smartphone applications. Healthcare 3.0 recognized healthcare-related complications to help to accelerate improvements in health outcomes for patients. A statistics approach ignores the emotional driving factors of individuals. Technology development and healthcare data analytics are key contributions to enhancing the effectiveness of treatment, reducing care expenses and, mostly significantly, treatment plans. Smart and information technologies have emerged to advance the crucial change from traditional knowledge to human-centered Healthcare 4.0.

Structural reforms to transform the health sector are also expected. Healthcare will be provided away from the hospital as a point-of-care, with a stronger emphasis on preventive and early diagnosis as a seamless continuum of care. The periodical changes from Healthcare 1.0 to Healthcare 4.0 are described in Figure 7.5. A recent digital revolution supported by advanced algorithms has provided the healthcare system with the Internet of Things, network computing devices, and wireless networks. Medical care advice programs have evolved under this framework as a catalyst for the provision of customized healthcare facilities that are patient-centric [8–12]. The different stages of Healthcare 4.0 have been demonstrated in Figure 7.6.

7.3   Development of AI in the healthcare sector

AI in healthcare is a broad term that refers to the analysis, understanding, and conceptualizing of complex medical, pharmaceutical, and/or financial data. It also refers to the use of machine-learning models and applications, as well as quantum computing, which uses AI to represent human intelligence. AI in healthcare applies

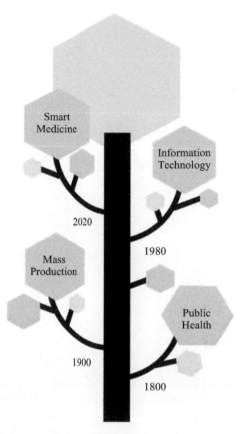

Figure 7.6 Traditional human-centered Healthcare 4.0

to anything within the diagnostic process seeking medical treatment using artificial intelligence systems/intelligent automation.

AI investigates information in order to explore, optimize, and forecast procedures in a medical system. It can be used to forecast intensive care unit (ICU) transfers, optimize patient outcomes, and also classify the risk of care facility infections from an individual. AI improves the ability to understand the daily routines or plannings of an individual, as the individuals will be providing excellent input and assistance. The various fields of healthcare using AI that can be used for advanced treatments and diagnostic tools are shown in Figure 7.7.

7.3.1 Areas in which AI is used across healthcare

- **Radiology:** Radiology is the healthcare facility used to assess and manage disorders using medical imaging of patients. AI techniques are being implemented in order to improve image recognition and treatment. This will serve to improve the radiologist's issues or interests by improving productivity and

Figure 7.7   Industry 4.0 in healthcare

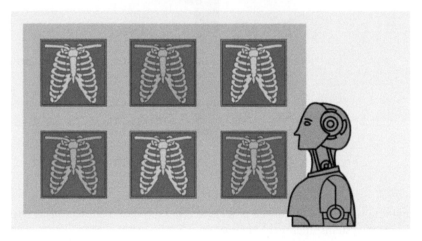

Figure 7.8   Innovations in healthcare development

reducing mechanical failure. There is also the prospect of highly automated approaches requiring less human oversight to read and understand a scan remotely, which could enable immediate analysis. Updated observations of improved tumor detection through MRIs as well as CTs indicate progress with current innovations for preventing cancer.

It is widely assumed that AI, also known as machine learning or deep learning, can and will improve radiologists' work processes, promote computational radiology, and help in the discovery of genomic markers. It is indeed interesting to see specific examples of just how automation in radiology will provide professionals to work on the most serious circumstances. Figure 7.8

shows how a robot can discover brain diseases or other unusual problems in the human brain. Automated machines can perform complicated tasks with more accurate outcomes [13].

Benefits of AI in Radiology: AI enables a more specific diagnosis to be provided. Numerous AI solutions are centered on offering additional data. This can be accomplished by measuring data contained in an image, which are currently only recorded in a qualitative manner. Alternatively, the program should provide normative principles, enabling doctors to equate patient outcomes to a population-wide average.

The issue with this advantage is that we may not always understand how to deal with the extra data. What does a particular value imply? What would it imply whenever a patient deviates greatly from the general population, and what does this mean for the treatment? Since we have little familiarity with quantitative data, there is frequently no guidance for what these data mean or what a radiologist can do with them. Getting an AI system running makes getting a second opinion easy. The outcomes of the algorithm can be used as a quick back-up check on the physician's diagnosis. Another advantage of using AI software as a second opinion would be that it helps the radiologist to eventually become open to dealing with it and gain confidence however they see the value it brings. It is vital that the program performs well but does not generate large false-positive or false-negative rates in order to successfully serve this function. Furthermore, protocols must be in effect in the event that the AI program makes a different diagnosis to that of the specialist. Even well-skilled radiologists will disagree with their diagnoses from time to time. Furthermore, different radiologists can place different emphasis on individual aspects of their records. This can be difficult for prescribing doctors, who must account for these differences while analyzing all of the data they have before reaching a final diagnosis. This variance among radiologist records can be reduced or even eliminated with AI technology [14–18].

- **Virtual Nurse:** A modern primary healthcare method is implemented by a digital nurse. Despite putting enormous pressure on nurses, automated nursing would double the productivity of a service and enhance the quality of healthcare. Patients can be quite enthusiastic about obtaining treatment from a virtual nurse. Nearly 65 percent of research participants said AI virtual healthcare-assisting co-workers are enough for the patients due to various day-to-day activities to provide support and convey answers. With respect to the development of technologies, the lack of personal human care oversight as well as the capability for medical failures have been inherent anxiety-causing disorders.

  Using AI and the network of medical equipment in customer healthcare applications would be another effective execution. Figure 7.9 shows an example of a patient obtaining a virtual doctor consultation. To collect medical information including digital applications, such solutions utilize health-based IoT devices which analyze the data and propose changes to the patient's living situation.

Figure 7.9   AI virtual healthcare

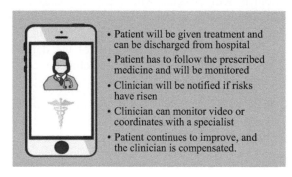

Figure 7.10   Patient instructions

- **Drug Discovery:** The standard clinical study system takes generations of studies which consumes millions and millions of dollars. About five in 5000 drugs which start clinical development studies actually makes it to human trials, as per the California Biomedical Research Association, "but only one of those five is always authorized and accepted for human consumption" [19] (Figure 7.10). AI will classify completely undiscovered triggers of different illnesses and enable further substances of greater precision and replication to be tested. Including AI in drug development will allow us to get away from the conventional approach and adopt further patient-driven science through the use of increasingly analytical predictions collected from questionnaires.

- **Health Monitoring:** Advancements have been focused on automation and ML to maintain records of the condition of patients. They monitor the heartbeat, temperature of the body, and some others to ensure the person is safe. These applications also submit warning updates for any changes to the patient's condition. Nearly every patient now has exposure to sensing devices, which can gather useful medical data. A large chunk of hygiene information is gathered out and about, through smartphones for steps tracking and wearable devices that can record the pulse all day and night. In obtaining meaningful data from such broad and complex sources of information, artificial intelligence will play a prominent part.

- **Diagnostic Tools:** Scientists claim that images captured through smartphones and some other healthcare platforms could be an essential complement to patient imaging, particularly in underserved communities or developing countries, following the tradition of creating a series of wearable electronics. Each year, the performance of smartphone cameras is expanding, and they can generate images which are suitable for artificial intelligence technology research. Figure 7.11 shows how doctors check patients' health conditions. These are more comfortable for capturing information about the patients' health condition and can prescribe treatments more accurately.

With the help of smartphones, we can capture images of injuries, diseases, and eye and skin problems, as well as other issues for diagnostic treatment while there is a shortage of experts in the medical field. The majority of people frequently come across various compact automated devices, with a wide range of various sensors built into them. Analysis proves that they are using AI information in mobile phones to provide even better customized, quicker, and

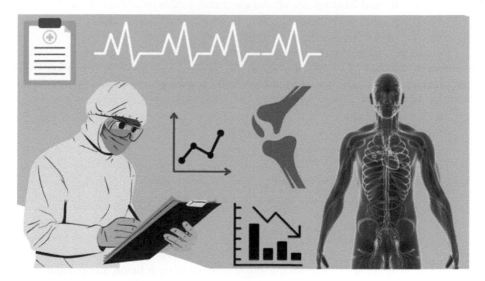

Figure 7.11 Health monitoring using AI

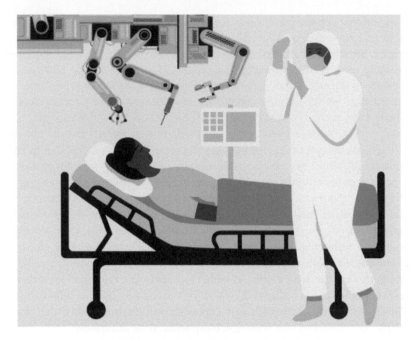

Figure 7.12   AI in diagnostic tools

intelligent services. AI in the medical field uses human-made machines, like computers, robots, and so on to perform complicated tasks precisely. As an example, Figure 7.12 depicts how surgery can be performed by a robot.

- **Health Record Management:** An electronic health record is the standard part of heavily encrypted medical records in an electronic medium for patients, doctors, and other healthcare professionals. It is possible to exchange these documents throughout numerous contexts of healthcare services. There are many manual errors that can occur during the collection of information from patients. AI is being used with electronic health records (EHRs) to eliminate repeated tasks which consume huge amounts and time and energy of healthcare staff. These people focus on three elements during their work: medical reports, appointments, and time management throughout the health records.

    Speech recognition and voice controls may help to improve a health reporting system, but still the natural language processing (NLP) resources would be insufficient. Obtaining regular questions from a database can also be part of AI, which includes these check-ups as well as result notifications.

7.4   AI challenges in healthcare

The study of AI is becoming increasingly advanced, with key features being seen around multiple medical fields. AI is often used for monitoring, quicker detection, and prediction. There are many challenges, explicitly, stored data challenges must be addressed by medical institutions.

- **Accidents and failures:** A far more immediate danger is often that AI may be incorrect and lead to medical injuries and other medical issues. When AI prescribes an individual the wrong medication, fails to recognize a disease on a radioactivity analysis, or makes a wrong decision such as assigning a bed in hospital for an individual who has less injuries than another patient who must be admitted to the hospital immediately, priority and decision-making become an issue [20].

    Even without the intervention of automation, several accidents arise through failures in the medical system. Care providers can respond better to software-induced accidents than those through human error. Second, unless AI technologies become prevalent, a single problem with one AI source could lead to thousands of patients being incorrectly treated, instead of the reduced percentage of patients harmed by a mistake from any single supplier.

- **Availability of data:** The professional development of AI devices involves vast amounts of information from databases such as EHRs, medical records, injury claims data, or details provided by customers such as wearable devices or documentation of purchases. However, there are also issues with health records [21]. Usually, data are distributed throughout several distinct structures. Generally, patients see various providers and change healthcare agencies, the data will be captured into various devices. This variability increases the probability of failure, reduces the integrity of databases, and increases the amount of data collection.

- **Adapting to modern society and environments poses major difficulties:** For most forms of medical data, the majority of AI technologies are far from achieving accurate generalizability, much less clinical applicability. Internal variations among websites (which include variations with software tools, programming languages, EHRs, scientific instruments, as well as evaluation) and also differences in regional medical and management practices make generalization difficult.

- **Impacts over confidentiality:** Private information raises a number of risks. The need for massive databases facilitates access for developers to obtain certain data from individuals. Some users may be worried that the confidentiality might be compromised by this database, and cases were filed provided by data sharing amongst large healthcare services and users of AI [6]. In another way, AI may enhance security: Although the methodology hasn't provided that data, AI may estimate personal data of patients.

    For example, an IoT device may be capable of detecting Parkinson's syndrome depending on the motion of a mouse pad, although the individual had never disclosed such details to anyone. This would be viewed by patient populations as a breach of confidentiality, particularly if the results of this AI model were open to third parties, such as banking or health insurance providers.

- **Change to the database:** It is highly relevant for EHR models to disregard the fact that certain analysis results are produced in a nonstationary environment of evolving healthcare providers, where business strategies change with time. In reality, the implementation of a new classification will trigger disruptions, leading to a new distribution to the trained models. Changes to detection methods and updating frameworks in reaction to worsening quality also are important. In addition to the probable need for regular additional training, preventive measures to handle this impact require diligent quantitative analysis of expected results to detect issues efficiently and effectively.

- **Implementing AI systems poses technical challenges:** The reality that almost all medical data are not readily available for machine learning is one of the current obstacles to converting AI systems for medical care. Data are frequently segmented into a number of different research processes of medical images, anatomy structures, EHRs, medication reconciliation applications, and clinical records, making it more difficult to combine all aspects. Standardized data types, such as fast healthcare interoperability tools, are being adopted.

- **Fitting confounding factors by mistake versus true signal:** AI techniques uses whichever inputs are accessible to obtain the best results throughout the dataset.

  This could involve some unspecified confounding factors that are not always correct, restricting some approaches for new data. For example, let's take a typical case, AI algorithms will not understand the fundamental comparison between a dog and a polar bear, though polar bears are typically portrayed like being with snow, and dogs are displayed being on a lawn.

- **Obtaining a good regulatory structure and a high degree of quality assurance:** The creation of the required regulatory structures is a key element to reaching secure and efficient AI algorithm deployment. Considering the current trend of technology, the major threat associated is the dynamic nature of AI techniques.

- **Healthcare professionals and patients' satisfaction and efficiency:** Large quantities of information are excellent and reliably calculated in many other sectors. Patient information is sometimes ambiguous and unreliable, with concerns such as:
  - Doctors' statements in patient health records being disorganized, making them difficult to understand or manage.
  - Incorrect data—an individual might be identified only as a nonsmoker, yet are they simply afraid to acknowledge that could not give up?
  - Several healthcare professionals have segregated databases, making it almost impossible to access a complete analysis and set of factors for a patient's condition.

- **Accomplishing effective supervision and strict monitoring of performance:** The establishment of the required regulatory structures is a fundamental element of ensuring secure and efficient implementation of AI. Despite the present speed of progress, a substantial cost inherent and the inherently dynamic existence of machine learning techniques, this presents unique challenges. Constructive control would give clinicians and health services trust. The technological effects of changes and enhancements which AI are responsible for supplying and are likely to generate over the life of a system are worth remembering. Some digital technologies may be aimed at improving through time, posing an obstacle to standard techniques of assessment.

- **The use of AI in healthcare is being hindered by human factors:** Human adoption hurdles were the most prominent successful technology which helps to solve every one of these obstacles. In making and implementing change, it is important to maintain a focus on the scientific usefulness and treatment options, for the system to improve through mathematical generalization, and gain a deeper understanding of technologies.
- **Ethical concerns:**
  The ethics of AI are described in Figure 7.13.
  - Some patients would be helped by the widescale launch of an innovative AI healthcare industry but subject to possible events. From that perspective, what really is the protection threshold—how often individuals should be supported?
  - Then how does that relate to a norm kept by a healthcare professional?
  - Who would be liable for injuries caused by automation errors: the computer engineer, the software firm, the administrator or the health professional?
  - Should a surgeon have a legal entitlement over the assessment or judgment of a device? Can the reverse similarly apply?

- Practical challenges:
  - Autonomous medical opinion and a wearable sensor system could facilitate the control of individuals and assisted personality, and may contribute to improved medical development.

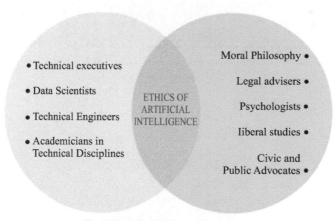

The Ethical Challenges, a Diversity of
involvement of stakeholders

Figure 7.13   Venn diagram for the ethics of AI

- o   Limited face-to-face communication could adversely affect the ability of patients to attend health promotion programs.
- o   AI systems are becoming critical assets for malicious attacks as patients become increasingly reliant on automated systems. How can we protect them from being scammed?
- o   The significance of the cost of suffering variables and usability is ignored. Also, from a design perspective, the community, healthcare workers, and professionals must be involved and not left generally as final users.
- o   Is there really a serious danger that perhaps people will oppose the use of AI technology entirely if chatbots are "over-sold" by developers?
- o   Clinicians must always be offered the choice on why a doctor or perhaps a method allows them any remedy for them?

- **Benefits of using advanced computers or robots in medicine through artificial intelligence:** AI is a popular factor in medicine, with continuing controversy over its legal, medical, and economic benefits and the drawbacks of using technologies to provide clinical outcomes (Figure 7.14) [22,23].
  - o   The possibilities for AI in healthcare appear infinite, and deep learning algorithms which is interpreted in CT scans are smarter than people which uses natural language processing to search data in electronic health records.
  - o   Artificial intelligence, like many other innovations at the height of interest in them, is met with skepticism from some as well as fervent support from others.

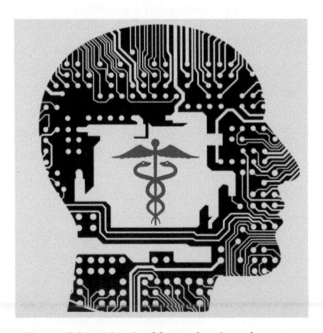

Figure 7.14   AI in healthcare for clinical services

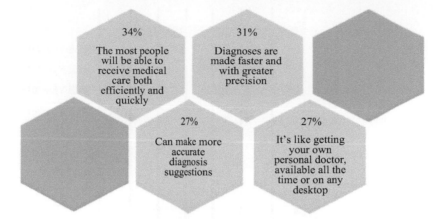

Figure 7.15 Analysis of medical instructions. Image source: [22]

o   People's ability to uncover fresh perspectives and standardize how patients and providers communicate to health records, AI can pose significant risks in terms of security, morality, and medical mistakes.

o   Analyzing the benefits and risks of AI in healthcare will necessitate collaboration among experts, authorities, and the final customers. The benefits of using advanced technologies with AI in the medical field have been analyzed and described in Figure 7.15.

7.5   AI developments in healthcare

Machine learning methods for structured data, including support vector machine and neural network technology, deep learning, and also natural language processing for an undifferentiated dataset, are all popular AI methods. Some medical areas such as cardiology, cancer, and neurology use advanced AI techniques. AI applications are now explored in greater depth, with an emphasis on the major aspects of early diagnosis, care, and resulting prognosis and diagnosis assessment. We end with a review of early AI systems, such as IBM Watson, as well as barriers to AI implementation in the real world. As in the early twentieth century, technical advances, mainly in the field of computer technology, have sparked a rampant consumerism movement in medicine. Figure 7.16 shows the development of AI in the medical sector through the years 2013–2016.

Disadvantages of artificial intelligence include the following:

• Increased cost;
• Difficulty in software development;
• Need for experienced programmers;
• Less availability of some products.

The advantages of using advanced technologies with AI in the medical field have been analyzed and described in Figure 7.17. People believe that technological

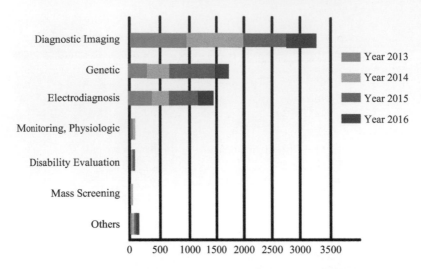

Figure 7.16   Developments in AI from 2013 to 2016

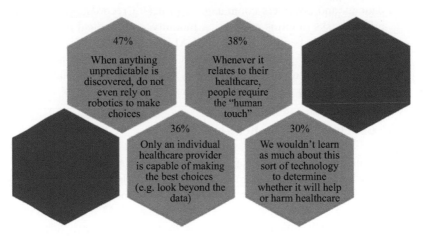

Figure 7.17   Analysis of healthcare technology. Image source: [22]

advances are more important in the medical field but they feel that machines are not safe for surgery or any other consultations, as machines lack emotions. When a person is stressful or fearful during surgery it is not advised to continue with the surgery immediately, we must make the patient feel comfortable and the robots or automated machines used must be able to understand the feelings or pain of patients.

7.6   AI opportunities in healthcare

• **Implementing a deeper understanding of the research into human–algorithm interactions:** There is little awareness about how analytics in clinical research influences individuals. In a review of precision medicine screening, automation showed improvement than those using human power. Technologies that reflect health information more substantively, include enhanced engagement for patients. The constantly evolving interaction between practitioners and human-centered AI instruments throughout the live medical setting is expected to always achieve better results.

- AI technology could pave the way or allow advancements in fields such as medical data analytics, which could tackle four particular areas:
  o **Descriptive**—to find out what went wrong.
  o **Diagnostic**—to determine why it occurred.
  o **Predictive**—to predict what will happen.
  o **Prescriptive**—to determine how we might make that happen.

- **Black-box technology**: Black-box AI is an AI device whose sources and actions are concealed from the client and even other relevant individuals. In a broader perspective, a black-box is an impenetrable device. The system is usually self-directed, making it more difficult to analyze with data analysts, developers, and clients.

- AI-based technology is increasingly shifting its focus into targeting scientific practitioners and researchers in order to improve their accuracy, efficiency, and expertise. Doctors might have confidential and ethical information to diagnose using the developed AI technologies. Some of the real-time applications designed based on AI technology include the following:
  o Google Maps and ride-hailing applications;
  o Face detection and recognition;
  o Text editors and autocorrect;
  o Search and recommendation algorithms;
  o Chatbots;
  o Digital assistants;
  o Social media;
  o e-Payments.

Deep learning networks are considered as black-box AI systems; they provide clarity about how the AI in a black-box is helpful in the medical field. When the transparency is hidden within black-box frameworks, it creates a threat to generating confidence in patients, but also is helpful for preventing technology bias in professionals. The principles used by AI in decision-making have been mentioned in Figure 7.18. This figure shows that explainability, transparency, and provability are the most important principles in decision-making. Almost, AI professionals provide exposure to black-box technology internal communications: for an automated decision-making technology outcomes (Figure 7.19).

- **AI techniques:** In the health sector, several AI methods are used to evaluate sensitive conditions in a clinical situation. Some of the AI techniques involved are:
  o **Fuzzy logic**: This has developed into a smart and confident approach for solving complicated real-world problems.

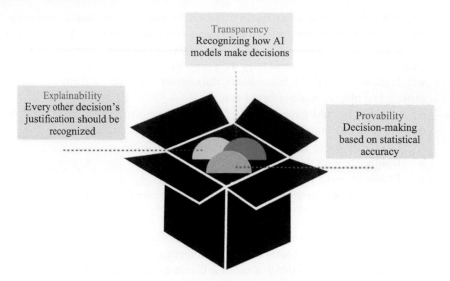

Figure 7.18   Three key principles to understand when it comes to AI decision-making

Figure 7.19   Black-box technology using AI in healthcare

o   **Artificial neural networks:** These are often used in circumstances in which we have a large amount of data to ensure that our observations do not include "flukes".

o   **Algorithm of genetics:** The details in the healthcare area contain a large amount of knowledge that could be blurred at times, making calculations easier.

o **Fuzzy neural:** The aim of fuzzy neural is to use various machine learning estimation technologies to identify the variables of a fuzzy inference system.

o **Particle swarm optimization (PSO):** Experiments have shown that a bio-inspired technique can be used to diagnose dangerous situations in patients. With a fuzzy method, PSO has been suggested for improving correct diagnosis.

• **AI in the construction of automation technologies:** Anna Sliwon-Stewart, a research expert at IHS Markit, reported that AI seems to have the ability not just to automate buildings but to also allow them to be fully flexible, intelligent, and scalable, through the use of AI technology to optimize processes, eliminate shortfalls, and reduce prices throughout building platforms in a wide variety of sectors (Figure 7.20).

Computer "bots" are a versatile automated resource which can perform in the back story to assist doctors or administrative staff. The growth in affordable healthcare, enhanced by the baby-boomer generation which has increased demand for immediate treatment, also has resulted in a massive rise in the quantity of patient information that programs must collect as well as the quantity of insurance payments which must be processed. Most hospitals were finding it hard to keep track of these data. In medicine, robotic process automation can be a key step which can lead to the right direction. Robotic process automation (RPA) is a

Figure 7.20   Robotic process automation

technique that provides anyone to set up computer code, or even a "automaton", to replicate and incorporate the behaviors of the person communicating to complete a business operation [24–26]. Throughout the healthcare sector, as shown in the latest trends report survey, "more than 40 percent of the total companies surveyed can build expert jobs via integrating artificial intelligence with Robotic Process Automation".

This analysis investigated the consequences of automation in smart buildings, and a pathway demonstrating both business benefits and challenges to the broader implementation of digital technologies across a variety of end industries [27,28].

- **Development of diagnostic technologies at universities and research institutes using AI:** AI is constantly attempting to address the needs of the health sector to fix problems which include enhancing job performance, boosting diagnosis accuracy, and making a positive impact on medical assistance. One of fields of medicine regarded to be the first to use a realistic AI system was diagnostic scanning.
  - o DeepMind, in conjunction with Moorfield Eye Hospital in London, revealed an AI approach to identifying symptoms of eye problems as accurately as globe physicians and specialists.
  - o The medical imaging company Arterys demonstrated its broad range of digital imaging systems and products in AI with MRI and CT treatment of liver and lung cancers, and also MRI cardiac perception, covering large possible areas of medical problems.
  - o Google Health allows clients to be assessed for their fitness routine and offers health history, the closest healthcare facilities, and prescription updates for their health conditions.
  - o Icometrix is an organization aiming to improve patient safety using AI scanning. The business is already well on path to altering the ways in which anomalies are detected inside the brain with MRI brain analysis used only to minimize errors in medical diagnosis.
  - o Including deep learning in clinical diagnosis to detect cancer was a big AI development in healthcare. A new research published by the National Cancer Institute indicates that a breast cancer detection rate equivalent to that of a regular breast radiologist has also been obtained by an AI model.
  - o AI-Rad Companion Chest CT is a Siemens Healthiness AI-powered medical system which can translate the CT scans of the body, conduct automated assessments, and compose valuable diagnostic images and measurements for the medical history.
  - o Another approach from Siemens Healthiness, AI-Pathway Companion, was developed to enhance treatment pathways by collecting all patient information and promoting treatment and medicinal plants along disorder pathways.
  - o Watson for Health from IBM helps hospitals, government services, scientists, and clinicians by providing solutions to enhance their efficiency, simplify the life choice process, safeguard against fraud, and enable studies to be approached cost-effectively.

7.7 Discussion and conclusion

AI will be used in all aspects of life in the future to drastically alter people's lives. it is now on the way to affecting all areas of the healthcare sector. Machine learning is also assisting experts and doctors in analyzing vast amounts of data in order to predict the spread of the COVID-19 virus. Thus, it behaves as an alert system for potential disease outbreaks, and aids in classifying vulnerable people. From the point of view of COVID-19, AI is assisting leaders in making good decisions. COVID-19 is also being researched for ways to reduce its spread, especially among children. Some AI start-ups are now using their health information knowledge to classify the COVID-19 patients that are most at risk of major problems. Closedloop.ai is a healthcare data science tool that created and open-sourced a COVID risk matrix, an AI-based predictive model that predicts those most likely to experience serious COVID-19 symptoms [29–31]. Healthcare programs, patient care agencies, and insurance plans are using the "C-19 Index" to identify high-risk patients, then contacting people to discuss the value of washing hands and social distancing, as well as promising to provide food, toilet paper, and other emergency goods so that they can remain at home if needed. We can assume that AI in Healthcare 4.0 can assist people in the healthcare sector in living increasingly satisfying lives. Healthcare 4.0 is about gathering large amounts of information and using it in healthcare-based applications. This would further enable effective healthcare decisions as well as major improvements in productivity by AI. There are several enhancements that can be done in the Healthcare 4.0 [32–40]. In this chapter, we have discussed a variety of challenges and opportunities for AI in healthcare which will help several stakeholders and policy-makers to make informed decisions [41–44].

References

[1] D.B. Neill, "Using Artificial Intelligence to Improve Hospital Inpatient Care", IEEE INTELLIGENT SYSTEMS, 1541–1672, 2013 IEEE.

[2] https://bmcmedicine.biomedcentral.com/articles/10.1186/s12916-019-1426-2#:~:text=Main%20body,necessary%20sociocultural%20or%20pathway%20changes, Nov 2021.

[3] https://www.linkedin.com/pulse/surgery-40-patrick-riley, Nov 2021.

[4] https://bdtechtalks.com/2021/02/17/ai-healthcare-tina-manoharan-philips/, Nov 2021.

[5] https://www.ncbi.nlm.nih.gov/pmc/articles/PMC7332220/, Nov 2021.

[6] https://www.healthcareitnews.com/news/3-charts-show-where-artificial-intelligence-making- impact-healthcare-right-now, Nov 2021.

[7] https://www.internationalsos.com/client-magazines/in-this-issue-3/how-ai-is-transforming- the-future-of-healthcare, Nov 2021.

[8] S. Srivastava, M. Pant and R. Agarwal. Role of AI techniques and deep learning in analyzing the critical health conditions. *International Journal of System Assurance Engineering and Management volume*, 6 Nov 2019.

[9]   E. Racine, W. Boehlen, and M. Sample. Healthcare uses of artificial intel-
       ligence: challenges and opportunities for growth. *Healthcare Management
       Forum*, pp. 1–4, 2019.

[10]   Z. Abedjan, N. Boujemaa, S. Campbell, *et al.* Data science in healthcare:
       benefits, challenges and opportunities. *Data Science for Healthcare*,
       Springer Nature Switzerland AG, 2019.

[11]   S.Y. Park, P.-Y. Kuo, A. Barbarin, *et al.* Identifying Challenges and
       Opportunities in Human-AI Collaboration in Healthcare, CSCW'19, 9–13
       Nov 2019, Austin, TX.

[12]   O. Iliashenko, Z. Bikkulova, and A. Dubgorn1. Opportunities and challenges
       of artificial intelligence in healthcare. E3S Web of Conferences 110, 0, 2019.

[13]   https://collaborativeimaging.com/how-artificial-intelligence-is-improving-
       radiology-workflows/ Nov 2021.

[14]   H. Asri, H. Mousannif, H. Al Moatassime, and T. Noel. Big data in health-
       care: challenges and opportunities. In Proceedings of the international
       Conference on Cloud Technologies and applications (CloudTech), pp. 1–7,
       Marrakech, Morocco, June 2015.

[15]   https://industrywired.com/robotic-surgery-is-at-the-forefront-of-tomorrows-
       healthcare/, Nov 2021.

[16]   https://cmajnews.com/2019/03/26/task-force-launching-to-examine-national-
       licensure- for-virtual-care-cmaj-109-5738-2/, 6 Oct 2021.

[17]   https://www.nanalyze.com/2019/11/ai-remote-patient-monitoring/, Nov 2021.

[18]   https://www.information-age.com/augmented-intelligence-distributed-ledger-
       technology- healthcare-123485246/, Nov 2021.

[19]   https://www.simplilearn.com/ai-in-healthcare-article, Nov 2021.

[20]   https://www.brookings.edu/research/risks-and-remedies-for-artificial-intelli-
       gence-in-health-care/, Nov 2021.

[21]   https://www.aiin.healthcare/topics/diagnostics/6-risks-ai-healthcare-artificial-
       intelligence, Nov 2021.

[22]   https://www.pwc.com/gx/en/industries/healthcare/publications/ai-robotics-
       new-health/survey-results.html, Nov 2021.

[23]   P. Dhingra, N. Gayathri, S.R. Kumar, V. Singanamalla, C. Ramesh, and B.
       Balamurugan. Internet of Things–based pharmaceutics data analysis. In
       *Emergence of Pharmaceutical Industry Growth with Industrial IoT
       Approach* (pp. 85–131). Academic Press, 2020.

[24]   https://allzonems.com/robotic-process-automation-in-healthcare-will-lead-to-
       better-patient- outcomes/, Nov 2021.

[25]   G. Nagasubramanian, R.K. Sakthivel, R. Patan, A.H. Gandomi, M. Sankayya
       and B. Balusamy. Securing e-health records using keyless signature infra-
       structure blockchain technology in the cloud. *Neural Computing and
       Applications* 2020;32(3):639–647. https://doi.org/10.1007/s00521-018-3915-1.

[26]   S.R. Kumar, N. Gayathri, S. Muthuramalingam, B. Balamurugan, C. Ramesh
       and M.K. Nallakaruppan. Medical big data mining and processing in e-
       healthcare. In *Internet of Things in Biomedical Engineering* (pp. 323–339).
       Academic Press, 2019. https://doi.org/10.1016/B978-0-12-817356-5.00016-4.

[27] S.K. Sharma, N. Gayathri, R.K. Modanval and S. Muthuramalingam. Artificial intelligence-based systems for combating COVID-19. In *Applications of Artificial Intelligence in COVID-19* (pp. 19–34). Springer, Singapore, 2021.

[28] V. Kavidha, N. Gayathri, and S.R. Kumar (2021). AI, IoT and Robotics in the Medical and Healthcare Field. *AI and IoT-Based Intelligent Automation in Robotics*, 165–187.

[29] https://closedloop.ai/c19index/, Nov 2021.

[30] G. Nagasubramanian and M. Sankayya. Multi-variate vocal data analysis for detection of Parkinson disease using deep learning. *Neural Computing and Applications* 2021;33(10):4849–4864. https://link.springer.com/article/10.1007/s00521-020-05233-7.

[31] G. Nagasubramanian, M. Sankayya, F. Al-Turjman and G. Tsaramirsis. Parkinson data analysis and prediction system using multi-variant stacked auto encoder. In *IEEE Access*, 2020;8:127004–127013, 10.1109/ACCESS.2020.3007140.

[32] M. Sathiyanarayanan and S. Rajan. MYO Armband for physiotherapy healthcare: A case study using gesture recognition application In 2016 8th International Conference on Communication Systems and Networks (COMSNETS). IEEE, 2016.

[33] T. Mulling and M. Sathiyanarayanan. Characteristics of hand gesture navigation: a case study using a wearable device (MYO). In Proceedings of the 2015 British HCI Conference (pp. 283–284), 2015.

[34] M. Sathiyanarayanan and S. Rajan. Understanding the use of leap motion touchless device in physiotherapy and improving the healthcare system in India. In 2017 9th International Conference on Communication Systems and Networks (COMSNETS) (pp. 502–507). IEEE, 2017.

[35] D. Ganesh, G. Seshadri, S. Sokkanarayanan, S. Rajan, and M. Sathiyanarayanan. IoT-based Google duplex artificial intelligence solution for elderly care. In 2019 International Conference on Contemporary Computing and Informatics (IC3I) (pp. 234–240). IEEE, 2019.

[36] S. Rajan, M. Sathiyanarayanan, S. Prashant, S.B. Prashant and P.L. Nataraj. Prevention of avoidable blindness and improving eye healthcare system in India. In 2018 10th International Conference on COMmunication Systems & NETworkS (COMSNETS) (pp. 665–670). IEEE, 2018.

[37] S. Rajan and M. Sathiyanarayanan. Breast cancer awareness through smart mobile healthcare applications from Indian doctors' perspective. In 2017 International Conference On Smart Technologies For Smart Nation (SmartTechCon) (pp. 607–612). IEEE, 2017.

[38] D. Kavitha, A. Murugan and M. Sathiyanarayanan. Deep analysis of dementia disorder using artificial intelligence to improve healthcare services. In 2021 International Conference on COMmunication Systems & NETworkS (COMSNETS) (pp. 378–380). IEEE, 2021.

[39] K. Mohanty, S.A. Subiksh, S. Kirthika *et al.* Opportunities of adopting AI-powered robotics to tackle COVID-19. In 2021 International Conference on

COMmunication Systems & NETworkS (COMSNETS) (pp. 703–708). IEEE, 2021.

[40] D. Ganesh, G. Seshadri, S. Sokkanarayanan, P. Bose, S. Rajan, and M. Sathiyanarayanan. Automatic health machine for COVID-19 and other emergencies. In 2021 International Conference on COMmunication Systems & NETworkS (COMSNETS) (pp. 685–689). IEEE, 2021.

[41] https://amfg.ai/2019/03/28/industry-4-0-7-real-world-examples-of-digital-manufacturing-in-action/, Nov 2021.

[42] https://undark.org/2019/12/04/black-box-artificial-intelligence/, Oct 2021, Nov 2021.

[43] https://elearningindustry.com/robotic-process-automation-in-india-experts-embrace, Nov 2021.

[44] https://svn.bmj.com/content/2/4/230, Nov 2021.

Chapter 8

Impression of artificial intelligence in e-healthcare medical applications

D. Kavitha[1], R. Sathya[1], V. Surya[1], C. Deepanjali[2] and P. Bhuvanashree[2]

Abstract

The aim of Artificial Intelligence (AI) is to depict human intelligence. It's causing a pattern change in healthcare, due to the ease of electronic medical records and the rapid growth in analytical tools. Not long ago, AI techniques sent shockwaves through the healthcare industry, encouraging a lively debate as to whether AI doctors could eventually treat patients suffering in the future. Human doctors are difficult to be replaced by machines anytime soon, but AI can help physicians in good clinical decision-making and even substitute human judgement in some areas of healthcare. The notable recent implementations of AI in healthcare have been achieved by the widespread availability of health information and the rapid increase in availability of big data analytic methods. Medically important information hidden away in vast amounts of data can be revealed using effective AI methods, which can aid in medical decision. Until AI systems could be used in healthcare, they must be "educated" using data produced from patient evaluation, such as transmitting, diagnostics, and medication assignment, so that they might learn related groups of subjects, correlations among subject features, and expected results. Demography, patient records, electronic records from surgical equipment, physical exams, and established testing laboratory and digital images are all examples of medical studies. AI has been utilized in a range of technological areas, including IoT, computer vision, automated vehicles, and natural language processing, according to the rapid advancement of AI operating systems technologies. Most excitingly, biomedical researchers are now consciously attempting to use AI to enhance diagnosis and patient outcomes, thus increasing the overall utility of the healthcare sector. The increase in interest is evident, particularly since the past 5 years, and strong development can be expected in the near future. The impact AI can have on the medical sector in the future is significant.

Keywords: Artificial intelligence; e-Health; Healthcare 4.0

[1]SRM Institute of Science and Technology, Ramapuram Campus, Chennai, India
[2]Computer Science and Engineering, Specialization in Big Data Analytics, SRM Institute of Science and Technology, Ramapuram Campus, Chennai, India

8.1   Introduction

Artificial Intelligence (AI) in medicine is a broad term referring to the need for machine-learning techniques and software systems to resemble the human brain in interpretation as well as understanding of complicated healthcare information. AI allows computer programmes to make predictions simply based on information provided in the dataset. The organizations to capture information, processing the data, and providing an excellent result to the end user is just what distinguishes AI from conventional health-care services. Machine learning techniques and deep learning techniques are used along with AI to address advanced healthcare problems. Such advanced technologies are capable of developing and detecting patterns in the given data. Machine learning methods should be developed to gain valuable opinions and forecasts.

In two different ways, AI systems vary from living beings: (1) algorithm are descriptive: when a goal has been achieved, the algorithm teaches itself entirely from the inputs and could only explain what has already been programmed for doing a particular job; (2) many deep learning models are black boxes; they may forecast with significant accuracy but provide little if any unclear or complex jus-tification given for the reasoning between their actions other than the data and algorithms is utilized. The main goal of healthcare AI technologies is to investigate the links between treatment or prevention approaches and clinical outcomes. Diagnoses, medication technology innovators, drug discovery, precision treatment,

Health Apps   Remote Monitoring

Smaller Implants

Digital Platform Integration

Artificial Intelligence

Surgical Robots

Device Connection

Additional Services

3D Printing   Less Invasive Diagnostics

Figure 8.1   Various applications of AI in healthcare

and patient care and management are all areas where AI programmes are being used. AI is a way of proving expertise in systems in addition to human intelligence [1]. Figure 8.1 describes the several medical sectors wherein AI is playing a predominant role. Among the technological and scientific advancements, which have allowed the adoption of AI-related applications in the last half century, are:

- Higher computer power allows for quick data gathering and processing [2]
- The number of gene sequencing systems is increasing [3]
- Regarding the adoption of electronic medical record (EHR) systems [4]
- Advances in processing of the languages as well as the vision of computer for allowing the machines to resemble a human brain
- Robot-assisted surgeries have become more precise
- Deep learning methods and dataset logs for serious conditions have improved

8.2   e-Healthcare

e-Healthcare is a medical platform that utilizes modern information and communication technologies to offer a variety of medical services for the customers, such as doctors, nursing staff, physicians, and clients. Use of information communication technology in medicine is referred to as e-Health. The term e-Health (also known as Electronic Health) refers to how digital technologies will be used to promote better healthcare throughout the medical sector. However, at the time of COVID-19 outbreak, information technology was becoming pretty prevalent, since it enabled healthcare providers to provide front-line clinical care to patients amid the closure of local therapy facilities and clinical divisions. Usage of emerging communication technologies to enhance community advancement or medical facilities requires software, the Web, and smartphones.

For the transmission of data to physicians and healthcare customers, e-Health is frequently used in combination with conventional "off-line" (non-digital) methods. Figure 8.2 depicts the different interconnections of digital health with

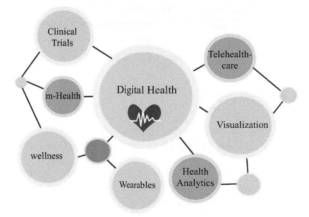

Figure 8.2   e-Healthcare

telehealth, mHealth, and so on. e-Health emerged from the need for better recording and monitoring of patients' care and diagnostic procedures, especially for premium payment requirements. Customarily, medical professionals stored paper copies of their patients' medical histories and current conditions. Through medical expenses and technical developments, but on the other hand, motivated the implementation of innovative monitoring devices.

8.3   Application of e-Healthcare

e-Health seems to be a vast concept that includes telemedicine, electronic documents, hiring, going digital, service delivery, medical necessary implication, inspections, and data management. The technology used here develops, manages, and measures, which is applicable to either an individual or even a medical professional and is known as e-Healthcare application. Information can also be used for medication management, clinical outcome measures analysis, medical health information production, or healthcare insurance payment tools.

Web-based e-Health or mobile health apps introduce effective treatment options regarding medical conditions. Patients may often use technology to bring awareness regarding any signs or regulate that disorder. Mobile health applications are among the largest segments throughout the medical sector for future development. These apps include users with quite an efficient and timely manner to monitor their own health.

The electronic medical record (EMR), which really is an electronic form of a medical history of patient, is among the most commonly utilized e-Health applications. Other groups, on the other hand, use software that enable several health services to access a patient's data. Something you'd notice in a paper chart, like health information, symptoms, medicines, diseases or disorders, and vaccinations, is included in the EMR. Previous health records, blood pressure, treatment plans, medications, prescriptions, allergies, laboratory information, and scanning records are also included in EMRs. Many related data, like insurance records, statistical factors, or even information acquired by prescribed treatment tools can be used. The research might be more productive and address the needs of many other representatives of in healthcare sector with a perfectly working EMR system, enabling users to:

- Improve care management
- Increase patient participation in treatment
- Enhance the standard of treatment
- Cost-cutting and increased profitability

Computerized physician order entry (CPOE) is also another e-Health platform that helps medical professionals insert medical information or orders digitally. Medical practitioners can write prescriptions or book appointments for clinics, radiology, and other services. Clinical decision support (CDS) systems provide doctors and nurses with knowledge required to assist them in accurately diagnosis.

CDS includes a variety of resources, such as automatic warnings and notifications for patients and physicians, clinical instructions, condition-specific instructions set, clinical care materials, medical assistance, and reporting layouts.

mHealth (mobile health) is a subset of e-Health that enables electronic devices to connect with healthcare professionals and patients. Mobile telemedicine, emergency, health tracking and domestic spying, or access to data for medical practitioners at the point of service are all standard techniques. Smartphones, laptops, medical monitoring equipment, and personal digital assistants are examples of mobile devices. mHealth is often used by hospitals or organizations to enter patient's information and relay important treatment to clinicians and other service providers. Emails and texts, protected hospital services, SMS, or instant message or virtual talk through phone can all be used to communicate with a person. In certain cases, it reduces the need for more doctor appointments. Given the historically slow acceptance of technology in the healthcare industry, this idea regarding telemedicine and telehealth may be unfamiliar to professionals and physicians. Telemedicine is described as "the provision of healthcare services from a distance."

Telemedicine is classified by the World Health Organization (WHO) as "healing from a distance." With the help of telecommunication services and information systems, physicians can aim at providing remote health services. Telemedicine is used by doctors to send digital scans, virtual consultations, and mobile treatment options. There seem to be three forms of telemedicine that are being used, which are enlisted below:

- *Interactive medicine:* Interactive medicine, often considered as "live telemedicine," helps patients and doctors communicate in actual environments, thus staying compliant with HIPAA. Mobile appointments and online chats are examples of effective communication. It allows doctors to evaluate patient history, conduct clinical examinations, and more.
- *Back-up and forward:* Services may exchange patient data with a doctor in another place using this method of telemedicine. A primary care doctor, in particular, could now exchange patient history and medical details with such a professional without meeting the patient in person.
- *Patient monitoring via the Internet:* Telemedicine, which allows physicians to monitor the patients in their own homes, is probably a common phenomenon for aging patients. Figure 8.3 shows the relationship between telehealth, electronic health, and telemedicine. A doctor may use medical records to collect and exchange information with their patients. Medical equipment may also transmit symptoms and other information to clinicians, allowing us to make changes to treatment if required.

8.3.1 *Application of telemedicine*

- Medication administration
- Chronic disease management
- Health information exchange
- Emergency room diversion

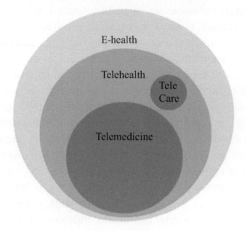

Figure 8.3   Telemedicine

- Neonatal intensive care unit (NICU)
- Intensive care unit (ICU)
- Disaster relief

8.3.2   Telehealth (upcoming years)

Hospital clinics on a Web: Consider a patient, supplier, and employees collabora-tion portal that is available for accessing at any time. The community with virtual doctors treating patients with chronic from throughout the states may be the vision of telemedicine. Health professionals can prescribe medications in lesser duration utilizing remote surveillance systems and teleconferencing.

Borderless telehealth: Again, with the advancement in technology, telehealth's growth has included global cooperation. Few regions have technological advances, which the American Government doesn't really (and vice versa), but telehealth will help to overcome these obstacles.

Responsiveness is exceptional: Patients' concerns about telehealth may decrease when they encounter shorter response time as well as quicker adherence to healthcare. Doctors would see improved health outcomes and improved economy despite not adding to their workforce. In fact, by developing methodologies, private insurers, healthcare, and health insurance providers can respond to the request.

Collaborative work between healthcare systems: Sharing electronic data with such a healthcare programme that utilizes a particular EHR system software is still challenging nowadays. Improved networking technologies would definitely be part of future telemedicine, enabling patients receiving appropriate care regardless of wherever they are.

Mirrors in virtual reality: Virtual reality mirrors are expected to be part of the development of telemedicine services. For diagnosis and treatment and research methodology, the device can use virtual reality and image enhancement

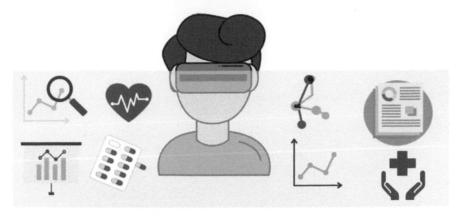

Figure 8.4   Use of virtual reality in healthcare

transformation. Assistants can help detect eye conditions, skin conditions, or even cancer using virtual reality mirrors' improved visualization. The new requirements for cardiac monitoring and guided respiration for the severely ill, combined with the effectiveness of advanced medical technology, such as MRI and PET scanning, have only strengthened the superiority of clinics and offices as patient care sites. Whereas modern hospital facilities and advanced technology that the medical profession depends on have undoubtedly improved patient health, there are a few drawbacks with regard to specific aspects of care [5]. Figure 8.4 shows how a doctor utilizes the virtual reality in for the complicated cases for patients.

8.4   Artificial intelligence

The knowledge of virtual agents or computers, as well as the technology in developing it, is known as AI. Though AI is among the most recent areas of engineering, it has been the focus for existing investigations since 1950s [6]. It is a fascinating field where software helps devices or computers that function complex tasks human experience and reasoning, such as visual processing, voice recognition, prediction, and language interpretation. In addition, AI systems even have understanding, logic, and consciousness capabilities. AI is indeed a big field that includes anything from mobile calculators to self-driving automobiles to world-ruling robotics. Figure 8.5 shows various AI applications in medical industry, such as early detection, advanced treatments, and various decision-making approaches for patients.

8.5   Significant advancements of technology

Over the past few months, there have been some developments in the technical field.

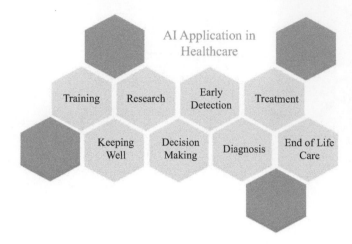

Figure 8.5   Artificial intelligence applications in healthcare

- Fast information gathering as well as analysis leading to enhanced performance characteristics
- Database management systems for genetic research are expanding
- Machine learning, data analysis, as well as the potential to imitate human processes also have strengthened
- Automaton surgeries that are extremely accurate
- Significant amount of information via medical applications are readily available

8.6   Artificial intelligence in medical sector

AI has the potential to outperform human doctors in terms of detecting, predicting, and diagnosing illnesses with greater accuracy or rate. In the case of recognizing neuropathy, AI systems have been proven to be more reliable and precise in high-quality diagnosis and treatment, and moreover profitable. The pros and advanced technologies of AI in the field of medicine are constantly increasing everyday, some of these are provided in Figure 8.6.

AI robots: Throughout the medical industry, robots are actively participating in delivering the integrated alternative for medical sector as well as other sectors. Big data and other important assets from medical industry are already being used by companies for training the robots in performing various tasks. Knowledge through real clinical experiences may be used by conceptual robotic technology to enhance current treatment methods. Health workers may receive information via pre-operative patient history to gain real-world information. This strategy will help save time and money by reducing the amount of time you spend on medication.

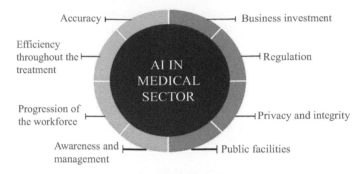

Accuracy

Business investment

Efficiency
throughout the
treatment

Regulation

AI IN
MEDICAL
SECTOR

Progression of
the workforce

Privacy and integrity

Awareness and
management

Public facilities

Figure 8.6   Artificial intelligence in medicinal field

8.6.1   Artificial intelligence and robotics are transforming healthcare

Remote diagnosis: DARPA (Defence Advanced Research Projects Agency) suggests using a robot for medicinal reasons since the 1990s; however, at that period,
communication systems were unable to provide the necessary resources to treat
soldiers on the battlefield. This is no longer an issue thanks to existing 4G and
future 5G standards. DARPA continues to support these attempts, but it appears
that surgical procedure also needs human assistance for hygiene as well as other
activities, which complicates the situation and makes it financially unviable.
Another method AI and AR will assist clinicians in is by developing a real-time,
personalized overlay throughout treatment, illustrating internal organs as well as
other critical areas. In the case of a robotic arm, the information library will
recommend different resources given current quality standards. A simple bot-pill is
yet another solution for remote medical robot that performs an endoscopy.

Auxiliary robots are robots that assist the main robot: In a clinic, there seems
to be a lot of work to be done, and physicians could just use any assistance. Nursing
staff and hospital staff will profit from the assistance of robots like Diligent
Robotics' Moxi. This robot handles overstock, carrying objects, and cleaning,
allowing nurses to spend more time with clinicians and have a human connection,
whereas the computer handles them altogether. An Ultraviolet Irradiation antiseptic
robot is yet another outstanding auxiliary robot that enters a patient's room but does
not exit until it becomes germ-free [19].

Enhancing human capabilities: In relation to clinical professionals, several
healthcare robots support patients. Exoskeleton robots, for instance, will support
injured people in walking and being self-sufficient. An intelligent stimulator is yet
another amazing feature in motion. Such cybernetic implants include sensors that
allow themselves very sensitive but precise than normal parts of the body, with
both the option of covering them in prosthetic skins and attaching themselves to the
user's muscles. With time, the medical industry witnessed many possibilities, such
as technological innovations, Intelligent Systems, Internet of Things, Data Science,
neural networks, and robots, that laid the foundation for advanced medicinal

progress. Figure 8.7 shows how robots help doctors during surgery in some complicated cases. The robots perform their job more precisely than human experts [7].

Promoting psychological health as well as day-to-day activities: Human-like tasks, such as helping hospitalized or aged patients feel more better, could be performed by robotic systems. Communicative and companion robots may assist such clinicians in maintaining a healthy attitude, reminding them to take their medications, and performing basic regular checks, such as measuring body temperature or glucose levels. It is like support staff, and they also have personality and sentiment classification designed, which would be particularly beneficial for hospitalized patients.

Increasing precision: Robots lack feelings and therefore are incapable of boredom, and never grow tired of what they've been doing. That's because this was the motivating factor behind a variety of robots that are now in operation in some of the world's most prominent hospitals. This was referred to as Waldo surgeons, and this shows the difference between people and robots by performing work with greater precision and enhanced strength. The individual doctor assumes a subordinate, supervisory task, as well as the technology, which is correctly set for the experiencing operation.

Accurate diagnosis: The ultimate strength of AI exists in identifying defects that define different symptoms by analyzing health data as well as other related data. The computer will search millions of reports and search for connections

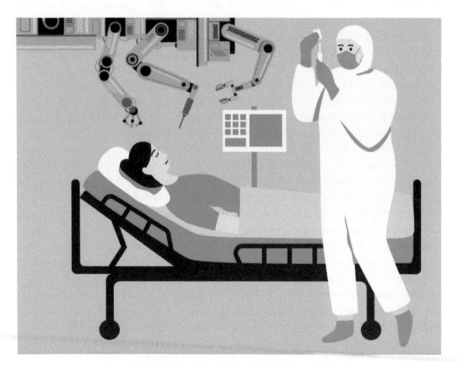

Figure 8.7   Robotics in healthcare

among thousands of variables, including some that are not even mentioned in existing scientific journals. Thus, we would have come across many informations that some experiments have also shown that robotics can compete or it would perform well than the other best surgeons in this medical field. A Japanese endoscopic system, for example, can detect colon cancer in the current situation and is 86% accurate [20].

In terms of speed and depth when performing precise indentations, intelligence and interactive robotics also transformed surgical procedures. Although robots are never exhausted, they never get ill throughout the process of long and critical procedures. Information from previous surgeries can be used by automation technologies to generate better medical techniques. The precision of such devices eliminates the problem of disturbances or unwanted or unintentional gestures during the surgery. A variety of AI robots are deployed throughout the healthcare industry. Some of the robotics are:

- *Transporting health services with robots*: These certified robots now provide medical supplies and other critical products for hospitals and medical centers. Actually, self-navigation technology can be used to build robots that can navigate around the hospital without the support of humans to walk around the hospital or any other locations. To improve the navigational capabilities of transportation robots, some AI robots are instructed with a huge volume of training data and image processing technologies. One of them is analytics, which requires great training sets for AI-based robots. Qualified workers will concentrate on greater roles according to the automated robotic system [8].
- *Disinfection and sanitization robots*: Robots are the top choices for disinfecting or sanitizing contaminated areas to prevent human interaction and minimize the spread of highly infectious diseases like COVID-19 and many others. It can quickly and efficiently inject chemicals and clean vast areas, saving a lot of time. Since AI robots are exposed to polluted areas and may cause infection, they must be sanitized. When people are exposed to diseased environments, they become ill or develop health problems.

  As a result, robots can be used to sanitize or disinfect various areas. The first thing during this disease outbreak is to get rid of infection from any clinics or hospitals. The important thing around the world is to prevent the spread of this COVID-19. Some robots have been developed to kill the coronavirus in the hospitals. Robots like the one shown in Figure 8.9 are being widely used in many hospitals as there are many COVID-19 cases with different variants [9].
- *Augmented reality doctors using robots*: They are often used to treat patients in rural or remote areas. Telepresence robots can give the impression of being treated by a medical professional, allowing for two-way contact between them. In emergency situations, however, specialists can be summoned through robots to respond to questions and provide care guidance remotely. These AI robots also have AI cameras as well as other features that enable them to physically examine patients and provide a practical diagnostic.

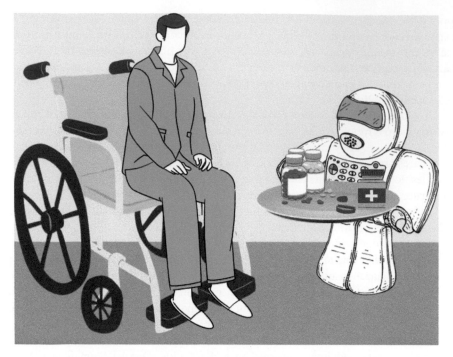

Figure 8.8   Autonomous service robots for medical centers

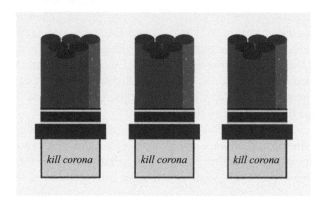

Figure 8.9   Robots to kill coronavirus in hospitals

Surgeons now have access to a wealth of biological image details, but they still rely on two-dimensional visuals prior to treatment. Since photographic data is captured from the viewpoint of the imaging system, doctors must interpret the images using their abilities, creativity, and training. AR vision systems hold a ton of potential for developing imaging techniques in medical applications. AR vision devices have a lot of potential for accessing healthcare imaging techniques [10].

- *Medicine prescribing services with robotics*: AI robots can perform more effectively and at a faster rate, which is critical for the healthcare sector in terms of providing reliable information and working quickly for providing appropriate treatment for patients. Similar to the previous one, additional technologies in an automated dispensing device are being introduced such that robots now can manage powder, liquids, and viscous items with greater accuracy [11,12]. When installed in hospitals and care centers, such robots could distribute a variety of other products.
- *Robots as a surgical assistance*: Surgeons may use AI-enabled robots to help them with a variety of tasks. AI robots for surgery are expected to make massive gains in medicinal field all over the globe, despite the fact that several surgeons have potential for future growth [13]. More sophisticated 3-Dimensional High-Definition technology provides surgeons with the spatial examples they need to conduct massively complicated surgeries. These robots are outfitted with improved natural audio visualization, as well as virtual reality. And, using computer vision, these robots are taught various forms of training data in order for them to comprehend the situation and take appropriate action. Healthcare facilities in few foreign countries have approved for surgical robots for the treatment of a variety of disorders [14].

The following are some of the advantages of surgical procedures:

- There are fewer risks, like disease at the surgical site
- Pressure and loss of blood are minimized
- Faster recovery
- Scars that are smaller or less can be noticed

Cybersecurity: Indeed, their responsibility at a hospital is to keep each of their patients' information private and protected as no one can hack information. If you've found how the device is vulnerable to hacking, an intelligence security software will save us. This can provide an additional level of protection because this is efficient and careful. As the amount and seriousness of cyberattacks has been increased in healthcare, AI is assisting providers in detecting vulnerabilities and responding to privacy violations quicker and more precisely [17].

AI can help identify falls in seniors and detect early symptoms of infection as a medical instrument. It will also have an effect on several other areas, such as clinical diagnosis and administrative work. As a response, suppliers are incorporating AI into a wide range of security devices, according to Miller. Cisco, for example, utilizes a combination in its next-generation firewalls, Cloud network access broker, cognitive threat analytics, and Cisco Advanced Malware Protection, among many other products or services. IBM's Watson uses AI platform in assisting in the speeding up of regular system reviews, reducing reaction time and negative results, and giving suggestions based on the deep evaluation.

Cybercrime impacts businesses in such a wide variety of sectors, including IT, economic, learning, production, and business. The approach of AI in cybersecurity among the medicinal field has been depicted in Figure 8.12. Among the most

Figure 8.10   Augmented reality used by the doctors during the surgery

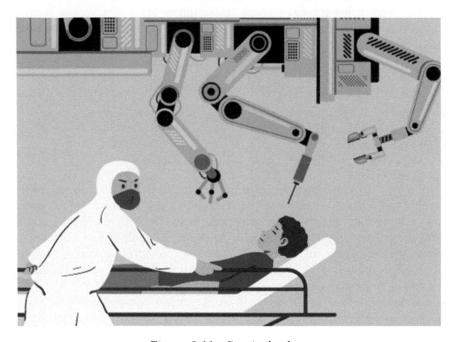

Figure 8.11   Surgical robots

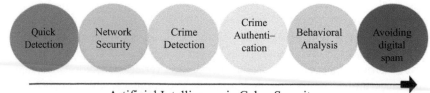

Artificial Intelligence in Cyber Security

Figure 8.12   Use of AI in cyber security

priority sectors is medicine, which depends upon its constant sharing of large amounts of useful information.

Detecting and predicting crime: As individuals become more competitive for quality medical care at such a cheaper price, the majority of instances of abuse are already on the rise. Fraud may bring injury to doctors as well as damage care organizations. This AI system can assist users in navigating complex transactions or business abuse strategies. Various AI technologies assist law enforcement officials in detecting suspicious trends that are not identified by individuals. It is used to forecast a convict's illegal activity using "Artificial Neural Networks."

Consultation via the Internet: Few digital applications could provide doctor's treatment based on a user's clinical problem and general scientific knowledge. Users will be able to edit their complaints into software, which further compares that information with such a repository of diseases using voice recognition. The frameworks, therefore, recommend therapies. Healthcare facilities could be capable of minimizing unexpected hospital stays and reduce the burden for clinical professionals also with support of digital nursing assistants. AI personal assistants are ideal for patient care since they can hold healthcare professionals in constant communication.

Rather than looking for reasons for signs you're experiencing, it is better to query the virtual nursing assistant to assist users. Once you have common diseases or problems, they will not only give you professional advice, but will also assist you in making a doctor's appointment. Furthermore, the digital assistant will be available 24 hours a day, 7 days a week, allowing it to respond to your queries in real time. The benefits of online consultation include [15]:

- No need for hospital visits
- Advanced approaches for diagnosis
- Saves money
- Less risk of getting infections from hospital
- More precise
- More secured

AI could be used to promote better involvement and personality skills to avoid medical illnesses from progressing. Certainly, a virtual health assistant or a chatbot may assist doctors, therapists, visitors, patients, or their relatives in a variety of ways. Chatbots for medical care are now being used to address various problems. Some of the Chatbots are as follows:

- *Cancer chatbot*: On Facebook Messenger, it's a useful resource for cancer patients, nurses, colleagues, and relatives. The chatbot provides some tips and facts for health. They provide caregivers support to help them cope with the stress of caring as well as make their lives more comfortable and easier. Furthermore, it would provide advice to some known persons about what to tell and how to better assist cancer patients. It is a really sophisticated approach.

    Since the healthcare chatbot market is booming, nobody will ever possibly accumulate all of them, as new bots are about to get approved and come in use every day. It also demonstrates the future of AI chatbots in healthcare, as well as the wide range of situations in which they can assist both patients and physicians.

- *Gyant chatbot*: It is a healthcare chatbot that asks queries to and learn about their issues and then transfer the message to doctors who can diagnose and prescribe in timely manner. Only Facebook Messenger and Alexa are supported by the bot. In addition to offering help to English-speaking patients, GYANT can interact with clients with their own native language. The organization stated in March 2019 that it had already completed a pre-diabetes screening programme for nearly 8 lakh people in Latin America. Following that, approximately 2 lakh high-risk people in the lower communities received daily diabetes tests at health stores.
- *Ada*: To improve the product quality of healthcare applications, this clinical chatbot takes together physicians, researchers, and technology experts. Ada correlates user requests to lots of different situations rather than depending exclusively on a database. It then compares its results to knowledge in the clinical library to come up with a much more specific and descriptive approach. Ada gives users control over their data. The user interface is once again harmed by limited natural language comprehension capacities.
- *Infermedica*: Machine learning technology powers the symptom-checker chatbot. This chatbot feature is available on both online and mobile platforms. It assesses the user's health and provides a possible diagnosis and actionable recommendations for treatment plan. This chatbot conducted three million patient screening interviews in 2017 and more than doubled its daily monthly revenue in 2018.
- *MAGe*: MAGe meets the needs of key customers within a healthcare service provider business, unlike with the number of physician medical chatbots. It analyzes visitor/patient feedback on various websites, such as Facebook, Twitter, MouthShut, and others. MAGe also offers in-depth analysis and classifies feedback using positive and negative emotion categories. It allows stakeholder groups to access and view reports for various regions and clinics. Senseforth's AI platform A.Ware was used to create this chatbot, which is based on the previous industry models. It delivers meaningful intelligence to the right person at right time. The number of data capturing point is small.
- *Babylon Health*: This chatbot belongs to the British, online medical consultation and health service, which was created in the year 2013. It is worth more than US$2 billion. The company provides AI consultations based on a patient's medical background as well as live virtual consultations with their doctor during any emergency. In the first scenario, patients provide their medical reports about the illness symptoms to software app, which uses speech recognition technology for comparing those medical informations with the database of diseases and then recommends a proper treatment for the patients. Doctors will focus closely to check the patient in the second phase, which would be more focused than the normal chatbot services. They either prescribe medication or refer the patient to a specialist if necessary.

For a trial time in 2017, the National Health Service (NHS) in the United Kingdom began using the chatbot to provide medical advice. The partnership is still going strong today, with the company providing remote appointments with doctors to NHS patients in the London and Birmingham areas. In the future, it intends to expand its operation to other cities in the United Kingdom.

- *OneRemission*: This chatbot belongs to the New-York company, which has the goal of making life easier for those fighting cancer by providing them with the required knowledge. The app empowers cancer patients and survivors by offering a detailed information for the patients being in diets, workouts, and cancer practices compiled through clinical research specialists, as people will be independent than depending on medicals experts every time. It allows patients to communicate with this chatbot doctor at any time if they need assistance [18].

- *SafedrugBot*: A good illustration of how a simple answer, such as a chatbot, could make a big difference. SafedrugBot provides healthcare practitioners with advice on drug use by breastfeeding. It assists physicians in accessing a massive information center to enhance their skills, from knowing the adverse effects of different medications to discovering healthier drugs. Telegram users can use this chatbot. SafedrugBot makes it easy for physicians to double-check medication details. It just works with one sided communication and does not have an omni-channel experience.

- *Sensely*: It works with employers, healthcare professionals, corporations, and pharmaceutical professionals to make custom applications that fill the gap among reduced chatbots and heavy social interaction. It has a wide variety of capabilities, including financing, claims management, and condition evalua-tion, and also customer support, employee health, and new treatments. With Sensely, you can create a specific company's brand by combining different characters. With AI, we are still a long way away from fully embracing com-passion. Although the idea is sound, how it would be applied remains to be seen [18].

- *NINA (AskNestlé)*: NINA is among the India's first AI-powered electronic nutrition experts, constructed with some AI platforms. This app guides new families through the process of creating a regular healthy diet to the kids. Elders would be able to personalize their food as per their dietary needs, come up with creative recipes to please picky eaters, as well as for maintaining a proper diet plan. The chatbot provides quite insightful and qualitative data. The material was chosen with the Indian audience in mind. As a result, much more contextual relevance is essential for the provision of a worldwide audience.

Reduced dosage error: Even just a small amount of medication may have a significant impact. As a result, it is indeed critical to maintain a patient's dose to something like a level, because otherwise recompense will be required. The fra-mework is developed to lower that risk of adverse events while dispensing treat-ment for patients. An extra dose of medicine could be dangerous to health. As just a consequence, it is indeed critical that the patient gets the right types of nutrients.

The aim of AI would be to reduce the chances of accidents mostly during dosage treatment phase.

Patients who consult a doctor through health providers and physicians are normally provided medication based on their questions and regular checkups. Since doctors are human, they do not have the time to listen to each individual personally due to the huge number of case scenarios they are required to treat, which creates scope for mistakes and incorrect treatment.

Layout of medication: In the medical field, there are many sophisticated AI structures that help collect and handle details. The software can assist one with narrowing down a particular or specific care course for a patient, whether that be observations and records from a patient's record, professional experience, or external analysis.

Clinical management: AI apps would be used to control how people take their medications. A monitoring system was put in place that constantly transmits details about how an individual performs managing certain prescribed medications. Unless the condition worsens, it therefore contributes to decent healthcare. AI is being used in a variety of purposes that tracks the status of a person's condition. They monitor a human's pulse rate and stress levels and ensure that they are in excellent condition. These apps can however give customers updates and reminders regarding changes. Few AI-based apps in the field of medicine are as follows:

- *ADA-AI doctor*: ADA is a medical app that has been used in 140 countries since its global launch in 2016. It was founded by physicians, scientists, and industry pioneers. Users may enter their symptoms using the app's instant messaging design. Easy questions are asked by ADA's AI to get a better understanding of the user's symptoms.

  ADA draws data from its integrated medical library using classification, clustering, and knowledge extraction to help patients prevent and treat their symptoms. The data in the virtual medical library makes it easy to align the issues raised with the available details. Its architecture is excellent, with the finest font and graphics, as well as UI and UX; the fonts can be found at FONTALIC. It was not a medical assessment. This is a secure app that requires users to log in with a unique password. If the user's symptoms worsen, they may seek medical help.

- *Analyze of Babylon Health*: Throughout the field of diseases and viral studies, AI is possibly the best assistant. This app will assist in the study and evaluation of diseases as well as predicting infectious diseases and hunting down infectious agents.

- *WebMD*: It is among the most well-known online symptom checkers. Every day, millions of citizens use it, which now has an app to expand its scope even further. Medication alerts, behavior and exercise monitoring, first aid tips, a prescription database, and other educational material are also included in the app, unlike with the online checker. Users may use the app to locate and schedule an appointment with a physician in their area. The WebMD framework is well-designed and easy to use, much like its online symptom checker.

All of the guidance has been double-checked by trained and experienced doctors, so you can trust the information it provides. Apps like these may be the way of the future when it comes to diagnosing and treating health issues.

- *Google Deepmind Health*: An app which can access and track specific medical data from a large number of health records is now available. As a result, the duration of effort consumed for manually analyzing the details is reduced.
- *K Health app*: It is a recent primary healthcare startup that just received a US $25 million Series B round of funding. It is hoped that the app would be able to provide users with more customized and appropriate health information. The app was created from the ground up to be a useful AI-powered triage and symptom checker tool. The app is based on the clinical history of over 2 billion health incidents gathered over a 20-year period.

  The app is backed by a team of seasoned and trained doctors, and it has established partnerships with about 40 New York-based health providers. The company was established in 2016 and now it has around 50 employees working to make it among the top most AI-driven medical heathcare companies throughout the industry. To determine what their ailment tends to be, users must complete a 3- to 4-minute questionnaire. The application is easy to provide an effective diagnosis based on this, and by reviewing its robust backend. It will also have recommendations on what to do next, ranging by seeing a medical professional to self-medication and care, if that is secure.
- *For diagnosis, IBM Watson Health, and Microsoft's InnerEye*: This eye diagnosis software detects eye disorders in real time. The app will illustrate damaged regions and sometimes even detect the disease or tumor the individual is experiencing by using desktop visualization of medical images.
- *SkinVision*: A Dutch startup has created an app that can detect skin cancer in its early stages. It is compatible with both iPhone and Android devices and provides an instant diagnosis. With the click of a button, you can be reassured or guided to seek medical attention by uploading a picture of your suspected skin issue to the app's database. Dick Uyttewaal, the company's CEO, has stated earlier that these types of applications will only become more relevant in the future since there is a clear lack of experience in some disciplines of medical. According to the CEO, as more photos are submitted, the online database is becoming broader and wiser enabling it to detect skin disorders.
- *Dr Now*: It aims to alleviate any stress by "separating the wheat from the chaff." Patients can speak to a doctor on demand via video conference on their mobile with this app. You have the option of paying a small monthly subscription or a one-time fee every consultation.
- *Careskore*: It is an app designed to keep track of a patient's vital signs when they are not in the hospital. It uses AI to measure and predict whether a medical case requires visit to medical center.
- *Precision medicine with the Splice Machine and QIAGEN Clinical Insight (QCI)*: The software is yet another stop for proper drug control and recognition. The application will effectively minimize prescription errors and help in drug delivery and control at the right time.

- *Sentrain & Babylon Health*: We could save time and reach more people through AI consulting apps like Babylon, which requires a private medical records and basic medical training. Sentrain provides remote clinical control.[18]
- *Zephyr Health*: Zephyr Health utilizes AI to assist in the development of customized care plans for clinician's information about medical records. Furthermore, if existing systems are also not effective, it will determine alternative care or available treatments for patients.[16]
- *Digital healthcare staff may use sensely*: The machine learning algorithms are used to power the virtual nurses. Data from people's clinical background may be fed into it. Considering the history, it can then easily detect the condition of the patient. The virtual medical assistant can also keep appointments, anticipate follow-up procedures, and bridge the gap among medical visits.

The numerous appropriate performance metrics often used assess m-healthcare efficiency [1]:

- Availability
- Efficiency
- Authenticity
- Participation
- Originality
- Customer appreciation

Drug development: Medical studies may take ages and cost too much money to develop new drug pathways. AI plays a critical role in drug development, from strategic planning to drug testing with the least amount of time and effort. AI will

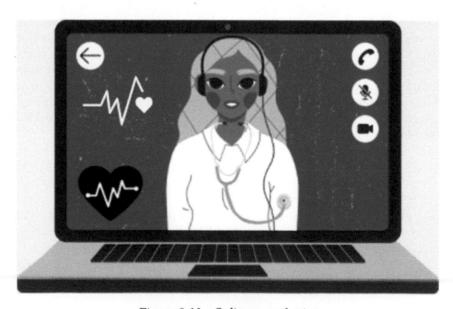

Figure 8.13   Online consultation

accelerate and reduce the cost of the process. The software would really be able to modify current drugs so that they should tackle the infection by screening it. The acceptance of drug has some proper steps to determine their quality and benefits for the patients. Few steps which are involved in the drug confirmation are mentioned in Figure 8.15. AI can distinguish between strike and result molecules, allowing for faster drug target confirmation and design process selection.

In the pharmaceutical industry, AI refers to the use of machine learning to execute activities that require human consciousness. AI has reshaped how researchers produce new medicines, therapeutic approach, and more in the

Figure 8.14   Health apps

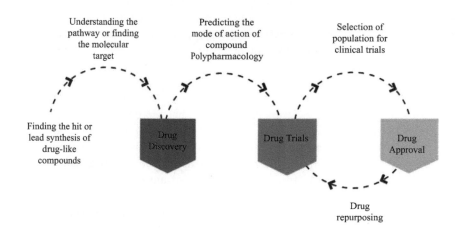

Figure 8.15   Selection and confirmation of drug

biotechnology and pharmaceutical sectors over the past few years. During the COVID-19 outbreak, AI was a positive addition to drug production. The architecture of enzymes was identified and replicated using AI. Via verification and molecular modelling, it aided in accelerating drug development. AI assists humans in drug development, research, and production, which require chemical equilibrium. Actually, AI is being used by some very renowned healthcare firms in drug development.

8.7   Pros of artificial intelligence in healthcare

- *An increase in ease of access*: Many developing nations that were facing issues with international advances in technology have little or no access to high-quality healthcare services and programmes. Such underserved places will benefit from AI advances to create a more competitive healthcare ecosystem. Automated smart digital devices can help with medical treatment and management. There are specific apps that have been utilized to treat foreign and national medical agencies in collaborating and providing critical support to someone in need.
- *Quick detection is essential*: People's personal data is used by digital applications to examine patients' past and current medical problems. Medicare workers can make more effective diagnoses by examining disorder data. So many mobile health apps' databases have reported thousands of signs and treatments. More importantly, it is capable of predicting future health problems that a person could face. Verily, for example, is indeed a software application that predicts inherited and non-contagious genetic abnormalities. With these resources available, medical practitioners can accurately anticipate and plan for potential risks by considering relevant measures today.
- *Improved productivity and lower costs*: Healthcare procedures now are simpler and cost a fraction of what they used to. From consultation session to treatment, AI has revolutionized companies in terms of time and efficiency. For example, AI can detect genetic markers in their bodies, which indicate disease. The physical effort required in determining such genetic markers has been reduced thanks to AI.
- *In treatment, reliable and one-of-a-kind support is provided*: In robotics, AI has advanced considerably. The same was said about the use of AI in operations. There are many AI medical devices that can perform even the smallest motions with 100% precision. It implies that we would perform complicated processes with little complications, internal bleeding, and discomfort. Post-surgery healing is often quicker and smoother. Antimicrobial nanorobots, for example, are used to eliminate possibility of any pathogens in bloodstream before surgery.
- *Human skills are improved, and personal development is supported*: Patients can now be assisted by robots in relation to clinical personnel. Exoskeleton robotics, for example, may assist people with disabilities in regaining

Figure 8.16   Advantages of AI in healthcare

movement with very little assistance from caregivers. Similarly, intelligent AI-powered prostheses have detectors that function as even more responsive limbs than conventional versions.

Machine learning-based automated systems can assist with daily activities and keeping people company. Figure 8.16 shows the various pros of AI in the medical industry. There have been devoted accompanying and communicative robots that perform essential scans and inspections, including blood glucose levels, heart rate, thermal insulation, or even pill administration. Due to their built-in analytics, robots are designed to assist people with depression.

8.8   Cons of artificial intelligence in healthcare

- *Lack of personal involvement*: Surgical robots are totally rational and will not be configured to have feelings for the people. It is considered as weakness by certain professionals. Some researchers say that there is always a trust between the doctor and patient due to human emotions, whereas the automated robots do not have any emotions for patients.
- *The healthcare sector has a high rate of unemployment*: There is a significant risk that all roles played previously by individuals will be replaced by robots once technology advances and AI is applied on different levels within a medical facility. As a result, many health workers are in danger of missing their jobs. Chatbots and robots can assist with mental health conditions, assess the state of such person's condition, and predict issues such as seizures, sepsis, heart attack, and so on. As a result, several individuals could quit their livelihood.
- *AI's scope of making an error*: There are rare cases of errors occurring, although in order with AI to accurately identify such diseases, it will require information from across thousands of individuals. If an information available is insufficient, the scope of making an error increases. If indeed the doctors may not have enough expertise to detect the error, they will probably provide incorrect care.
- *Social ramifications*: Since AI does not really recognize real emotions or purpose, it can offer approaches which may or may not be appropriate for specific individuals. For example, AI may prescribe an effective solution to a problem, however the person may not be from an affluent family who can afford it. Humans doctors prescribe care based on a client's societal and economic conditions.

Figure 8.17   *Disadvantages of AI in healthcare*

- *Change is hard*: The final advancement that is been supposed to reshape the medical industry, EMR, has left the healthcare community quite resentful. Mostly from billing clerk to the doctors, EMRs are designed to make everybody's work simpler. Despite its advantages, most people considered its introduction expensive as well as interruption to their routines. So, for AI to also be embraced by pharmaceutical industry as a whole, evidence are needed on its operations outlining advantages, as well as a project schedule that requires feedback from across all shareholders and proof that the project is profitable. Figure 8.17 shows the disadvantages of AI in medical field.

8.9   Discussion and conclusion

Over decades, medical distribution has become much more complicated and nuanced. The amount of information produced throughout patient journey, must be evaluated in an academic manner, responsible for a substantial portion of the complexity in providing healthcare. Through their major issue approach, AI systems can address various needs. Their intelligent design and construction combines understanding and analysis with the capacity to act in unexpected ways. It is enthralling without the need for people's interaction. As a result, the scientific domains have given fertile ground for AI researchers to establish their methods, which in many cases, AI systems have effectively addressed similar to human trials. Healthcare AI focuses on the development of AI programmes that aid in predictive modelling, diagnosis, therapy, and management.

References

[1]   Z. Faizal khan and S.R. Alotaib (2020). "Applications of Artificial Intelligence and Big Data Analytics in m-Health: A Healthcare System Perspective". *Journal of Healthcare Engineering.*   2020, Article ID 8894694, 15 pages. https://doi.org/10.1155/2020/8894694.

[2]   J. Koomey, S. Berard, M. Sanchez, and H. Wong (2010). "Implications of historical trends in the electrical efficiency of computing". *IEEE Annals of the History of Computing.* 33(3): 46–54. CiteSeerX 10.1.1.323.9505. doi:10.1109/MAHC.2010.28. S2CID 8305701.

[3]   B. Barnes and J. Dupré (2009). *Genomes and What to Make of Them,* University of Chicago Press, Chicago, IL.

[4]   A.K. Jha, C.M. DesRoches, E.G. Campbell, *et al.* (2009) "Use of electronic health records in U.S. hospitals". *The New England Journal of Medicine.* 360: 1628–1638.

[5]   https://www.medicaldesignandoutsourcing.com/how-ar-vr-devices-boosting-medicine/ Nov 2021.

[6]   S. Reddy, J. Fox and M.P. Purohit (2018). "Artificial Intelligence-Enabled Healthcare Delivery". *Journal of the Royal Society of Medicine.* 112: 22–28. doi: 10.1177/0141076818815510.

[7]   http://www.culturedose.net/category-php/ Nov 2021.

[8]   https://www.swisslog-healthcare.com/en-us/products-and-services/transport-automation/relay-autonomous-service-robot, Nov 2021.

[9]   https://spectrum.ieee.org/automaton/robotics/medical-robots/autonomous-robots-are-helping-kill-coronavirus-in-hospitals, Nov 2021.

[10]   https://www.visiononline.org/blog-article.cfm/How-Augmented-Reality-Vision-Systems-Benefit-Medical-Applications/182, Nov 2021.

[11]   S.K. Sharma, N. Gayathri, R.K. Modanval, and S. Muthuramalingam (2021). Artificial intelligence-based systems for combating COVID-19. In *Applications of Artificial Intelligence in COVID-19*, Springer, Singapore, pp. 19–34.

[12]   V. Kavidha, N. Gayathri, and S.R. Kumar (2021). AI, IoT and robotics in the medical and healthcare field. In AI and IoT-Based Intelligent Automation in Robotics, pp. 165–187.

[13]   https://fortune.com/2016/07/28/surgical-robot-development-intuitive-surgical-medtronic-google/, Nov 2021.

[14]   https://www.mayoclinic.org/tests-procedures/robotic-surgery/about/pac-20394974, Nov 2021.

[15]   https://www.diagnosio.com/blog/general/8-benefits-of-an-online-consulta-tion-with-a-doctor/, Nov 2021.

[16]   https://bigdata-madesimple.com/top-10-ai-apps-and-solutions-that-are-chan-ging-the-healthcare-industry/, Nov 2021.

[17]   https://data-flair.training/blogs/ai-and-cyber-security/, Nov 2021.

[18]   https://alan.app/blog/what-is-a-medical-chatbot/, Nov 2021.

[19]   https://www.roboticsbusinessreview.com/health-medical/6-ways-ai-and-robotics-are-improving-healthcare/, Oct 2021.

[20]   https://www.analyticssteps.com/blogs/artificial-intelligence-healthcare-applications-and-threats, Nov 2021.

[21]   S. Azzi, S. Gagnon, A. Ramirez, and G. Richards (2020). "Healthcare applications of artificial intelligence and analytics: a review and proposed framework". *Applied Sciences, MDPI.* 10(18): 6553. https://doi.org/10.3390/app10186553.

[22]   D.B. Neill (2013). "Using artificial intelligence to improve hospital inpatient care". *IEEE Intelligent Systems*, IEEE, New York, NY, pp. 1541–1672.

[23]   H. Asri, H. Mousannif, H. Al Moatassime, and T. Noel. "Big data in healthcare: challenges and opportunities". in *Proceedings of the International Conference on Cloud Technologies and Applications (CloudTech)*, Marrakech, Morocco, June 2015, pp. 1–7.

[24] https://www.investopedia.com/terms/a/artificial-intelligenceai.asp#:~:text=Artificial%20intelligence%20(AI)%20refers%20to,as%20learning%20and%20problem%2Dsolving.

[25] A. Agah (2017). *Medical Applications of Artificial Intelligence*. Agah A., ed. CRC Press, Boca Raton, FL,p. 461.

[26] G. Nagasubramanian and M. Sankayya (2021). "Multi-variate vocal data analysis for detection of Parkinson disease using deep learning". *Neural Computing and Applications*, 33(10), 4849–4864. https://link.springer.com/article/10.1007/s00521-020-05233-7.

[27] G. Nagasubramanian, M. Sankayya, F. Al-Turjman, and G. Tsaramirsis (2020). "Parkinson data analysis and prediction system using multi-variant stacked auto encoder". *IEEE Access*, vol. 8, pp. 127004–127013. 10.1109/ACCESS.2020.3007140.

[28] G. Nagasubramanian, R.K. Sakthivel, R. Patan, A.H. Gandomi, M. Sankayya, and B. Balusamy (2020). "Securing e-health records using key-less signature infrastructure blockchain technology in the cloud". *Neural Computing and Applications*, 32(3), 639–647. https://doi.org/10.1007/s00521-018-3915-1.

[29] S.R. Kumar, N. Gayathri, S. Muthuramalingam, B. Balamurugan, C. Ramesh, and M.K. Nallakaruppan (2019). "Medical Big Data mining and processing in e-healthcare". In *Internet of Things in Biomedical Engineering,* Academic Press, London, pp. 323–339. https://doi.org/10.1016/B978-0-12-817356-5.00016-4.

[30] P. Dhingra, N. Gayathri, S.R. Kumar, V. Singanamalla, C. Ramesh, and B. Balamurugan (2020). "Internet of Things–based pharmaceutics data analysis". In *Emergence of Pharmaceutical Industry Growth with Industrial IoT Approach*, Academic Press, London, pp. 85–131.

Chapter 9

Heterogeneous recurrent convolution neural network for risk prediction in the EHR dataset

Anand Javali[1] and R. Suchithra[2]

Abstract

The increasing adoption of electronic health record (EHR) systems has brought tremendous opportunities in medicine while enabling more personalized prognostic models. Predicting the risk of chronic diseases using EHRs has attracted considerable attention in recent years. Diabetes is a chronic disease, and using EHRs to predict the onset of diabetes could improve the quality and efficiency of medical care. However, most work to date has investigated the binary classification problem for predicting the onset of diabetes, but little attention has been given to assessing the risk of developing comorbidities that are major causes of morbidity and mortality. Leveraging massive EHRs brings tremendous promise to advancing clinical and precision medicine informatics research. However, it is very challenging to directly work with multifaceted patient information encoded in EHR data. Deriving effective representations of patient EHRs is a crucial step to bridge raw EHR information and the endpoint analytical tasks, such as risk prediction or chronic disease subtyping. To overcome these problems two new approaches, Heterogeneous Recurrent Convolution Neural Network (HRCC) and Multi Level Spatial Coherence Optimization Approach (MLSCO), are developed in this work. To understand the predictive performance of this approach several performance metrics are used. Compared with traditional machine learning models, the deep learning-based approach achieves superior performance on risk prediction tasks. The experimental results show that this method provides a superior predictive effect than other traditional machine learning models.

Keywords: Smart health; EHRs; Machine learning; Diabetes; Risk Prediction Analysis; MLSCO; HRCC

[1]Computer Science and Engineering, Jain University, Bangalore, India
[2]MCA Department, Jain University, Bangalore, India

9.1   Introduction

Diabetes is responsible for considerable morbidity, healthcare utilization, and mortality in both developed and developing countries. Globally, in 2017, it was estimated that 425 million people had diabetes, and this is predicted to increase to 629 million by the end of 2045. Type 2 diabetes mellitus (T2DM) is the most common type of diabetes (95%) in the United States (US), where more than 30 million people had diabetes in 2017. The high costs of hospital treatment and the high rate of readmission associated with diabetes mean that early prevention and effective treatment are crucial. The early prediction of the onset of diabetes using routinely available data such as electronic health records (EHRs) is therefore important.

The broad adoption of EHR systems has provided clinicians and researchers with an unprecedented resource and opportunity for conducting health informatics research. EHRs are systematic collections of longitudinal patient health information, such as diagnoses, medications, lab tests, procedures, and other information to characterize patient health, generated by one or more encounters across multiple healthcare providers or organizations. While EHR data provide a unique opportunity to characterize chronic disease patterns and imminent risk of chronic disease, they also present many challenges due to their heterogeneity, high-dimensionality, sparsity, irregularity, and bias. To overcome these challenges, previous studies have developed various methods for feature extraction and representation from EHR data. The processing pipeline generally approaches the problem by first defining the representation structure of the data, then adjusting the learning infrastructure, and finally conducting prediction experiments according to the available data and target label. Research in feature representation spans from vector, sequence, tensor, temporal matrix, to graph representations. Once the primary representation is selected, the adapted learning infrastructure is developed for different representations with different techniques including support vector machine, regression, and tensor factorization, etc.

Despite the advances in representation learning techniques for EHR data, one of the most important issues has not been given enough examination. Particularly, it is nontrivial to preserve the information completeness to capture the correlation between features. For example, some of the feature representations including vector and sequence lose the information about the temporal transitions between diagnoses. Moreover, the correlation between features is critical to the spatial arrangement in some deep learning approaches, such as convolutional neural networks. To overcome this drawback this work introduces a novel approach for feature representation with complete information that captures the temporal correlation from EHR features and a deep learning infrastructure to further extract features in a supervised manner. This method is called the Heterogeneous Recurrent Convolution Neural Network (HRCC). After extracting the features, to enhance the prediction accuracy this method is developed into the Multi Level Spatial Coherence Optimization Approach (MLSCO) to select the best features.

Specifically, this method can employ all the existing deep learning-based approaches as the basic predictive model, such as recurrent neural networks (RNNs) and convolutional neural networks (CNNs). This not only makes the training process of the model more efficient, but also learns different weights for different constraint features. This work conducts experiments on three medical datasets. The results show that the framework PRIME is able to incorporate heterogeneous prior medical knowledge and outperforms existing risk prediction models. It is worthwhile highlighting the contributions of this framework as follows:

- To the best of our knowledge, this is the first attempt to take prior medical knowledge into account for a risk prediction task.
- This is a novel framework HRCC, which models prior medical knowledge as posterior regularization and learns the desired posterior distribution with a log-linear model.
- The HRCC is a general model, which can be easily applied to any predictive models in health care. Moreover, it is able to distinguish the importance of different prior knowledge contributed to risk prediction using MLSCO.
- Experimental results on three medical datasets demonstrate that the MLSCO is effective for the task of risk prediction.

9.2   Related work

In this section, existing studies are briefly reviewed which are closely related to our work, including machine learning and deep learning-based models for healthcare applications and posterior regularization techniques with deep learning models.

Machine learning methods have been applied to EHRs for predicting a number of different outcomes, both for specific diseases and also for the risk of mortality and hospitalization, also, the number of studies using EHR data for creating risk prediction models is increasing [1]. Zhao and Weng [2] used 20 variables known to be related to pancreatic cancer and weighted them using PubMed abstracts. The variables included symptoms, lab results, and comorbidities, and were extracted from EHRs for 98 cases and 196 controls. Each selected variable was assigned a weight according to whether the association to pancreatic cancer mined from the abstracts was positive or negative and a Bayesian Network Inference model using the assigned weights gave a better predictive performance compared to not using the weights derived from PubMed.

In their study on using machine learning to develop risk prediction models from health record data, Mani *et al.* [3] aimed to identify patients at risk of type 2 diabetes. They extracted 16 variables representing demographic information, clinical findings, and laboratory values for over 2000 patients, of whom 10% were patients with a diabetes type 2 diagnosis and the remaining were controls. Three datasets representing different time intervals were created. In the first one, all data up to the diagnosis date were included, while in the second and third ones, data were included from over 365 days and over 180 days before the diagnosis.

A number of classifiers were evaluated for predicting which patients would develop type 2 diabetes, and an AUC (area under the curve) of >0.8 was achieved for each of the three time intervals.

Huang *et al.* [4] aimed to predict future cases of depression, the severity of the depression, and the response to treatment. In brief, 5000 patients with a future depression diagnosis and at least 1.5 years of data before the diagnosis were matched to six times as many controls. Diagnosis codes, medication codes, demographics, and free text from EHRs belonging to the cases and controls were used as input and their model could predict depression diagnoses 12 months in advance with an AUC of 0.7, and when including all available data up to the diagnosis data, the corresponding result was an AUC of 0.8.

Kop *et al.* [5] used structured data from EHRs to predict future cases of colorectal cancer (CRC). Six months of data for over 260,000 patients, of whom 0.5% were CRC cases, were extracted from primary care health records. The data included ICPC codes (International Classification of Primary Care), ATC codes (Anatomical Therapeutic Chemical Classification System), and laboratory values. Temporal and co-occurrence patterns were mined from the dataset and used as input for three different classifiers, CART decision trees, logistic regression, and Random Forest. An AUC of 0.891 was achieved and the input features were ranked according to the importance factor provided by the logistic regression model. Most of the features with high ranks corresponded to events known to be linked to colorectal cancer, providing validation of their model.

Chen *et al.* [6–8] proposed a healthcare system using smart clothing for sustainable health monitoring. Qiu *et al.* [9] thoroughly studied the heterogeneous systems and achieved the best results for cost minimization on tree and simple path cases for heterogeneous systems. Patients' statistical information, test results, and disease history are recorded in the EHR, enabling us to identify potential data-centric solutions to reduce the costs of medical case studies. Qiu *et al.* [10] proposed an efficient flow-estimating algorithm for the telehealth cloud system and designed a data coherence protocol for the PHR (Personal Health Record)-based distributed system.

Bates *et al.* [11] proposed six applications of big data in the field of health care. Qiu *et al.* [12] proposed an optimal big data sharing algorithm to handle the complicated dataset in telehealth with cloud techniques. One of the applications is to identify high-risk patients which can be utilized to reduce medical costs since high-risk patients often require expensive health care. Moreover, in the first paper proposing a healthcare cyber-physical system [13], it innovatively brought forward the concept of prediction-based healthcare applications, including health risk assessment. Prediction using traditional disease risk models usually involves a machine learning algorithm (e.g., logistic regression and regression analysis, etc.), and especially a supervised learning algorithm by the use of training data with labels to train the model [14,15].

In the test set, patients can be classified into either high-risk or low-risk groups. These models are valuable in clinical situations and are widely studied [16,17]. However, these schemes have the following characteristics and defects. The dataset is typically small for patients and diseases with specific conditions [18], and the characteristics are selected through experience. However, these preselected characteristics may not satisfy the changes in the disease and its influencing factors. With the development of big data analytics technology, more attention has been paid to disease prediction from the perspective of big data analysis, various researches have been conducted by selecting the characteristics automatically from a large amount of data to improve the accuracy of risk classification [19,20], rather than the previously selected characteristics.

Recently, deep learning-based models have shown their superior ability to learn complex patterns from high-dimensional, noisy, and temporal EHR data. Multilayer perception (MLP) is used to learn the representations of phenotypes and medical codes [21]. However, MLP-based models do not consider the temporal nature of the EHR data. To model the temporal EHR data, recurrent neural networks (RNNs) are applied to predict patients' health status and patient subtyping. Convolutional neural networks (CNNs) focus on capturing local temporal dependency among EHR data and are used for predicting multiple diseases and other related tasks [22]. Risk prediction is an important yet challenging task in the healthcare domain. Choi *et al.* [23] tried to use attention-based recurrent neural networks to predict the risk of heart failure disease. Cheng *et al.* [24] applied the CNN model to analyze discrete patient EHR data. Che *et al.* [25] proposed using the pretrained embeddings of medical features in the CNN model to improve the prediction performance. In Ref. [26], the authors built a semi-supervised deep learning model with generative adversarial networks for the risk prediction task.

Compared with all the aforementioned predictive models, the PRIME framework has the following advantages:

1. It takes prior medical knowledge into account, and
2. It is a general model that can include any state-of-the-art predictive model when modeling patients' visits. The prior knowledge guides the predictive models to learn better suboptimal parameters, which finally leads to good predictive performance.

9.3   Methodology

This section illustrates the procedure of data collection, processing, feature retrieving schemes for presenting datasets, prediction schemes, and combining knowledge-gathering methods employed in experimental examination. An illustration of the work is depicted in Figure 9.1. It consists of the following five modules:

1. Gathering of the dataset;
2. Data cleaning;
3. Attribute selection;
4. Feature extraction;
5. Prediction of risk model generation.

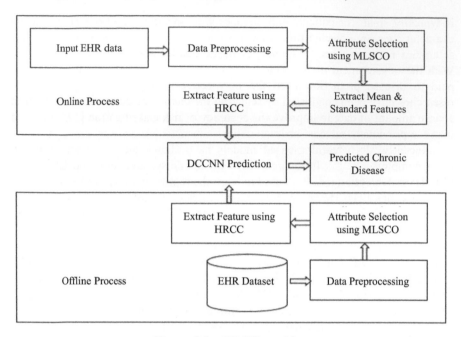

Figure 9.1　HRCC workflow

9.3.1　Gathering of the dataset

We used a publicly available dataset from the United States released by Practice Fusion in 2012. The dataset consisted of the de-identified electronic health records of 9948 patients, with 1904 diagnosed with T2DM over a 4-year period (2009–2012). The dataset also included doctor transcripts with diagnoses, laboratory tests, and medications.

9.3.2　Data cleaning

EMR databases usually have different hereditary data sources, and the data extracted from the MRR database are incomplete and unnecessary, which will ultimately affect the final output [27,28]. Therefore, EMR data must be prepared in advance to ensure that they are accurate, complete, consistent, and confidential. Incomplete, noise-free, and incompatible EMR data should be optimized by meeting noise standard settings and correcting inconsistencies when cleaning data.

When collecting EMR data, some data attributes may be lost due to manual errors and system failures. For default data, there are several ways to work. We can ignore the missing data, complete the default value manually, use the average value, fill the default value with the most likely value, or download another data source. When missing values have a significant impact on processing, the missing data are usually ignored. For example, when retrieving patient information, if the name of the operation is lost, the data must be ignored. However, if the bed number information is lost, the data cannot be ignored. In the case that the dataset is small, the default settings can be filled manually.

In conclusion, if one attribute can be derived from another attribute, then the attribute is no longer needed and must be deleted. Surplus is mainly reflected in many records of data attributes or inconsistencies in the way the attributes are displayed. For example, when a patient needs to be transferred to another hospital for treatment, some check-ups will be repeated at the last hospital, resulting in many unnecessary medical records. These obsolete records are removed when cleaning data.

9.3.3 Attribute/feature selection through MLSCO

Once the database has been cleared, the next step is to select the important attributes from the cleaned dataset. This process can be used to reduce the dimensions of the dataset by selecting the main and important features. We grouped 1312 features into (1) basic and fixed features [age, sex, body mass index (BMI), and blood pressure], (2) adjustable features (diagnostic features based on ICD-9 codes, medication, and laboratory tests) with labels encoded into binary vectors corresponding to three embeddings, and (3) crossed features by selecting top diagnosis features to cross with top medication features. Embeddings are a mapping of a categorical variable to a vector of continuous numbers which are useful for reducing the dimensionality of categorical variables and meaningfully represent categories in the transformed space. Three types of features (diagnoses, medications, and laboratory tests) were label encoded into binary vectors.

Steps taken for feature extraction and selection are described below.

1. Outliers of BMI, height, and weight variables were cleaned for each patient.
2. BMI-related features were generated from BMI data for each patient including BMI median, minimum, and maximum values, isOverweight, isObese, and difference between BMI min and BMI max values. isOverweight and isObese features were determined based on some cut-offs (ranges) of the BMI median value of each patient. BMI data were already calculated from the height and weight of each patient. Each patient could have more than one BMI data record. These data were used to generate six BMI-related features.
3. Systolic and diastolic blood pressures were calculated to generate blood pressure features (median, minimum, and maximum values), difference between minimum and maximum values of blood pressures, whether a patient had high blood pressure (HBP) in the first or second stage, or not. These HBP features (1/0 ~ yes/no) were determined based on a range of threshold values of blood pressures for each patient which were ranked in medical research.
4. Diagnosis data were analyzed to extract ICD-9 codes, excluding the data in 2012, there was a total of 3903 different codes for all patients. These diagnosis features were encoded with labels as a sparse binary vector (each ICD-9 code was labeled with value 1, otherwise 0) for each patient.

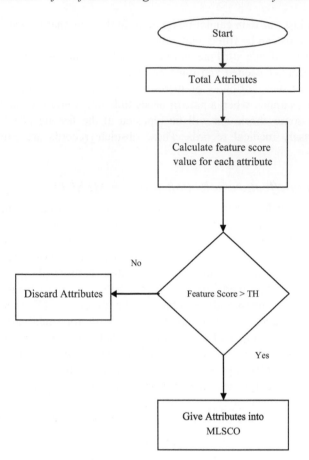

Figure 9.2   Flow chart of the MLSCO algorithm

To reduce the dimensions of diagnosis feature vectors for all patients, each column vector corresponding to one column ICD-9 code feature was assigned an important feature score by measuring cosine distance between column feature vector and label column vector (target) (labeled as 1/0 corresponding with yes/no diabetes, respectively). Then these feature scores are given into the input MLSCO approach.

The flow chart of the MLSCO is shown in Figure 9.2.

9.3.3.1   MLSCO algorithm

Input: attributes and their values, correlation probability (CRP), transmutation probability (TP).

Output: Best attributes B.

1. Select random attribute values from each attribute and consider as the initial attribute A.

2. Evaluate the feature score f(x) of each attribute x in the attribute A by using the below formula

$$f(x) = \frac{1}{N}\sum_{i=1}^{N} X_i$$

where X_i is the *i*-th attribute values in the attribute X and N is the total values in the attribute.

3. Create a new attribute NA by repeating following steps until the new population AP is complete.

4. Select attributes from an attribute NA according to their fitness. Select the attribute if the fitness value is high. otherwise reject the attribute.

5. With a correlation probability, CRP, the selected attributes form a new attribute. If no correlation was performed, the new attribute is an exact copy of selected attributes.

6. With a transmutation probability MP mutate selected attribute.

7. Place selected attribute in a new attribute AP.

8. Use new generated attribute AP for a further run of the algorithm.

9. If the end condition is satisfied, stop and return the best solution B in the current attribute.

10. Go to step 2.

11. Finally, the output of the algorithm is the fitness value F and the best attribute B.

12. In addition, give the best attribute B as the weight value of the ML and execute MLSCO.

13. From the MLSCO, return the best attribute B as the output.

9.3.3.2　Extraction of features using HRCC

In this module the features are extracted from the best attributes. The first-order features, such as mean and standard deviation, are used. The mean features are calculated by using the following formula:

$$M = \sqrt{\frac{1}{N}\sum_{i=1}^{N}(x_i)}$$

where x_i is the value of each best attribute and N is the total number of patients.

The standard deviation formula is calculated by using the following formula:

$$\sigma = \sqrt{\frac{1}{N}\sum_{i=1}^{N}(x_i - \mu)^2}$$

where x_i is the value of each best attribute, μ is the mean value, and N is the total number of patients. Then, the features of all three transforms are combined to form a single feature vector and then these features are given as the input to HRCC.

In this section, a new method is introduced for extracting features. This new method is called the Heterogeneous Recurrent Convolution Neural Network (HRCC). Although RNN produces better results than the existing feature extraction approaches, adding deep learning with RNN surely increases the detection accuracy. Deep learning uses the deep features by increasing their size. The generally supervised classification result is based on the total number of features given to it. If the number of features is increased the classifier produces the best results. Therefore, in this section to improve the detection accuracy of the RNN the deep features are added to the RNN. To extract the deep features, CNN is used. The CNN is applied after extracting the RNN feature map from the input features.

A CNN consists of one or more convolutional layers and pooling layers. Normally, CNNs are used for classification purposes. However, in this work CNN is used to extract the deep features from the GOLOF feature map image. Therefore, in this work, CNN is designed with three convolutional layers, with pooling layers.

Convolution layer
In a CNN, convolution layers play the role of the feature extractor. In this work, deep features are extracted from the convolution layers. To extract these, first the filter is generated and then the convolution operation is applied by using the following formula to extract the features:

$$FI(i,j) = \sum_{m=-1}^{1} \sum_{n=-1}^{1} FMI(i+m, j+n) \times K(m,n)$$

where $FI(i,j)$ is the convolution output of the RNN feature map FM. Here i and j are variables that represent the position of the feature value. K is the convolution filter of dimensions $m \times n$.

Pooling layer
The pooling layer performs downsampling, that is, it reduces the computation time by reducing the number of extracted features. There are two kinds of pooling layers: max pooling and average pooling. In max pooling, we take only the value of the largest attribute among all the attributes in the receptive field of the filter. In the case of average pooling, we take the average of all the values in the receptive field. The output of the pooling layer is given as the input of the next convolution layer. After completing three layers the outputs of the three pooling layers are combined and become the output features. These features are called deep features. Finally, these deep features are given into the classifier for risk prediction.

9.3.4 Prediction of risk using HRCC

To build a prediction model, this work uses the same HRCC approach. An explanation of the HRCC is given in the above section. Figure 9.3 presents the HRCC processing flowchart graphically.

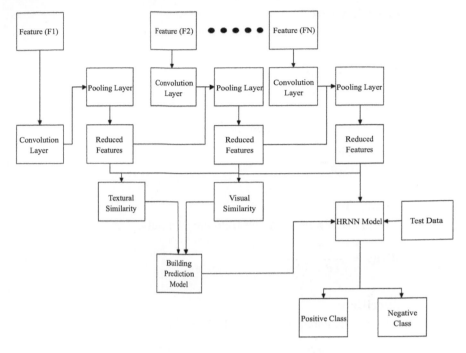

Figure 9.3 The flowchart of HRCC

9.4 Result and examination

9.4.1 Examination parameters

To examine the effectiveness of the prediction methods, several examination parameters are available. This work considers the detection accuracy, precision rate, recall rate, sensitivity, specificity, F-measure, and error rate to examine the effectiveness.

9.4.1.1 Detection accuracy

The detection accuracy metric finds the percentage of accuracy between the original disease and the predicted disease.

$$\text{Accuracy} = \frac{TP + TN}{TP + FP + TN + FN} \tag{9.1}$$

9.4.1.2 Error rate

The error rate finds the percentage of inaccuracy between the original disease and the predicted disease.

$$\text{Error Rate} = \frac{\text{No of Images of Falsely predicted disease}}{\text{Total No. of Records}} \tag{9.2}$$

9.4.1.3   Precision rate
The precision value is calculated by using the following formula:

$$\text{Precision} = \frac{TP}{TP + FP} \tag{9.3}$$

9.4.1.4   Recall rate
The recall rate is calculated by using the following formula:

$$\text{Recall} = \frac{TP}{TP + FN} \tag{9.4}$$

9.4.1.5   Sensitivity
The sensitivity is calculated using the following formula:

$$\text{Sensitivity} = \frac{TP}{(TP + FN)} \tag{9.5}$$

9.4.1.6   Specificity
The specificity is calculated using the following formula:

$$\text{Specificity} = \frac{TN}{(FP + TN)} \tag{9.6}$$

9.4.1.7   F-measure
The F-measure is calculated using the following formula:

$$F_m = (1 + \alpha) * \frac{\text{Precision} * \text{Recall}}{\alpha * (\text{Precision} * \text{Recall})} \tag{9.7}$$

9.4.2   Experimental examination
The efficiency of the model is validated in multiple experiments. Evaluation of the efficiency of prediction is done with the accuracy, precision rate, recall rate, sensitivity, specificity, F-measure, and error rate measures.

9.4.2.1   Experiment No. 1
Examination of prediction approaches using accuracy
Accuracy is evaluated for various techniques through operating indicators. The results are recorded in Table 9.1.

The graphical representation of the previous result set indicates the trend with individual techniques and the highest value obtained is 98.34% for DT and heuristic combination. This is comparatively more powerful than other techniques. The result set is illustrated in Figure 9.4.

Table 9.1   HRCC prediction techniques using accuracy

Feature selection	Prediction approaches—Accuracy				
	ELM	**NN**	**RNN**	**CNN**	**HRCC**
Genetic	86.24	88.14	88.28	91.05	97.35
PSO	87.15	89.05	89.19	91.96	98.26
Fuzzy	85.23	87.13	87.27	90.04	96.34
MLSCO	87.67	89.42	90.33	92.41	98.34

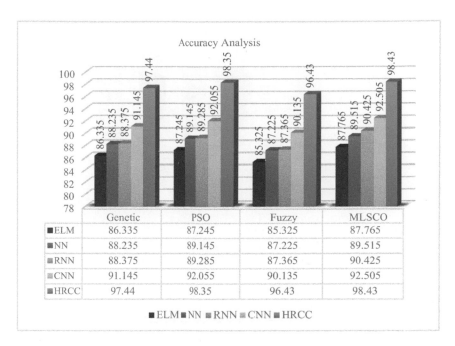

Figure 9.4   HRCC accuracy analysis

9.4.2.2   Experiment No. 2

Evaluation using the precision rate

The precision rate is evaluated for various techniques through operating indicators. The results are recorded in Table 9.2.

The graphical representation of the previous result set indicates the trend with individual techniques and the highest value obtained is 98.34% for DT and heuristic combination. The results are more efficient than other techniques. The result set is illustrated in Figure 9.5.

Table 9.2   HRCC prediction techniques using the precision rate

Rules	Prediction approaches—Precision rate				
	ELM	NN	RNN	CNN	HRCC
Genetic	86.27	88.17	88.31	91.08	97.38
PSO	87.18	89.08	89.22	91.99	98.29
Fuzzy	85.26	87.16	87.3	90.07	96.37
MLSCO	87.7	89.45	90.36	92.44	98.37

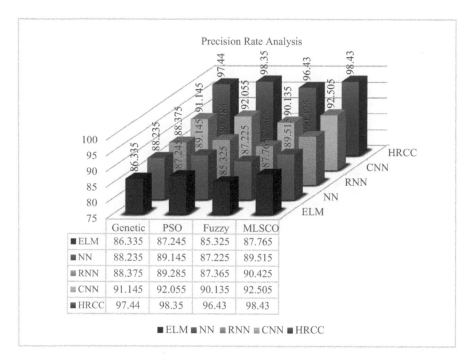

Figure 9.5   HRCC precision rate analysis

9.4.2.3   Experiment No. 3

Examination of prediction approaches using the recall rate
This section uses the recall rate to examine the performance of the approach and the performance values are included in Table 9.3.

Table 9.3 shows that the highest specific value of 98.39% was found for this method, and it is more effective because it has the highest value compared to other techniques. The results of these indicators are shown in Figure 9.6.

Table 9.3   HRCC prediction techniques using the recall rate

Feature selection	Prediction Approaches—Recall rate				
	ELM	**NN**	**RNN**	**CNN**	**HRCC**
Genetic	86.29	88.19	88.33	91.1	97.4
PSO	87.2	89.1	89.24	92.01	98.31
Fuzzy	85.28	87.18	87.32	90.09	96.39
MLSCO	87.72	89.47	90.38	92.46	98.39

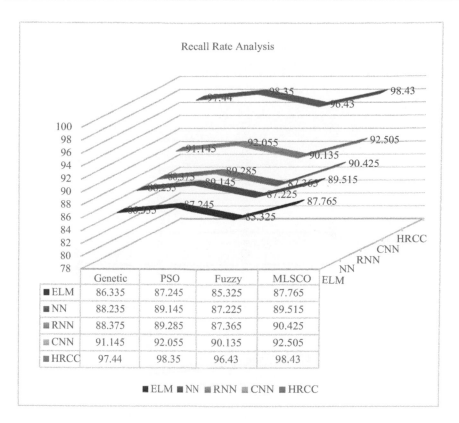

Figure 9.6   HRCC recall rate analysis

9.4.2.4   Experiment No. 4

Examination of prediction approaches using sensitivity

Sensitivity is one of the metrics used for analyzing performance. Therefore, this section uses this metric to evaluate the prediction scheme. The output for sensitivity is shown in Table 9.4.

From Table 9.4, it can be seen that the highest sensitivity value of 98.40% is found for HRCC which higher than the others. The resultant values are drawn in Figure 9.7.

Table 9.4   HRCC prediction techniques using sensitivity

Feature selection	Prediction approaches—Sensitivity				
	ELM	**NN**	**RNN**	**CNN**	**HRCC**
Genetic	86.3	88.2	88.34	91.11	97.41
PSO	87.21	89.11	89.25	92.02	98.32
Fuzzy	85.29	87.19	87.33	90.1	96.4
MLSCO	87.73	89.48	90.39	92.47	98.4

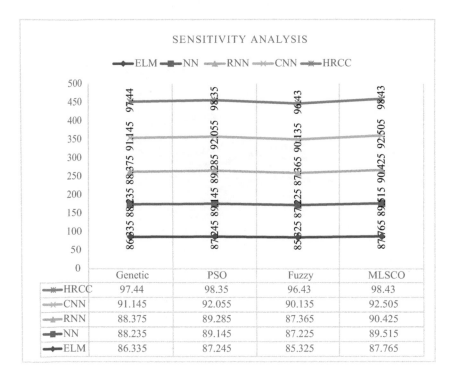

Figure 9.7   HRCC sensitivity analysis

9.4.2.5   Experiment No. 5

Examination of prediction approaches using specificity

In this section, the approach's performance is inspected through the specificity and the values are tabulated in Table 9.5.

Table 9.5 shows that the highest value of 98.41% was found for HRCC, which is higher than for the other techniques. The values obtained are plotted in Figure 9.8.

Table 9.5   HRCC prediction techniques using specificity

Feature selection	Prediction approaches—Specificity				
	ELM	**NN**	**RNN**	**CNN**	**HRCC**
Genetic	86.31	88.21	88.35	91.12	97.42
PSO	87.22	89.12	89.26	92.03	98.33
Fuzzy	85.3	87.2	87.34	90.11	96.41
MLSCO	87.74	89.49	90.4	92.48	98.41

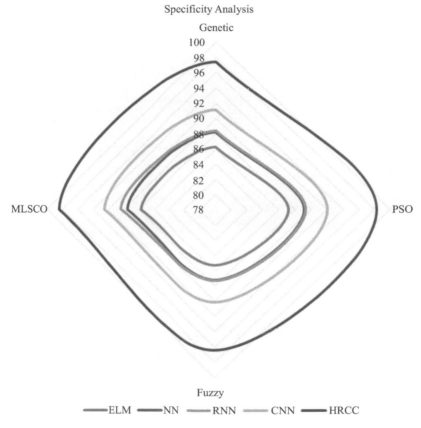

Figure 9.8   HRCC specificity analysis

9.4.2.6   Experiment No. 6

Examination of prediction approaches using the F-measure
This section employs the F-measure for analysis of the performance of the approach, and the performance values are included in Table 9.6.

Table 9.6   HRCC prediction techniques using the F-measure

Feature selection	Prediction approaches—F-Measure				
	ELM	NN	RNN	CNN	HRCC
Genetic	86.335	88.235	88.375	91.145	97.44
PSO	87.245	89.145	89.285	92.055	98.35
Fuzzy	85.325	87.225	87.365	90.135	96.43
MLSCO	87.765	89.515	90.425	92.505	98.43

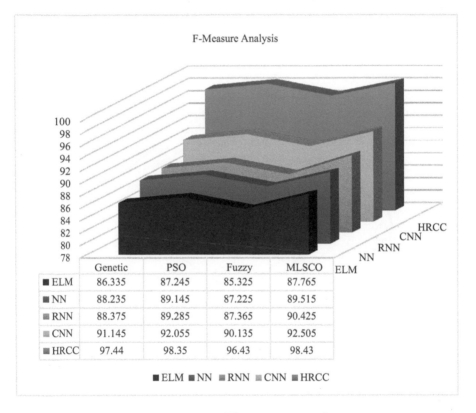

Figure 9.9   HRCC F-measure analysis

In this section, specificity is successfully assessed and Table 9.6 shows that the peak specificity value of 98.43% is found for HRCC, as shown in Figure 9.9.

9.5   Conclusion

In this chapter, the focus is on prediction of chronic disease risks in which the EHRs are used largely as data sources along with other supporting datasets for knowledge extraction and value mappings. Multiple deep learning techniques are implemented in this approach. Through experiments, it was proven that individual feature labeling is low in accuracy and performance. Considering several feature variables and rules, implementation produced greater accuracy and better efficiency of predicting risk. Evolution of these algorithms with multiple experimental results has shown the highest accuracy of 97.44%. A novel algorithm is designed for prediction, and a generic framework is designed for analyzing disease progression and risk prediction by combining multiple algorithms. Therefore, this method and the combination of rules and features performs best in risk prediction analysis of disease.

References

[1] B.A. Goldstein, A.M. Navar, M.J. Pencina, and J. Ioannidis. Opportunities and challenges in developing risk prediction models with electronic health records data: a systematic review. *Journal of the American Medical Informatics Association.* 2017; 24(1): 198–208. pmid:27189013.

[2] D. Zhao, and C. Weng. Combining PubMed knowledge and EHR data to develop a weighted Bayesian network for pancreatic cancer prediction. *Journal of Biomedical Informatics.* 2011; 44(5): 859–868. pmid:21642013.

[3] S. Mani, Y. Chen, T. Elasy, W. Clayton, and J. Denny. Type 2 diabetes risk forecasting from EMR data using machine learning. In: AMIA Annual Symposium Proceedings, vol. 2012. Washington, DC: American Medical Informatics Association; 2012. p. 606.

[4] S.H. Huang, P. LePendu, S.V. Iyer, M. Tai-Seale, D. Carrell, and N.H. Shah. Toward personalizing treatment for depression: predicting diagnosis and severity. *Journal of the American Medical Informatics Association.* 2014; 21 (6): 1069331075. pmid:24988898.

[5] R. Kop, M. Hoogendoorn, A. Ten Teije, *et al.* Predictive modeling of colorectal cancer using a dedicated pre-processing pipeline on routine electronic medical records. *Computers in Biology and Medicine.* 2016; 76:30–38. pmid:27392227.

[6] M. Chen, Y. Ma, Y. Li, D. Wu, Y. Zhang, and C. Youn. Wearable 2.0: enable human-cloud integration in next generation healthcare system. *IEEE Communications*, 2017; 55(1): 54–61.

[7] M. Chen, Y. Ma, J. Song, C. Lai, and B. Hu. Smart clothing: connecting human with clouds and big data for sustainable health monitoring. *ACM/ Springer Mobile Networks and Applications* 2016; 21(5): 825–845.

[8] M. Chen, P. Zhou, and G. Fortino. Emotion communication system. *IEEE Access*, 2016; 5: 326–337, DOI: 10.1109/ACCESS.2016.2641480.

[9] M. Qiu and E.H.-M. Sha. Cost minimization while satisfying hard/soft timing constraints for heterogeneous embedded systems. *ACM Transactions on Design Automation of Electronic Systems (TODAES)*, 2009; 14(2): 25.

[10] J. Wang, M. Qiu, and B. Guo. Enabling real-time information service on telehealth system over cloud-based big data platform. *Journal of Systems Architecture*, 2017; 72: 69–79.

[11]   D.W. Bates, S. Saria, L. Ohno-Machado, A. Shah, and G. Escobar. Big data in health care: using analytics to identify and manage high-risk and high-cost patients. *Health Affairs*, 2014; 33(7): 1123–1131.

[12]   L. Qiu, K. Gai, and M. Qiu. Optimal big data sharing approach for tele-health in cloud computing. In IEEE International Conference on Smart Cloud (SmartCloud), IEEE, 2016, pp. 184–189.

[13]   Y. Zhang, M. Qiu, C.-W. Tsai, M.M. Hassan, and A. Alamri. Healthcps: Healthcare cyber-physical system assisted by cloud and big data. *IEEE Systems Journal*, 2015; 11: 1–8.

[14]   K. Lin, J. Luo, L. Hu, M.S. Hossain, and A. Ghoneim. Localization based on social big data analysis in the vehicular networks. *IEEE Transactions on Industrial Informatics*, 2016; 13: 1932–1940.

[15]   K. Lin, M. Chen, J. Deng, M.M. Hassan, and G. Fortino. Enhanced finger-printing and trajectory prediction for IoT localization in smart buildings. *IEEE Transactions on Automation Science and Engineering*, 2016; 13(3): 1294–1307.

[16]   D. Oliver, F. Daly, F.C. Martin, and M.E. McMurdo. Risk factors and risk assessment tools for falls in hospital in-patients: a systematic review. *Age and Ageing*, 2004; 33(2): 122–130.

[17]   S. Marcoon, A.M. Chang, B. Lee, R. Salhi, and J.E. Hollander. Heart score to further risk stratify patients with low TIMI scores. *Critical Pathways in Cardiology*, 2013; 12(1): 1–5.

[18]   S. Bandyopadhyay, J. Wolfson, D.M. Vock, *et al.* Data mining for censored time-to-event data: a Bayesian network model for predicting cardiovascular risk from electronic health record data. *Data Mining and Knowledge Discovery*, 2015; 29(4): 1033–1069.

[19]   B. Qian, X. Wang, N. Cao, H. Li, and Y.-G. Jiang. A relative similarity based method for interactive patient risk prediction, *Data Mining and Knowledge Discovery*, 2015; 29(4), 1070–1093.

[20]   A. Singh, G. Nadkarni, O. Gottesman, S.B. Ellis, E.P. Bottinger, and J.V. Guttag. Incorporating temporal EHR data in predictive models for risk stratification of renal function deterioration. *Journal of Biomedical Informatics*, 2015; 53: 220–228.

[21]   E. Choi, M.T. Bahadori, E. Searles, *et al.* Multilayer representation learning for medical concepts. In Proceedings of the 22nd ACM SIGKDD International Conference on Knowledge Discovery and Data Mining (KDD'16), 2016, pp. 1495–1504.

[22]   I.M. Baytas, C. Xiao, X. Zhang, F. Wang, A.K. Jain, and J. Zhou. Patient subtyping via time-aware LSTM networks. In Proceedings of the 23rd ACM SIGKDD International Conference on Knowledge Discovery and Data Mining (KDD'17), 2017, pp. 65–74.

[23]   E. Choi, M.T. Bahadori, J. Sun, J. Kulas, A. Schuetz, and W. Stewart. Retain: An interpretable predictive model for healthcare using reverse time attention mechanism. In Proceedings of Advances in Neural Information Processing Systems (NIPS'16), 2016, pp. 3504–3512.

[24] Y. Cheng, F. Wang, P. Zhang, and J. Hu. Risk prediction with electronic health records: a deep learning approach. In Proceedings of the 2016 SIAM International Conference on Data Mining (SDM'16), 2016, pp. 432–440.

[25] Z. Che, Y. Cheng, Z. Sun, and Y. Liu. Exploiting convolutional neural network for risk prediction with medical feature embedding. In Proceedings of NIPS Workshop on Machine Learning for Health (NIPS-ML4HC'16), 2016.

[26] Z. Che, Y. Cheng, S. Zhai, Z. Sun, and Y. Liu. Boosting deep learning risk prediction with generative adversarial networks for electronic health records. In 2017 IEEE International Conference on Data Mining (ICDM). New York, NY: IEEE, 2017, pp. 787–792.

[27] S.K. Sharma, N. Gayathri, R.K. Modanval, and S. Muthuramalingam. Artificial intelligence-based systems for combating COVID-19. In *Applications of Artificial Intelligence in COVID-19*. Springer, Singapore, 2021, pp. 19–34.

[28] V. Kavidha, N. Gayathri, and S.R. Kumar. AI, IoT and robotics in the medical and healthcare field. In *AI and IoT-Based Intelligent Automation in Robotics*, 2021, pp. 165–187.

Chapter 10

A narrative review and impacts on trust for data in the healthcare industry using artificial intelligence

S. Dayana Priyadharshini[1], M. Arvindhan[2] and M. Sivakumar[3]

Abstract

Artificial intelligence (AI) and robotics are quickly entering the healthcare industry, assuming several important responsibilities, including the capability to diagnose and treat patients. Although the majority of research in its technological development has been focused on interpersonal contact, this has led to a slew of technological challenges. As a result, the scope of technologies' effect on human–human interactions and relationships in the healthcare industry is limited rather than treating healthcare information technology. The hypothesis of AI in health care is that trust is critically important for healthcare partnerships, and because of this, healthcare AI could have dramatic consequences on these bonds of trust. In helping the technology of healthcare in AI, it is believed that data from the traditional task and medical devices have been classified into various levels for maintaining healthcare in the AI domain. Despite this, the application of AI will necessitate successful planning and strategy implementation to help and comprehensively apply these technologies.

Keywords: Artificial Intelligence; Healthcare Analytics; Machine Vision; Machine Learning

10.1 Introduction

Information and communications technology (ICT) is a vital aspect of digitalized enterprises, capable of facilitating operating efficiency and enhancing competitiveness.

[1]Independent Researcher, Greater Noida, India
[2]Galgotias University, Greater Noida, India
[3]Department of Information Technology, Mookambigai College of Engineering, Keeranur, India

In the current 4th Industrial Revolution, advanced digital technology and devices for innovation and value development are widely utilized in all industries, and the medical industry is no exception. Hospitals and healthcare providers worldwide, particularly in advanced economies, widely use digital technologies to improve health care quality and operational performance. For example, artificial intelligence (AI), machine learning, smart sensors, robots, big data analysis, and the Internet of Things [1].

AI refers in general to an electronic system combined with either hardware or software that is capable, without explicit human instructions, of autonomously carrying out a task physically and with cognitive functions, solving innumerable issues, or making choices. The broad AI umbrella includes various methods and applications which includes different algorithms, such as genetic neural networks implementing machine learning methods with pattern recognition. AI can address human routine duties and activities with their impact on productivity and performance within a wide range of industrial, intelligent, and community applications [2].

AI can take over some of the computer-intensive and intellectual constraints of humans as a nonhuman intelligence programmed for certain activities. In order to assist with patient-specific diagnostics and therapeutic solutions and undertake demographic risk prediction analysis, AI can be used as another clinical decision system (CDS). The promotion of AI-based services has been a focal point for the plans of many companies. Recent investigations have led to significant changes made by AI to investigate the effects of the technology and to study the results of AI. However, this goal requires a thorough understanding of the elements which affect acceptance by potential consumers in diverse production and service sectors of AI-based services [3]. The reputation of AI for healthcare, mostly in health informatics, has been emphasized in previous studies. Various tools like kuberneets and AI stimulation tools can address the AI enabled tools. However, the history of risk studies in the use of AI-based devices for broad public treatment is little understood. Theoretical and qualitative research results show certain contributing elements to risk beliefs and the withdrawal of individuals from the use of AI clinical devices. However, empirical research into the good and negative aspects of the use of AI in medicine from the standpoint of customers remains sparse (Figure 10.1). It has also not been investigated how significant and widespread this excellent understanding is and its apparent association and AI's desire to be utilised in healthcare. AI in today's medical processes could be quite difficult. This study aims mainly to explore the perceived benefits, hazards, and usage of AI-based products by future users. The perceptions of the benefits and risks to future consumers could influence the future uptake of AI instruments [4]. Primarily because it is important to pick whichever medical tool practitioners should use in daily routine practice, it has to be identified by considering the most potential concerns and challenges in the medical domains with impediments that can hinder them from backing and using clinical tools.

10.2   Hypotheses development

Three issues (technical, regulatory, and ethical) directly influence the general perceived hazards of AI according to the research model. There are two elements of

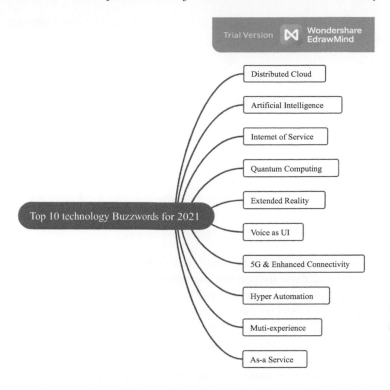

Figure 10.1 Top technology list for 2021

technical concern: perceived worries over performance and perceived impediments to communication. Three components are included in the ethical concerns, viz.: perceived worries about privacy, a perceived lack of confidence in AI systems, and social bias. There are two regulatory concerns: uncontrolled standards viewed and liability problems perceived. In addition, both risk beliefs and perceptions of benefits affect the intentions of individuals to utilize AI-based products [5]. The impacts of demographics and technology experiences have to be controlled. The maximum variables of controller include age, income, gender, jobs, race, education, general computer abilities, and technical knowledge about AI technology and AI services, which are identified and tested as reasons affecting the acceptance of AI evidences through past studies.

Machine learning is a technology used for the fitting of data models and the training of data models. As a bridge between supervised and unsupervised learning, "Instruction is aspired after by a few." Based on the output obtained from electronic health records (EHRs) of hospitals, the results were pre- dictated with machine learning [6]. Clinical data from patients' electronic health records are used to training the data set and make short-term predictions about the consequences if it follows the clinical situation in the present (Figure 10.2). Another term, deep

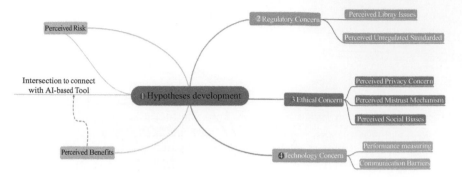

Figure 10.2   Developments in the hypothesis model for healthcare in AI

learning, is the machine learning area used to train a huge neural network with massive amounts of data. It supports the practitioner in making prescriptions and treatments more tailored to the individual recipient. It enables a more accurate diagnosis of disease based on past knowledge. When it comes to the trial's patient relative risk and personal compensation, there is only one software provider to consider. Software producers give professionals with reliable genetic information. The topic of research on how to use and interpret the natural language texts and speech of a computer is called natural language processing (NLP). Different activities such as speech recognition, text translation and processing, natural language processing and summarization, and the collection of information from different languages around the world are performed by natural language processing. Two different processes are focused on NLP: language processing and language generation. Processing language is a matter of listening to/reading the information that is presented, whereas generating language is linked to the author/speaker who interprets the information processed. N Clinical Text Analysis and Knowledge Extraction System (cTAKES) and also another toolkit that helps with data gathering are two examples of NLP software applications that can be used to extract knowledge and access from individual healthcare data. An Annotation and Modeling, Processing Toolkit for Clinical Language (CLAMP) [7].

Healthcare AI and robotics are promising for the future, offering: diagnosis of patients; simple operation performance; tasks that are clearly delineated in more complex operations (e.g., suturing or staple closures incisions), as well as long-term care supervision of patients' well-being and emotional health, are essential.

Both AI and robotics have the potential (but not the need) to redefine human communication and human relations in healthcare at all levels. As an example, the choice to use an AI or a robot to care for oneself or for one's loved ones could potentially affect the patient, the family, and human connections. The decision to utilize a robot to take care of an aged parent's health at home should, therefore, not "only" rest on the safety of the robot, but should include other possible consequences. As an example, by allowing significant interactions (while the robot deals with menial jobs), or alternatively by decreasing the amount of interactions, it could improve the parent–child bond [8].

10.2.1 Roles for healthcare artificial intelligence

Patients' diagnosis, minor surgery, likely the greatest activities inside complex measures (e.g. closing incisions with sutures or staples), diagnostic health and well-being surveillance in facilities ranging from short-term to long-term care, basic physical support to increase patient independence all through physical or emotional decline have been the concentrate of this media attention on public healthcare robotics and artificial intelligence (e.g., using physical aids, or reminding the customer to take their prescribed medication) [9].

10.3 The inconvenient truth about AI in healthcare

The rapid expansion of AI has opened the door to the use of aggregated data from healthcare to produce powerful diagnostic models and also to enhance the precision of medicine by promptly and dynamically adjusting treatments and targeting the resources with the greatest efficiency. The way healthcare is supplied is determined by the underlying politics and economics, as well as the proximity of medical norms and business interests that all interact in shaping trade agreements. Adding additional AI to a broken system will not result in enduring change. Additionally, numerous healthcare facilities are missing the infrastructure to obtain the information necessary for efficient procedures, especially in relation to local demographic and/or practicing trends (Figure 10.3). Otherwise, the advancement of cloud computing, the protected general data usage organization, and Internet-based demand for services toward the cloud have been a major enabler, providing considerably lower fixed costs and presentation for large and small technology companies alike and supporting the above-mentioned AI opportunities. In theory, health care with its wealth of data is ideally situated to take advantage of the expansion in cloud computing [10]. Additionally, there appears to be a correlation between cloud computing, which is described as a protected, high-performance asset, with huge general-purpose data systems and facilities that are accessible on the Internet (the "cloud"), and the development of AI; these additional advantages could lead to reduced infrastructure and maintenance costs while still enhancing performance.

10.4 Role of cloud storage with AI in healthcare

Cloud computing alone would not be sufficient to address these issues; public debate and policy involvement will be required (Figure 10.4). Public-private partnerships and, perhaps most significantly, the public's confidence in organisations and individuals to treat their healthcare information with acceptable regard for economic and financial perverse incentive schemes will determine the exact course forward from which this pathway is based [11].

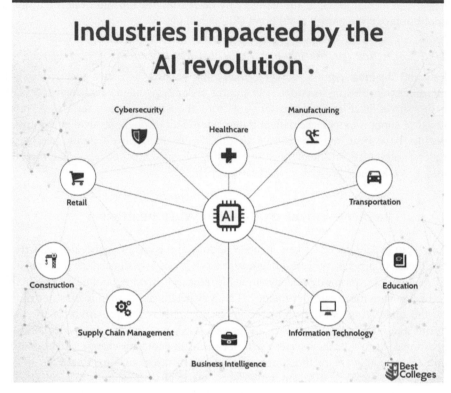

Figure 10.3   Different role of AI in various technologies

Possible Applications for Artificial Intelligence

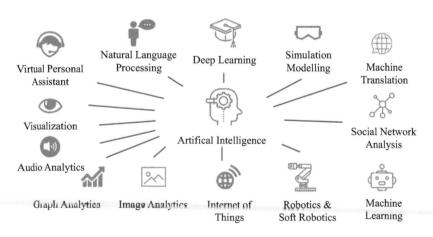

Figure 10.4   Data collection and storage using various applications

In the private sector, similar concerns are heightened by the fact that cloud computing is provided by a limited number of huge technology corporations that wield great market influence and have significant business benefits external to health care in which healthcare data may be valuable. Specific agreements are required to confirm that appropriate data sharing provides sufficient protection including, if applicable, material benefits to healthcare institutions and the patients they care for. In the absence of a consistent approach to hiring, public trust in just this area has been lost. AI can be used in routine clinical practice, or to overcome concerns of information sharing and trust, as well as to invest in the necessary data infrastructure. Now that cloud computing has bridged the computing divide in the broader economy, the same opportunities exist to incorporate population health while also realizing the potentiality, if governments are willing to foster a productive compromise of healthcare data ownership issues to complete a method that must transcend selection sequences as well as encompassing all AI interest in patient data [12].

10.5 Finally grasping the enormous potential of AI in healthcare

To really be fully welcomed and incorporated into healthcare, artificial intelligence and machine learning must be thoroughly recognized and implemented (Figure 10.5).

10.5.1 Prediction

There are currently technologies in place that monitor data in order to forecast disease outbreaks. This is frequently accomplished by combining real-time data

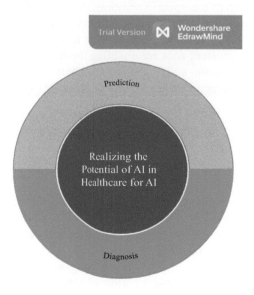

Figure 10.5 Potential of AI in healthcare

sources which collect huge datasets such as from social media with statistical information from the Web and other sources [13].

10.5.2   Diagnosis

Numerous digital technologies give alternatives to nonemergency medical care. With this approach, combining genome-employing machine learning algorithms would help in the understanding of illness risks and provide better pharmacogenetics.

10.5.3   Personalized treatment options and behavioral interventions

The fast developing subfield of digital health is known as digital therapeutics. In exchange for being able to avoid endless changes in behavior, digital healthcare should be tailored to the particular situation. Digital treatment designed by Diabetes Digital Media encounters noncommunicable disorders by focusing on the four important foundations of health: physical, mental, social, and spiritual well-being (modifiable risk). Leveraging AI and remote access, intelligent knowledge and help can be provided in the areas of food, activity, sleep, and mental health according to the user's intention, disease profile, ethnicity, age, gender, and region. The program integrates health tracking and personalized education to continually improve and meet the needs of users and the community as a whole [14].

10.5.4   Drug discovery

Machine learning offers a variety of applications in basic drug discovery, ranging from first transmission of therapeutic combinations to predicting achievement rates based on biological parameters. Next-generation sequencing (NGS) research and development (R&D) expertise. The application of digital therapies and the gathering of real-world persistent data are enabling the treatment of ailments that were previously seen as chronic and progressive. There is a significant disconnect between stakeholder perceptions of AI and its actual uses.

10.6   Several key challenges to the integration of healthcare and AI

10.6.1   Understanding the gap

Communication of concepts, methodology, and evaluations is critical to advancing methods for AI and machine learning in the healthcare domain. Data, including their exchange and integration internally and externally, are critical for advancing healthcare closer to precision medicine.

There is a significant disconnect between consumer understanding of advanced automation applications. The dissemination of concepts, procedures, and evaluations is critical also to the necessary innovations to advance AI and machine learning in health-care.

It is critical to transform healthcare toward value-based care, which includes data exchange and integration implementing precision medicine [15].

10.6.2   Fragmented data

Numerous obstacles must be overcome including for data that are scattered and impossible to merge. Patients gather information via their smartphones, Amazon Fitbits, and smart watches, whereas clinicians collect physical biomarker and demographic data on a routine basis. Such data are never combined during the patient experience, nor do institutions exist to meaningfully and robustly interpret and evaluate this greater set of data. Additionally, electronic health records (EHRs), which are currently disorganized and fragmented across databases, require digitization in a manner that is convenient for patients and clinicians. The COVID-19 pandemic has accelerated the process of connecting data sources, but work toward a real-world, sophisticated statistical fabric remains in its infancy. Data fabric is a term that refers to a unified environment for the collection of architecture, technology, and services that enables a person to maintain and advance their decision-making (Figure 10.6). All of a patient's medical information could be made public by a healthcare information provider in a nation [16].

10.6.3   Appropriate security

Simultaneously, enterprises face security and compliance concerns, particularly with regard to the handling of patient data and confirming their availability at all times. During the COVID-19 pandemic, national health services have come under scrutiny for discarding Apple and Google's COVID-19 tracing plans in favor of developing their own, which had significant security issues.

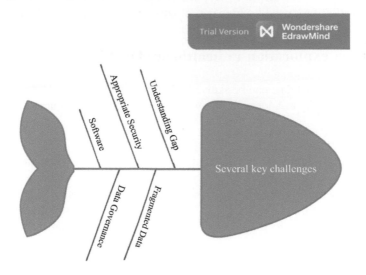

Figure 10.6   Several key challenges to AI use in health-care

10.6.4   Data governance

Healthcare administrations require network arrangement modernization to guarantee that they are sufficiently organized to provide the best possible care over the long term. Several medicare beneficiaries have gained the ability to contact patients during the COVID-19 pandemic. This may sound trivial, but it has fundamentally altered the way care is delivered throughout the world. As a result of patients being encouraged to approach healthcare workers, and the fact that return calls were promptly received, treatment delivery was altered. COVID-19 satisfies everyone else by allowing them to complete tasks through their own pace, moving expectations away from time and toward tasks [17].

10.6.5   Software

Embedded devices traditionally have been created in Lisp, as well using machine learning and Lisp. Thanks to the availability of a wealth of mathematical foundations for machine learning in the Python libraries, the bulk of machine learning techniques are implemented in Python nowadays. While algorithms that "learn" can be implemented in numerous computer languages, such as C and Python Java, require different libraries.

Data are the information that an intelligent system requires to operate, and are the most crucial element of comprehensive AI [9].

Data are divided into five categories:

- Data from the web and social media: clicks, histories, especially health communities;
- Data sent between machines: sensors, wearables;
- Billing records and health claims: huge transactions;
- Biometric data: fingerprints, DNA, and biomarkers gleaned from wearables;
- Information produced by humans: emails, physical papers, and patient data.

10.7   Data exploration in healthcare for AI

It is worth noting that data can be skewed. Unbalanced features might make it difficult for machine learning to understand how categories influence the output (Table 10.1).

10.7.1   Data cleansing

Data cleansing identifies and corrects values that are insufficient, redundant, missing, or inaccurate. The objective of data cleansing seems to be to optimize the value of the evidence used to train a model, perform analytics, or make a decision. This is the most time-consuming and difficult step of a machine learning project. These are some of the techniques followed during the data cleansing process [18].

10.7.2   Data that are inconsistent or duplicate

When there is uncertainty that the data are representative of the real world, it is necessary to investigate contradicting data in order to determine whether happenings

Table.10.1   Various types of healthcare data collections from devices

S. no.	Types of healthcare data	Data collection from devices and applications	Small and large use cases
1	Structured data	Smartphones, smartwatches, IoT devices, and embedded sensors	Diastolic blood pressure, steps taken, caloric intake, heart rate, or blood glucose levels
2	Unstructured data	Grammatically, emails letters, texts and emails, Facebook postings, and Tweeting tweets are all correct	Needs a machine learning method like NLP to organize
3	Semistructured data	Relational database data schemas	Structured data can be classified into three basic types of languages: JSON (JavaScript Object Notation), XML (Extensible Markup Language), and flat text

Figure 10.7   Cleaning up and formatting of data attributes

are explicable or random. For example, data indicating that a patient was admitted to hospital prior to their birth date indicate there might be an issue with the dating system or representation. It is usually preferable to delete data duplication (Figure 10.7).

10.7.3 Exploring anomalies in the data

Machine learning algorithms are only as accurate as the data used to train them. If the data are skewed (i.e., unrepresentative), the learning process will be skewed also. Simultaneously, while exploring datasets, caution should be exercised to prevent introducing human error. This is often accomplished by establishing proper description control [19].

10.8   Starting the cleaning up of typographical errors, clearing the values, and perfecting the formatting

Normalize textual headings to lowercase or uppercase. Analyze the information to see whether unique entities have multiple representations and to repair any misinterpreted strings or conceptual frameworks. For example, high blood compression might well be expressed in such a datasheet, including blood pressure and hypertension, where another category is correct, but data accuracy requires unification.

10.8.1   Aggregation

Clustering is used to refer to variables that can be combined into a single attribute. For instance, rather than showing each appointment separately, a log of specific patient participation at health education could have been aggregated into a tally of the total number of attendance figures.

10.8.2   Decomposition

Segmentation is the process of segmenting attributes in order to make them more relevant to a machine learning technique. For instance, a patient's records may indicate that they are Asian; nonetheless, it is much more accurate to understand the patient's country of origin and major language in order to forecast factors such as obesity more correctly [20].

10.8.3   Encoding

Compression converts categorical variables to a numerically represented, machine-readable format. Ordinal classifications will demand an input rating. For nonordinal categorizations, a column can be used to indicate whether a category is right or wrong for that object (Table 10.2).

10.9   Artificial intelligence (AI) in healthcare using an open science approach

Machine learning techniques such as artificial neural networks (ANNs) are other ways to tackle AI. An ANN approach is used to build statement networks of artificial "neurons" that function similarly to organic nervous systems. Machine learning artificial intelligence differs from neural network artificial intelligence in that the first is not explicitly stated by authorities but is generated through an automated repeated process that begins with formulating a hypothesis and that continuously improves until it is accepted as the truth (supervised or unsupervised

Table 10.2 Standardization of data types with examples

Data type	Characteristics	Example
Sentimental behavior of patients	Data in their rawest form, unstructured or semistructured Data are big and happening all the time. A chance to study, interact, and gain a better understanding. The default level of open source	Social media, smartphones, Web forums
Health data on the Web	Important metadata. This technology suggests that it is more likely to be professionally discovered than not.	Patient portals
Clinical data	Comprised of distinct elements. Under control of service providers	Image of patients
Transactional data	Requires preprocessing to become useful data	Health information exchanges
Patient health data	In the possession of the sufferer. Smartphone data are common. Typically, storage requirements are negligible. The amount of data required for storage varies based on the imagery being stored	The following sensors monitor blood glucose levels: meters, cellphones, wearables, and images
Clinical data	Physician data; the image captured with the registered format for the patients.	Structured data

by human experts). A machine learning algorithm can determine the network which could ensure the pattern with output by correlating patterns of outcomes (such as symptoms, medical imaging, or biological signals) with outputs (such as medical diagnoses) in "trained" databases. With all the progress that has been made in technology, there are a number of issues that have arisen with the application of AI in healthcare, bearing in mind that the healthcare industry is high risk [21].

10.9.1 What is the difference between open data and open research?

A more accurate and capable machine learning system requires a large amount of data. A definition of "open data" is as follows: informatics researchers, rather than healthcare organizations, are largely used for open datasets, which are generally as described above. This, however, opens up a wealth of fresh resources for machine learning, which include the CheXpert chest X-ray dataset derived from healthcare information. It is critical to provide patients with the confidence that their private health information is secure in EHR systems and other clinical systems. Identification is rarely done even after data have been de-identified. Because of this, sensitive healthcare data are typically not published due to the fact that open data and secure facilities are needed to perform machine learning analysis on vulnerable data sources [22].

The large and increasing body of research on AI and techniques/methodologies is centered on novel algorithms and their ability to predict outcomes. The clinical utility of automated clinical decision-making in real-world applications is little understood, as work on the algorithms themselves is scarce. Because black box machine learning systems are so complex that qualified programmers may have difficulty understanding how they make judgments, the term "black box" is widely used in centralized treatment. In order to evaluate specific healthcare applications, a balancing act will need to be struck between both the positive effects of the "black box" method (high numbers of components can be analyzed in a single choice) and the judgment component's associated challenge (there is mystery involved in using the black box).

10.10   Conclusion

The underlying nature of the patient–doctor relationship, as well as its basic trust, will be tested and may be transformed by the advances in AI and robotics. Many of the "trusted pathways" depend on healthcare AI or robotic technologies to be installed in the healthcare ecosystem. In order to ensure that treatment based on patient values and physician standards is administered in a consistent and effective manner, the medical community and AI developers must collaborate to establish rules that adhere to the principles of the representative democracy paradigm.

References

[1]   C. Sohrabi, Z. Alsafi, N. O'Neill, *et al.* World Health Organization declares global emergency: A review of the 2019 novel coronavirus (COVID-19). *International Journal of Surgery*, vol. 76, pp. 71–76, 2020. https://doi.org/10.1016/j.ijsu.2020.02.034.

[2]   P. Esmaeilzadeh, "Use of AI-based tools for healthcare purposes: a survey study from consumers' perspectives," *BMC Medical Informatics and Decision Making*, vol. 20, no. 1. BioMed Central Ltd, Jul. 22, 2020, doi: 10.1186/s12911-020-01191-1.

[3]   T. Lysaght, H. Y. Lim, V. Xafis, and K. Y. Ngiam, "AI-assisted decision-making in healthcare: the application of an ethics framework for big data in health and research," *Asian Bioethics Review*, vol. 11, no. 3, pp. 299–314, 2019, doi: 10.1007/s41649-019-00096-0.

[4]   V. Kalaiselvan, A. Sharma, and S. K. Gupta, "'Feasibility test and application of AI in healthcare'—with special emphasis in clinical, pharmacovigilance, and regulatory practices," *Health and Technology*, vol. 11, no. 1. Springer Science and Business Media Deutschland GmbH, 2021, doi: 10.1007/s12553-020-00495-6.

[5]   T. Panch, H. Mattie, and L. A. Celi, "The 'inconvenient truth' about AI in healthcare," *npj Digital Medicine*, vol. 2, no. 1, 2019, doi: 10.1038/s41746-019-0155-4.

[6] K. I. Zheng, F. Gao, X. B. Wang, *et al*. Obesity as a risk factor for greater severity of COVID-19 in patients with metabolic associated fatty liver disease. *Metabolism*, vol. 108, p. 154244, 2020.

[7] J. Born, D. Beymer, D. Rajan, *et al*. On the role of artificial intelligence in medical imaging of COVID-19. *medRxiv*, 2020.

[8] D. Hee Lee and S. N. Yoon, "Application of artificial intelligence-based technologies in the healthcare industry: opportunities and challenges," *International Journal of Environmental Research and Public Health*, vol. 18, no. 1, pp. 1–18, 2021, doi: 10.3390/ijerph18010271.

[9] R. Rodrigues, "Legal and human rights issues of AI: gaps, challenges and vulnerabilities," *Journal of Responsible Technology*, vol. 4, p. 100005, 2020, doi: 10.1016/j.jrt.2020.100005.

[10] S. Gerke, T. Minssen, and G. Cohen, "Ethical and legal challenges of artificial intelligence-driven healthcare," in *Artificial Intelligence in Healthcare*. New York, NY: Elsevier, 2020, pp. 295–336.

[11] M. Arvindhan and A. Anand, "Scheming and proficient auto scaling technique for minimizing response time in load balancing on Amazon AWS cloud," *SSRN Electronic Journal*, pp. 1–8, 2019, doi: 10.2139/ssrn.3390801.

[12] F. Jiang, Y. Jiang, H. Zhi, *et al*., "Artificial intelligence in healthcare: past, present and future," *Stroke and Vascular Neurology*, vol. 2, no. 4. pp. 230–243, 2017, doi: 10.1136/svn-2017-000101.

[13] J. B. Wagner, "Artificial intelligence in medical imaging," *Radiologic Technology*, vol. 90, no. 5, pp. 489–503, 2019, doi: 10.1016/b978-0-12-818438-7.00006-x.

[14] A. C. Chang, "The future of artificial intelligence in medicine," in *Intelligence-Based Medicine*, Elsevier, New York, NY, 2020, pp. 431–443.

[15] M. Almada, "Contesting automated decisions: limits to the right to human intervention in automated decision-making," *SSRN Electronic Journal*, 2018, doi: 10.2139/ssrn.3264189.

[16] M. Ananny and K. Crawford, "Seeing without knowing: Limitations of the transparency ideal and its application to algorithmic accountability," *New Media & Society*, vol. 20, no. 3, pp. 973–989, 2018, doi: 10.1177/1461444816676645.

[17] F. Doshi-Velez, M. Kortz, R. Budish, *et al*., "Accountability of AI under the law: the role of explanation," *SSRN Electronic Journal*, vol. 2, 2017, doi: 10.2139/ssrn.3064761.

[18] A. Meiliana, N. M. Dewi, and A. Wijaya, "Artificial intelligent in healthcare," *Indonesian Biomedical Journal*, vol. 11, no. 2. pp. 125–135, 2019, doi: 10.18585/inabj.v11i2.844.

[19] M. Matheny, S. T. Israni, M. Ahmed, and D. Whicher, editors. *Artificial Intelligence in Health Care: The Hope, the Hype, the Promise, the Peril*. National Academy of Medicine, Washington, DC, 2019.

[20] M. Dave and J. Kamal. Identifying big data dimensions and structure. In *2017 4th International Conference on Signal Processing, Computing and Control (ISPCC)*. IEEE, 2017, pp. 163–168.

[21] E. Gómez-González, E. Gomez, J. Márquez-Rivas, *et al.*, "Artificial intelligence in medicine and healthcare: a review and classification of current and near-future applications and their ethical and social impact," 2020. Accessed: June 27, 2021. [Online]. Available: www.etsi.us.es/gfihttps://5a8fe19c-a1f8-41fe-938d-8c3f23f975c9.filesusr.com/ugd/d42f6e_2fc902643d594faa8e80d82d7f43d2b6.pdf.

[22] J. Bae, Y. J. Cha, H. Lee, *et al.* Social networks and inference about unknown events: a case of the match between Google's AlphaGo and Sedol Lee. *PLoS One*, vol. 12, no. 2, p. e0171472, 2017.

Chapter 11

Analysis of COVID-19 outbreak using data visualization techniques: a review

Kishan Kanhaiya[1], Arpit Kumar Sharma[2],
Kamlesh Gautam[3], Aakanksha Jain[4], Surendra Sharma[5],
S. B. Goyal[6] and Shalini[7]

Abstract

Coronaviruses are a family of infections viruses that can cause sickness due to infection. They can shift from basic cold and hack to a more serious malady. The SARS-CoV and MERS-CoV syndromes are the most serious instances that the world has ever encountered. This pandemic is spreading worldwide, and it is critical for us to analyze and comprehend its spread using various approaches. Our work is primarily concerned with determining the global spread pattern of the virus. This groundbreaking work presents a study of the COVID-19 outbreak using various visualization techniques and data analysis techniques. This study also shows the comparison of cases between China, from where this pandemic actually arise, and the rest of the world. Additionally, this work analyzes the impact and dissemination of COVID-19 using several prediction and time-series forecasting techniques, such as SARIMA and ARIMA models.

Keywords: COVID-19; Linear regression; SVM; Polynomial regression; Time-series forecast; Holt's linear model; Holt's winter model; ARIMA; SARIMA; Facebook's Prophet model

[1]Computer Engineering, Netaji Subhas Institute of Technology, Delhi, India
[2]Computer and Communication Engineering, Manipal University Jaipur, Jaipur, India
[3]Poornima College of Engineering, Jaipur, India
[4]Poornima University, Jaipur, India
[5]Arya Institute of Engineering and Technology, Jaipur, India
[6]Faculty of Information Technology, City University, Malaysia
[7]Arya Institute of Engineering Technology and Management, Jaipur, India

11.1 Introduction

COVID-19 is a novel respiratory illness-producing virus. Fever, cough, sore throats, and shortness of breath are all its symptoms. Although the virus is contagious, proper hygiene can help prevent infection. However, COVID-19 is a non-fatal disease, and it spreads much more quickly than the common cold. Reproduction numbers are assigned to each virus (R0). This indicates the number of people who will contract the disease from an infected individual. According to preliminary research, the R0 value of COVID-19 is 2.7 [1]. As of now, "smoothening of the curve" is every country's main goal. In this study, we will learn more about the rapid spread of COVID-19 around the world. Leveling the curve typically implies that while confirmed cases are increasing, their transmission should be spread out over a longer period of time. That is, we should expect to infect 100,000 people in a year rather than one month. For the sole purpose of reducing the burden on the medical system and increasing the focus of research on finding a cure for illness, the curve should be flattened [2].

Each pandemic is divided into four stages:

Stage 1: Participation of confirmed cases come from various countries.
Stage 2: The beginning of local transmission.
Stage 3: Communities that have been impacted by close transmission.
Stage 4: Significant transmission forever.

The four countries that are currently in Stage 4 are Italy, the United States, the United Kingdom, and France, while India is on the edge of entering Stage 3. Other techniques to deal with infections like Corona include testing, contact tracing, and quarantine, in addition to a travel ban, cross-border shutdown, and ban on migrants.

11.2 Methodology

11.2.1 Objective

The purpose of this study is to consider the COVID-19 flare-up using some key perceptive processes, and also the correlation between China, where the COVID-19 began, and the rest of the world. Perform expectations and time-series estimates to account for the COVID-19's impact and spread in the following days [3].

11.2.2 Method

According to DFD, our proposed strategy is divided into two parts as follows:

1. Data analysis
2. Algorithm and modeling

In the first part, data analysis is also divided into three parts as follows: (1) analyze the data according to day-by-day and confirmed cases, (2) recovery rate, and (3) mortality and recovery rate analysis. In the second part, country-level and India-level analyses [4,5] are performed. All the existing methods and analysis techniques in DFD are shown as follows:

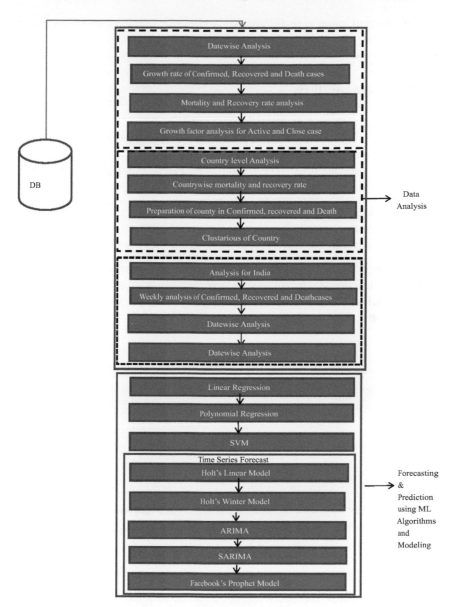

11.2.3 About dataset

Application program interface-based dataset, such as Kaggle, is available on the internet. In this dataset, update is done on daily basis and many columns contain a number of different cases with full details and can be extracted and used for prediction and analysis accordingly.

According to DFD explanation stepwise:

11.3   Datewise analysis

A date-by-date study based on the increase in the number of active cases is a hint that the number of recovered cases or death cases is rapidly decreasing in comparison to the number of confirmed cases. In this study, we will look for convincing evidence for the equivalent [6]. The formulas for calculating the active and closed cases are as follows:

Number of confirmed cases − Number of recovered cases − Number of death
cases = Active cases
Number of recovered cases + Number of death cases = Closed cases

An increase in the number of closed cases indicates that either more patients are recovering from their illnesses or that more people are dying as a result of COVID-19 [6,7].

Figures 11.1 and 11.2 depict the graphs of active and closed cases, respectively, by date.

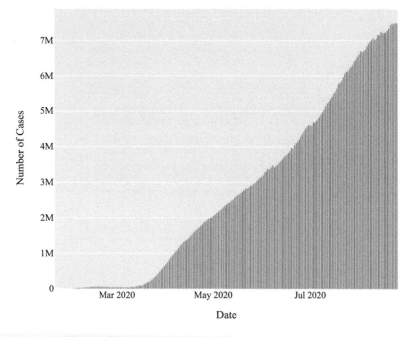

Figure 11.1   Distribution of number of active cases

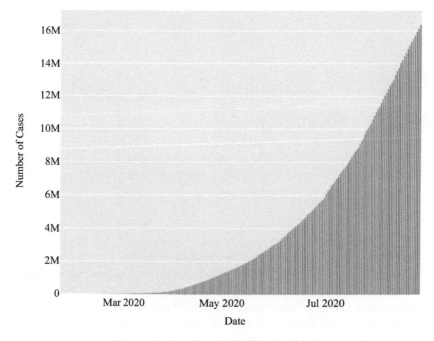

Figure 11.2   Closed case distribution

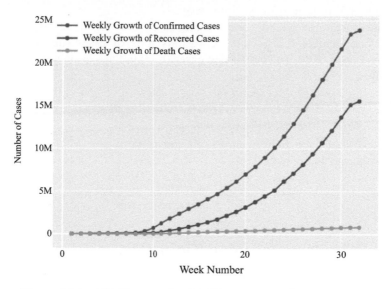

Figure 11.3   Weekly growth of different types of Indian cases

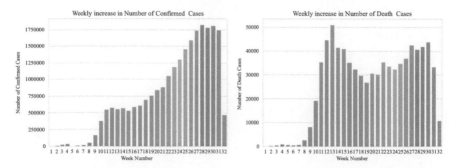

Figure 11.4   The number of death cases is increasing on a weekly basis

Case growth by type on a weekly basis: Beware the year 2020 week 26 has only recently begun. The mortality toll was low in the 14th week, which was expected given the recent trend of infection and death. The number of death cases has been continuously reducing from the 14th week to the 19th week. After that, it showed another spike for two weeks in a row. We have been able to cut death tolls in half or at least keep them in check, but new illnesses are spreading at breakneck speed, with 800,000 instances reported in the first week of the twenty-first century [8].

The number of infections rises every week, eventually reaching 1.2 million+ confirmed cases in the 24th week. The number of confirmed cases reached an all-time high (1.5 million+) in the 25th week.

Confirmed, recovered, and death cases are all increasing with rate. Figure 11.5 depicts the growth of various sorts of cases (death cases (DC), recovered cases (RC), and confirmed cases (CC)) in the section according to DFD guidelines.

11.3.1   Analysis of recovery rate (RR) and mortality rate (MR) throughout the world

Figure 11.6 shows the recovery rate (RR) and mortality rate (MR) around the world and their formulas are as follows:

$$Recovery\ rate\ (RR) = \frac{No.\ of\ recovered\ cases}{No.\ of\ confirmed\ cases} \times 100$$

$$Mortality\ rate\ (MR) = \frac{No.\ of\ death\ cases}{No.\ of\ confirmed\ cases} \times 100$$

The MR has been steadily decreasing for a long period of time, which is a positive development. The RR has begun to increase once more, which is a positive development and is another contributing factor to the increase in the number of closed cases [9].

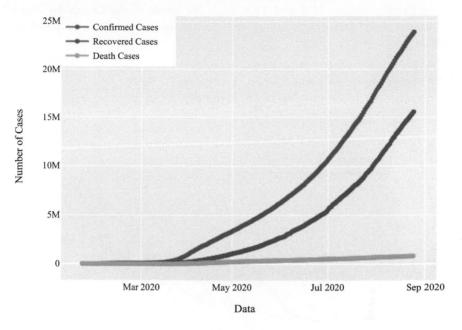

Figure 11.5   Growth of various sorts of cases

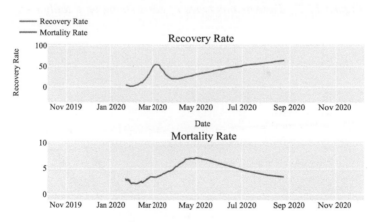

Figure 11.6   Analysis of MR and RR around the world

After the formulation calculation, the results of the analysis are:

- Average MR 4.656986414299647
- Median MR 4.453754169039291
- Average RR 38.675845311211425
- Median RR 41.28908480460453

Similarly, Figures 11.7 and 11.8 show the graph of the day-to-day rise of various cases and the 7-day rolling mean of the daily rise in CC, RC, and DC, respectively.

- Average rise in the number of CC every day: 110,086.0
- Average rise in the number of RC every day: 71,752.0
- Average rise in the number of DC every day: 3,776.0

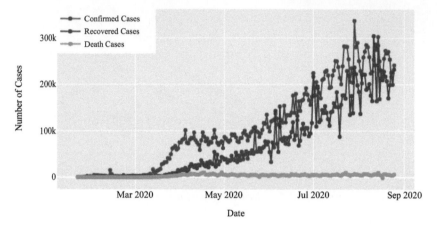

Figure 11.7   The various types of cases rising on a daily basis

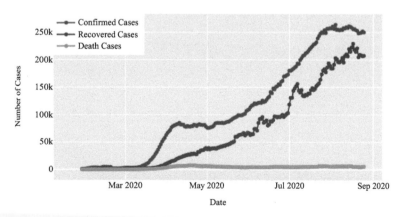

Figure 11.8   The 7-day rolling mean of everyday rise in CC, RC, and CC

11.4   Growth factor

The growth factor is essentially the rate at which an amount doubles in size with time [10]. The recipe is as follows:

Formula: Every day's recent (confirmed, recovered, deaths) / recent (confirmed, recovered, deaths) on the previous day.

The following conditions are indicated by the growth factor:

(a)   A development factor greater than one indicates an expansion in comparison to the previous case.
(b)   A development factor greater than one but trending downward is a good thing. A constant value greater than one indicates exponential development.
(c)   A constant growth factor of 1 indicates that there is no change in any situation.

Figure 11.9 illustrates the growth rate of confirmed, recovered, and death cases.

As shown in Figure 11.10, the growth factor of both closed and active cases consists of the mentioned durations in the figure.

In all conditions, an exponential growth rate that is constantly greater than one is a strong indicator of exponential growth. Globally, the rate of confirmed cases is increasing by a factor of two. Because of the substantial fluctuations in the doubling rate, it is projected to increase if the curve is suitably flattened [11–13].

The following are the daytime hours required to boost confirmed cases by 300,000. It only takes a few days or a few weeks for the number of cases to climb by 300,000, which is very compelling evidence that we have not yet been able to "flatten the curve."

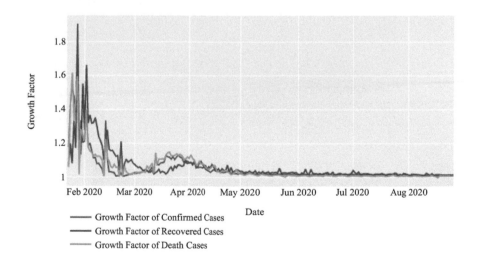

Figure 11.9   Growth factors for various types of situations on a date-by-date basis

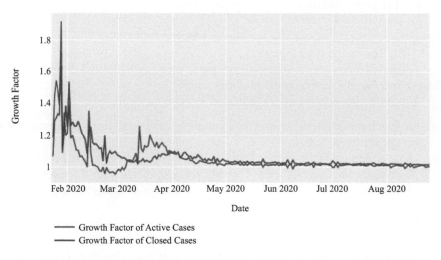

Figure 11.10   The growth factor of both closed cases and active cases

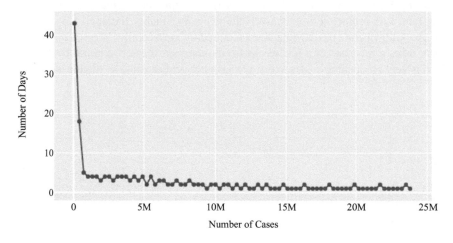

Figure 11.11   Number of daytimes required to increase the number of cases by 300,000 from the current level

11.5   Countrywise analysis

Figure 11.12 depicts the greatest number of confirmed cases, recovered cases, and death cases reported in the recent 24 h.

Figure 11.13 shows the confirmed and death cases of countrywise analysis.

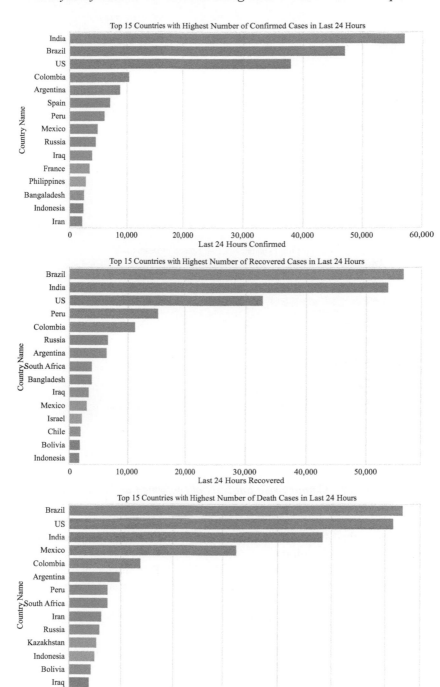

Figure 11.12   Countrywise analysis of last 24 h

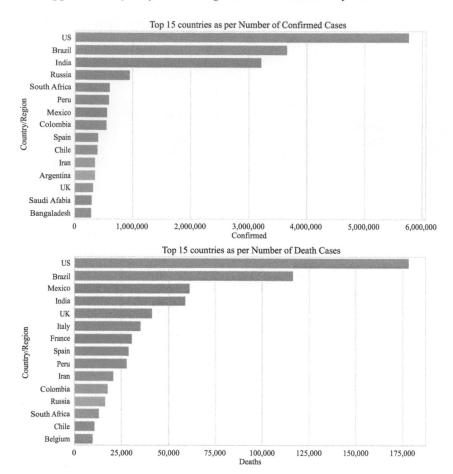

Figure 11.13   Countrywise analysis of confirmed and death cases

According to the MR and RR of cases with more than 500 confirmed cases, the following are the top 15 nations

The number of patients recovered with a high MR is shown in Table 11.2.

In Serbia, there have been over 50 documented cases for an extended period of time, with no recovered patients [14]. At this time, there have been no confirmed cases in any of the nations named above; however, there have been a small number of recovered patients [15,16].

Countries with over 100 confirmed cases and no fatalities have a significantly higher recovery rate (Table 11.3).

Cambodia has done an admirable job of containing COVID-19, with no deaths reported to date and a relatively high recovery rate. For the record, Cambodia was the first nation to report COVID-19 transmission from person to person to the WHO [17,18]. Mongolia and Cambodia are on the verge of being COVID-19-free.

Table 11.1   Number of cases and the required daytime for doubling

S. no	No. of cases	Daytime since the first case	Duration for doubling
0	560	0 Daytime	0 Daytime
1	1120	2 Daytime	2 Daytime
2	2,240	4 Daytime	2 Daytime
3	4,480	5 Daytime	1 Daytime
4	8,960	8 Daytime	3 Daytime
5	17,920	11 Daytime	3 Daytime
6	35,840	16 Daytime	5 Daytime
7	71,680	25 Daytime	9 Daytime
8	143,360	50 Daytime	25 Daytime
9	286,720	58 Daytime	8 Daytime
10	573,440	64 Daytime	6 Daytime
11	1,146,880	72 Daytime	8 Daytime
12	2,293,760	86 Daytime	14 Daytime
13	4,587,520	114 Daytime	28 Daytime
14	9,175,040	152 Daytime	38 Daytime
15	18,350,080	194 Daytime	42 Daytime

Table 11.2   No of recovered patients with a considerable mortality rate

Country/regions	Confirmed	Deaths	MR
MS Zaandam	9	2	22.2222
Sweden	86,891	5,814	6.69114
Serbia	30,820	705	2.28748

Table 11.3   Nations with over 100 confirmed cases but no fatalities and significantly huge RR

Nations/regions	Confirmed	Recovered	Deaths	Recovery
Cambodia	273	264	0	96.7033
Mongolia	300	289	0	96.3333
Seychelles	136	127	0	93.3824
Eritrea	315	276	0	87.619
Bhutan	173	118	0	68.2081

All of the aforementioned countries are healing at a breakneck pace and will shortly become entirely COVID-19-free.

The number of confirmed cases per day demonstrates unequivocally why the United States currently has the highest number of active cases. Each day, the number of cases exceeds 27,000. Every day, the value of that asset is increasing.

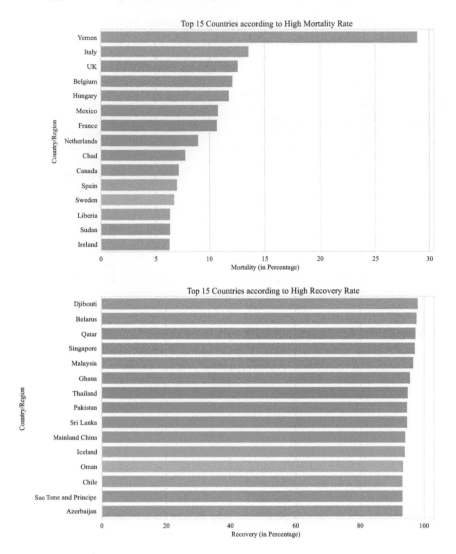

Figure 11.14   Countrywise highest mortality and recovery rate

A single graph that appears most promising is the survival probability graph! Having a survival chance of over 95% in all nations. The disparity among the mean and median death possibilities indicates that a few countries, including Italy, Algeria, and the United Kingdom, possess extremely high mortality rates [15].

11.5.1   Journey of different countries in COVID-19

It is difficult to read daily news stories about COVID-19 because the figures change so frequently, but that is expected with exponential development. Because almost

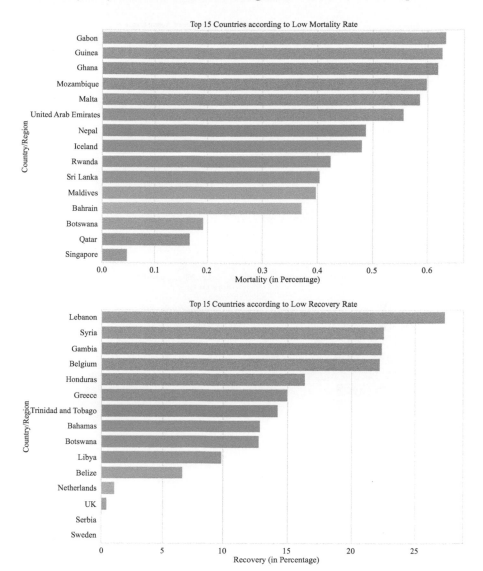

Figure 11.15   Countrywise low mortality and recovery rate

all pandemics spread exponentially, non-mathematicians or non-statisticians may struggle to understand [15].

Rather than focusing on the ever-increasing numbers, we are more concerned with our own progress and trajectory. The increase would not remain exponential forever. The curve will eventually flatten out because either everyone on earth is afflicted or we humans have mastered the disease [19,20].

While the illness is going to spread in the same manner worldwide, the graph illustrates the results of a nation's pandemic control efforts. The majority of

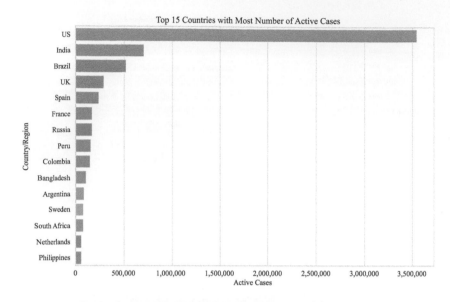

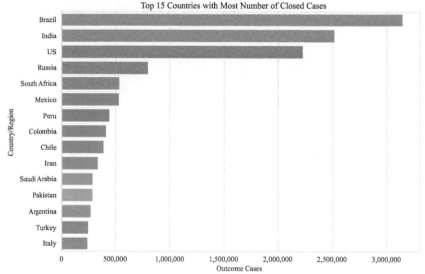

Figure 11.16   Countrywise topmost active and closed cases

countries will follow the United States' trend of "uncontrolled exponential growth" [15]. China, Germany, Italy, Spain, and Turkey have begun to show signs of decline, indicating that they have gained control of COVID 19. Countries such as the United Kingdom and Russia are expanding at the same rate as the United States, implying exponential growth.

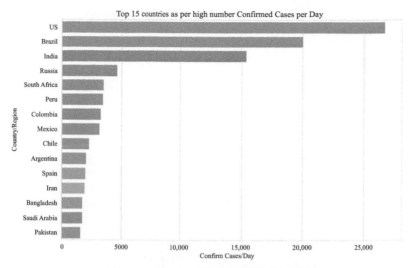

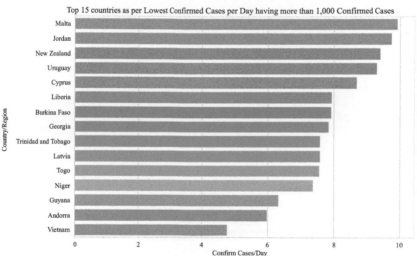

Figure 11.17   Countrywise high and low confirmed cases

11.5.2   *Proportion of each nation in CC, RC, and DC*

11.6   Clustering of countries

Various factors can be used to group countries. The study attempts to classify nations according to their MR and RR. As is well-known, COVID-19 has a variable MR and RR that varies according to the country's pandemic preparedness practices. Additionally, it encompasses all manners of cases: confirmed, recovered, and

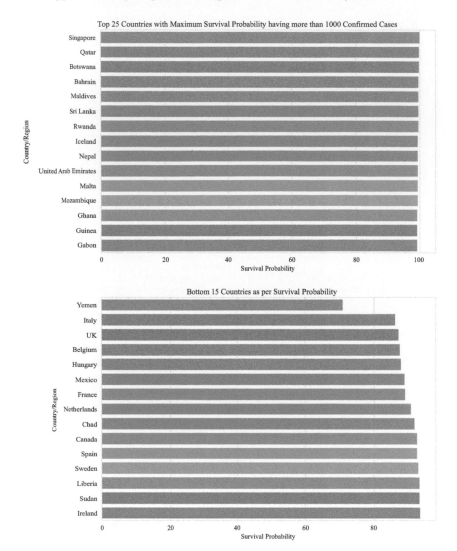

Figure 11.18   Topmost and bottom-most 15 countries survival confirmed cases

deaths. In the elbow method and hierarchical clustering, the number of clusters is K = 3.

Cluster 0 countries have a low mortality rate and a high rate of recovery. These are the countries that successfully contained COVID-19 through strict adherence to pandemic control practices.

Cluster 1 countries have a low mortality rate and a low rate of recovery. Several of these countries have a high rate of infection but a low rate of mortality, which is a positive sign.

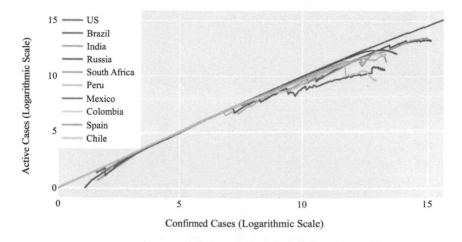

Figure 11.19   Journey of the 15 nations with the worst COVID-19 outcomes

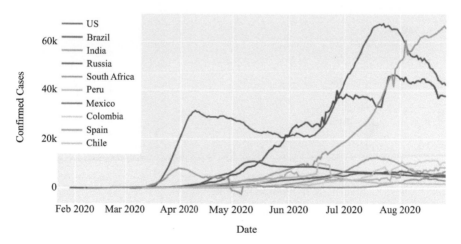

Figure 11.20   Seven-day rolling avg. of increase in CC on a daytime basis

Cluster 2 countries have a high mortality rate but a high rate of recovery. Several countries within these clusters have already endured the worst of the pandemic but are now recovering well.

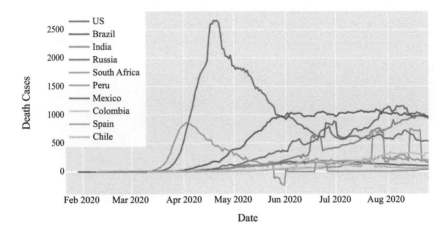

Figure 11.21   Seven-day rolling average of daytime DC rise

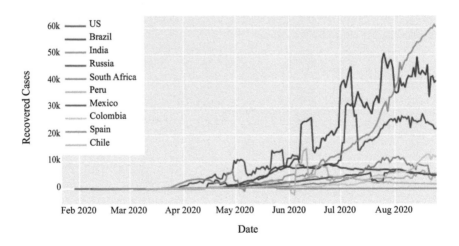

Figure 11.22   Rolling average of daily rise in RC during last 7 daytimes

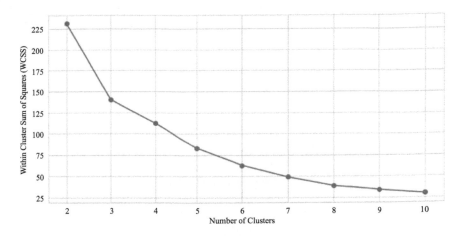

Figure 11.23   Clustering of countries by elbow method

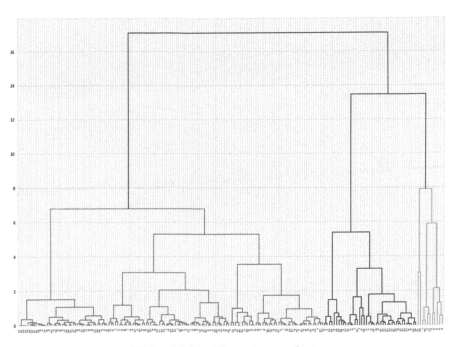

Figure 11.24   Clustering analysis

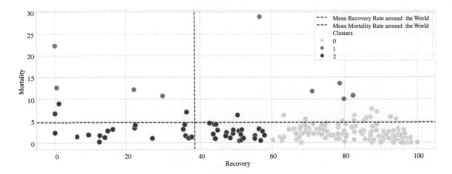

Figure 11.25   Clustering mortality and recovery

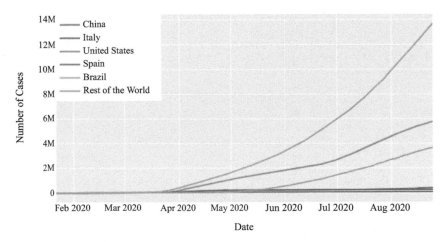

*Figure 11.26   Comparison of confirmed cases in China, Italy, the United States,
Spain, Brazil, and the rest of the world*

China has "flattened the curve" in terms of confirmed and fatal cases in comparison to Italy, the United States, Spain, Brazil, and the rest of the world. A surprisingly high rate of recovery in the United States appears to have a good handle on death rates, but the number of affected individuals is out of control.

Even if Spain's recovery rate is improving, it is still lagging behind in relation to the country's mortality rate. It is a concerning indicator for the United States and Brazil, as their recovery rates are increasing significantly when compared to other badly afflicted countries in the region.

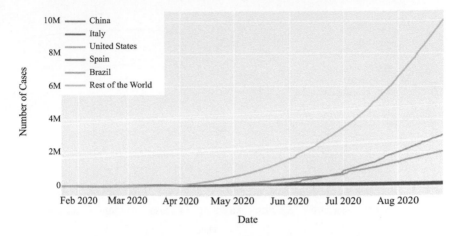

Figure 11.27 Comparison of recovered cases in China, Italy, the United States, Spain, Brazil, and the rest of the world

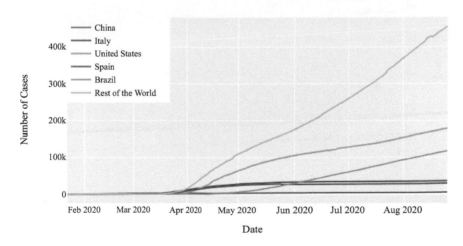

Figure 11.28 Comparison of death cases in China, Italy, the United States, Spain, Brazil, and the rest of the world

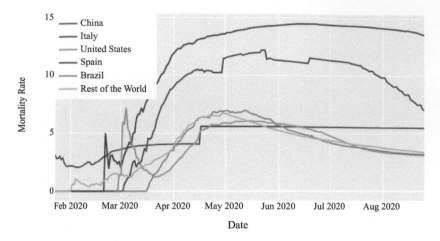

Figure 11.29   Comparison of mortality rates in China, Italy, the United States, Spain, Brazil, and the rest of the world

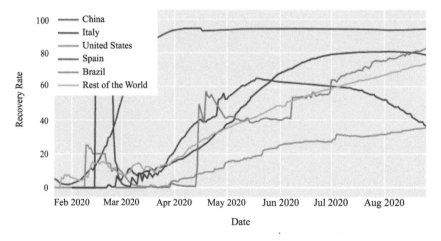

Figure 11.30   Comparison of the recovery rates in China, Italy, the United States, Spain, Brazil, and the rest of the world

As illustrated in Figures 11.31 and 11.32, Spain and Italy have seen a significant decline in the number of daily confirmed and fatal cases. That is a tremendously encouraging sign for both countries.

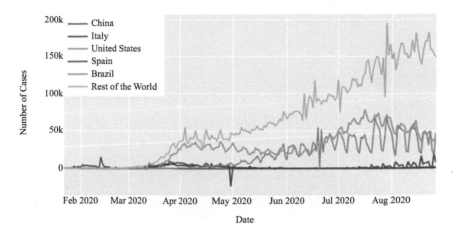

Figure 11.31   China, Italy, the United States, Spain, and Brazil are compared with the rest of the world in terms of daily increase in confirmed cases

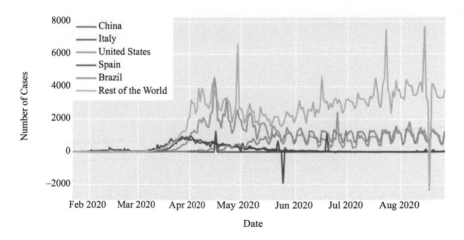

Figure 11.32   China, Italy, the United States, Spain, Brazil, and the rest of the world in terms of daily increase in death cases

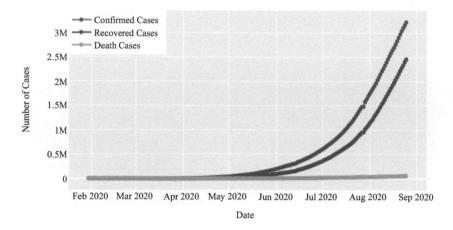

Figure 11.33 Data analysis for the increase in the number of various kinds of cases in India

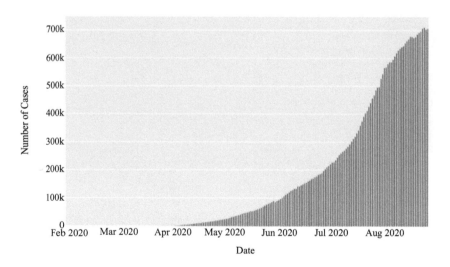

Figure 11.34 Data analysis for the distribution of cases and date in India

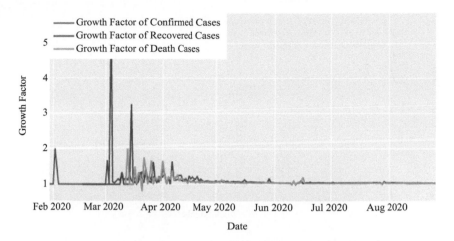

Figure 11.35   Data analysis of active and closed cases in terms of CC, RC, and DC in India

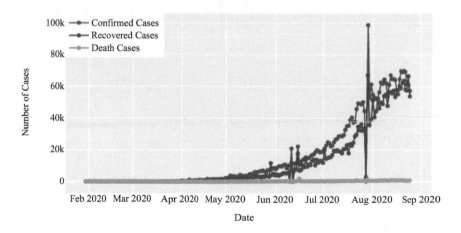

Figure 11.36   Data analysis of daily increment in CC, RC, and DC in India

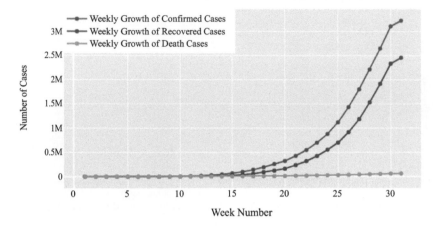

Figure 11.37   Weekly data analysis for the growth of different cases in India

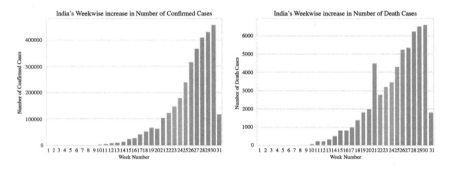

Figure 11.38   Weekly data analysis of CC and DC in India

This section includes a detailed analysis of Indian data, comparison with neighboring countries and the pandemic worst-affected countries, and attempts to build machine learning prediction, time-series, and forecasting models in order to gain a better understanding of how the numbers will change over time.

11.6.1   Weekly data analysis for India

Italy, Spain, the United States, and India are compared in terms of the daily rises in number of CC, where the maximum number of CC in Italy and Spain is equal to the maximum number of CC in India.

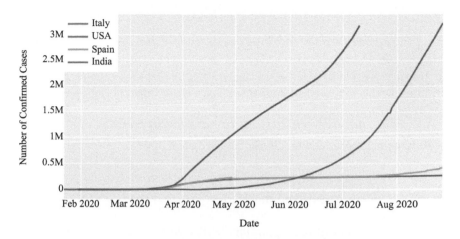

Figure 11.39   Weekly data analysis of growth for recovered cases in India

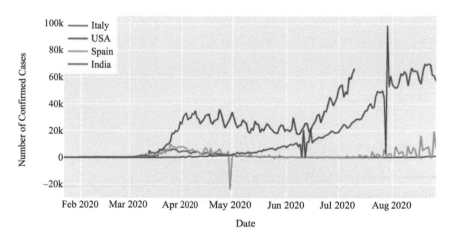

Figure 11.40   Comparison with other countries in the form of confirmed cases

11.6.2   Datewise/daily data analysis for India with comparison

Comparison of the daytime increase in the number of cases in Italy, Spain, the United States, and India

11.7   Machine learning models for prediction

11.7.1   *Linear regression model prediction for confirmed cases*

The linear regression model is on the verge of collapsing (Figure 11.41). As is readily apparent, the trend of confirmed cases is not linear [21].

11.7.2   *Polynomial regression for prediction of CC*

The polynomial regression model for the prediction of CC is given in Figure 11.42.

11.7.3   *SVM model regression for prediction of CC*

The SVM model regression model for the prediction of CC is given in Figure 11.43.

Time-series forecasting: According to previous research work concept of time-series analysis prediction techniques [22].

11.7.4   *Holt's linear model*

Holt's linear model for the prediction of CC is given in Figure 11.44.

11.7.5   *Holt's winter model for everyday time series*

Holt's winter model for the prediction of CC is given in Figure 11.45.

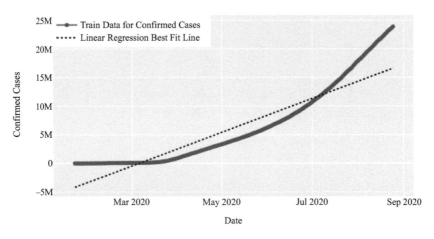

Figure 11.41   Linear regression prediction for CC

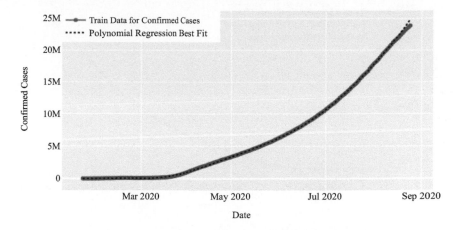

Figure 11.42   Polynomial regression prediction for CC

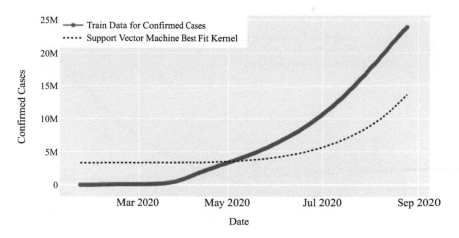

Figure 11.43   SVM regression prediction for confirmed cases

11.7.6   AR model (using AUTO ARIMA)

AR model for the prediction of CC is given in Figure 11.46.

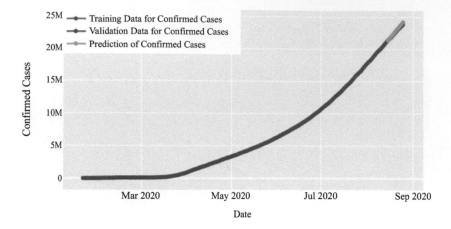

Figure 11.44   Holt's linear model prediction for confirmed cases

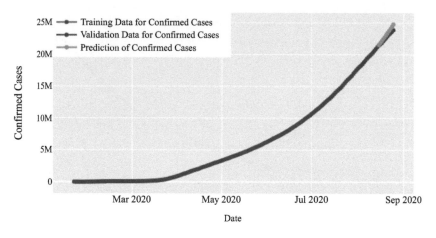

Figure 11.45   Holt's winter model prediction for CC

11.7.7   MA model (using AUTO ARIMA)

MA model for the prediction of CC is given in Figure 11.47.

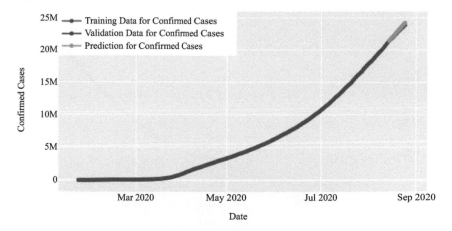

Figure 11.46   AR model prediction for confirmed cases

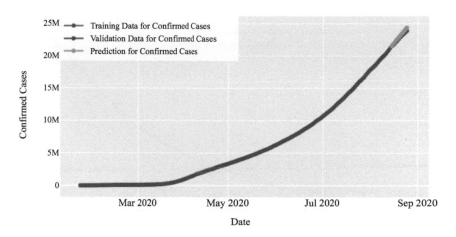

Figure 11.47   MA model prediction for confirmed cases

11.7.8   ARIMA model (using AUTO ARIMA)

ARIMA model for the prediction of CC is given in Figure 11.48.

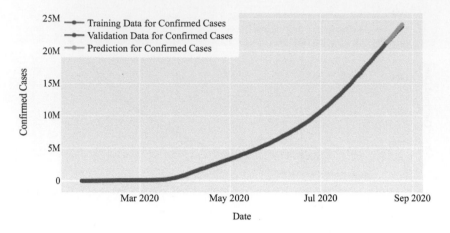

Figure 11.48   ARIMA model prediction for confirmed cases

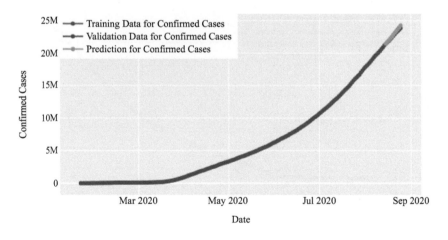

Figure 11.49   SARIMA model prediction for confirmed cases

11.7.9   SARIMA model (using AUTO ARIMA)

SARIMA model for the prediction of CC is given in Figure 11.49.

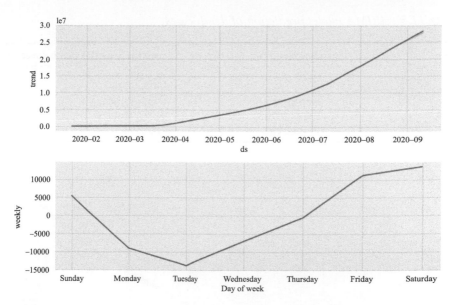

Figure 11.50   Forecasting graph according to Facebook's Prophet model

Table 11.4   All model comparison with root mean squared error

S. no.	Model title	RMS error
0	Linear regression	6,578,397.681
1	Polynomial regression	525,652.6806
2	SVM regression	10,151,499.74
3	Holt's linear	177,578.2446
4	Holt's winter model	499,567.0326
5	Auto regressive model (AR)	172,435.955
6	Moving average model (MA)	274,712.9864
7	ARIMA model	158,559.0719
8	SARIMA model	205,970.4068
9	Facebook's Prophet model	26,270.84619

11.7.10   Facebook's Prophet model for forecasting

The forecasting graph according to Facebook's Prophet model is given in Figure 11.50.

11.8   Forecasting results and summarizations using various models

Prediction of all application models and algorithm is given in Table 11.4.

Table 11.5   ARIMA model prediction of death cases

S. no.	Deaths	ARIMA model death forecast
0	26-08-2020	850853.5341
1	27-08-2020	859845.708
2	28-08-2020	868511.0955
3	29-08-2020	876070.8938
4	30-08-2020	882594.5224

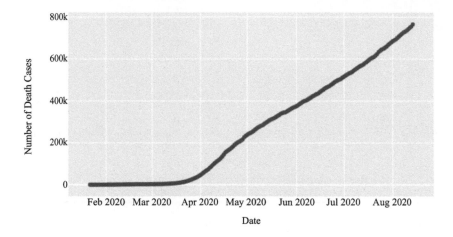

Figure 11.51   Time-series forecasting for death cases

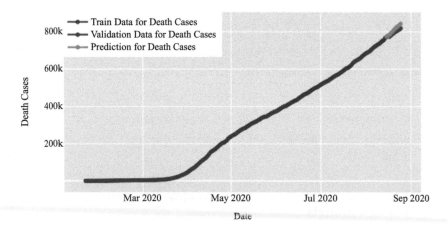

Figure 11.52   ARIMA model prediction of death cases

11.8.1 Time-Series forecasting for DC

The time-series forecasting and ARIMA model prediction are given in Figures 11.51 and 11.52.

11.9 Conclusion

As should be obvious from the fact that it is the most effective removal method, COVID-19 does not have an extremely high death rate. Aside from that, the high recovery rate indicates that the condition is curable. The exponential growth rate of contamination is the most serious source of concern at this time. Nations like the United States, Spain, and Italy are experiencing genuine difficulties in containing the illness, demonstrating how fatal the illness can be owing to carelessness. Performance of COVID-19 pandemic control practices such as testing, contact tracing, and quarantine at a rate that is commensurate with the rate at which the disease is spreading at the national level is critical.

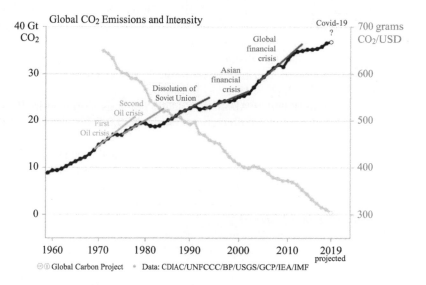

The reason for including this graph at the end of the paper is that it reveals an interesting pattern: every time the world's carbon emissions have decreased, the world economy has suffered a corresponding decline. The Great Recession of 2008 is a classic example. I believe the majority of you already know what's coming; COVID-19 is most likely just a large wave that will be followed by a Tsunami of recession or depression, as predicted. The number of confirmed and death cases appears to have slowed significantly over the last few days. This is an extremely positive sign. I am hoping this trend continues for a brief period. No new country should emerge as the new epicenter of COVID-19, as the United States did briefly when it was the original epicenter. If a new country becomes the epicenter of the epidemic, the number of confirmed cases will increase dramatically once again.

Availability of data/codes: Following the publication of the article, the author will make the code available to the public on Kaggle.

References

[1]   Hui DS, Azhar E, Madani T, *et al.*, "The continuing 2019-nCoV epidemic threat of novel coronaviruses to global health—the latest 2019 novel coronavirus outbreak in Wuhan, China," 2020.

[2]   Read JM, Bridgen JR, Cummings DA, Ho A, Jewell CP, "Novel coronavirus 2019-nCoV: early estimation of epidemiological parameters and epidemic predictions," medRxiv. 2020.

[3]   Corman VM, Landt O, Kaiser M, *et al.*, "Detection of 2019 novel coronavirus (2019-nCoV) by real-time RT-PCR,". *Euro Surveillance,* vol. 25(3), 2020.

[4]   Coronavirus Closures Reveal Vast Scale of China's Secretive Wildlife Farm, https://www.theguardian.com/environment/2020/feb/25/coronavirus-closures-reveal-vast-scale-of-chinas-secretive-wildlife-farm-industry.

[5]   Sharma AK, Nandal A, Dhaka A, Dixit R, "A survey on machine learning based brain retrieval algorithms in medical image analysis," *Health and Technology*, vol. 10, pp. 1359–1373, 2020.

[6]   Chinese Citizens Push to Abolish Wildlife Trade as Coronavirus Persists, https://www.nationalgeographic.com/animals/2020/01/china-bans-wildlife-trade-after-coronavirus-outbreak/.

[7]   Sharma A, Nandal A, Dhaka A, Dixit R, Medical image classification techniques and analysis using deep learning networks: a review. In: Patgiri R., Biswas A., Roy P. (eds) *Health Informatics: A Computational Perspective in Healthcare*. Studies in Computational Intelligence, vol. 932. Springer, Singapore, 2021.

[8]   Paul A, Chatterjee S, Bairagi N, "Prediction on Covid-19 Epidemic for Different Countries: Focusing on South Asia Under Various Precautionary Measures," April 2020.

[9]   Crokidakis N, "COVID-19 spreading in Rio de Janeiro, Brazil: do the policies of social isolation really work?" *Chaos, Solitons & Fractals*, vol. 136, July 2020.

[10]   Rubaiyat Hossain Mondal M, Bharati S, Podder P, Podder P, "Data Analytics for Novel Coronavirus Disease," Elsevier Public Health Emergency Collection, New York, NY, Jun 2020.

[11]   Bhargava N, Kumar Sharma A, Kumar A, Rathoe PS, "An adaptive method for edge preserving denoising," 2017 2nd International Conference on Communication and Electronics Systems (ICCES), 2017, pp. 600 604, doi: 10.1109/CESYS.2017.8321149.

[12] Nagasubramanian G, Sankayya M, "Multi-variate vocal data analysis for detection of Parkinson disease using deep learning," *Neural Computing and Applications*, 33(10), 4849–4864, 2021. https://link.springer.com/article/10.1007/s00521-020-05233-7.

[13] Nagasubramanian G, Sankayya M, Al-Turjman F, Tsaramirsis G, "Parkinson data analysis and prediction system using multi-variant stacked auto encoder," in *IEEE Access*, vol. 8, pp. 127004–127013, 2020, 10.1109/ACCESS.2020.3007140.

[14] Kirichu SK, "Short-Term Projection of COVID 19 Cases in Kenya using an Exponential Model," BMC Public Health, 2020.

[15] Said N, "Coronavirus Covid-19: Available Free Literature Provided by Various Companies, Journals and Organizations Around the World Journal of Ongoing Chemical Research," 2020.

[16] Nagasubramanian G, Sakthivel RK, Patan R, Gandomi AH, Sankayya M, Balusamy B, "Securing e-health records using keyless signature infra-structure blockchain technology in the cloud," *Neural Computing and Applications*, vol. 32(3), 639–647 2020. https://doi.org/10.1007/s00521-018-3915-1

[17] Kumar SR, Gayathri N, Muthuramalingam S, Balamurugan B, Ramesh C, Nallakaruppan MK, *Medical Big Data mining and processing in e-healthcare*. In *Internet of Things in Biomedical Engineering,* Academic Press, London, 2019, pp. 323–339. https://doi.org/10.1016/B978-0-12-817356-5.00016-4.

[18] Dhingra P, Gayathri N, Kumar SR, Singanamalla V, Ramesh C, Balamurugan B. Internet of Things–based pharmaceutics data analysis. In *Emergence of Pharmaceutical Industry Growth with Industrial IoT Approach*. Academic Press, London, 2020, pp. 85–131.

[19] Sharma SK, Gayathri N, Modanval RK, Muthuramalingam S, Artificial intelligence-based systems for combating COVID-19. In *Applications of Artificial Intelligence in COVID-19*, Springer, Singapore, 2021, pp. 19–34.

[20] Kavidha V, Gayathri N, Kumar SR, AI, IoT and robotics in the medical and healthcare field. AI and IoT-Based Intelligent Automation in Robotics, 165–187, 2021.

[21] Ghosal S, Sengupta S, Majumder M, Sinha B, "Linear Regression Analysis to predict the number of deaths in India due to SARS-CoV-2 at 6 weeks from day 0 (100 cases – March 14th 2020)," *Diabetes & Metabolic Syndrome: Clinical Research & Reviews*, vol. 14, issue 4, pp. 311–315, 2020.

[22] Reddy VK, Chimmula, L, "Time series forecasting of COVID-19 transmission in Canada using LSTM networks," *Chaos, Solitons & Fractals*, vol. 135, June 2020.

Chapter 12

Artificial intelligence-based electronic health records for healthcare

Aradhna Saini[1], A. Suresh Kumar[2] and Gaurav Dhuriya[3]

Abstract

Artificial intelligence (AI) is the ability of machines to perform tasks like a person and assist in solving existing real-life problems. These machines have their own ability to solve problems by constructive use of machine learning, deep learning, and neural network algorithms. AI created by persons adds many intelligent features through which they can resolve existing real-life problems. An electronic health record (EHR) is a collection of different types of documents generated by any health-associated body tests or wearable smart devices stored electronically in a digital format. Healthcare is a very vast structure and there are millions of health matters. So, it is very difficult to collect all health documents and keep them in a structured format for future use. It is a major concern because many deaths occur in a year since they do not have access to health documents. In this chapter, constructive use of AI in EHR structure is discussed.

EHR is the digital form of all documents in a single place. It is highly secure and is only pre-owned by authorized users. It assists to treat forbearing with multiple health matters and manage all their documentation for future use. In such cases electronic health documentation works like a key to saving several lives. AI is a very advanced technology that assists in collecting all advices about the forbearing and how keep them secure. According to Gartner's report, AI grew between 2018 and 2019 from 4% to 14%, and in the 2020 Report it increased to 40%. AI plays an important and huge role in e-healthcare and also assists to keep the information secure in EHR. This chapter describes the role of AI in e-healthcare and EHR with the architecture of healthcare documentation. We study the requests, use of AI in EHR, healthcare, and privacy of all health documents.

Keywords: Electronic health documentation; Healthcare; Artificial intelligence

[1]Department of Computer Science and Engineering, Noida Institute of Engineering and Technology, Greater Noida, Delhi-NCR, India
[2]Department of Computer Science and Engineering, Graphic Era (Deemed to be University), Dehradun, Uttarakhand, India
[3]Department of Computer Science and Engineering, Noida Institute of Engineering and Technology, Greater Noida, Delhi-NCR, India

12.1   Introduction

12.1.1   Overview of artificial intelligence

The man-made reasoning term "artificial intelligence" was instituted by John McCarthy in 1956. He characterized it as "the science of designing and making insightful machines." AI is a part of software engineering that manages the study and plan of astute specialists who see its climate and constructive moves that amplify its odds of achievement. Artificial intelligence (AI) might be characterized as "The ability to hold a kind contemplations at the highest point of the need list at the same time besides, still stay the ability to work." Yet, AI must incorporate the gain from experience, thinking about the dynamic, derivative force and speedy reaction. Likewise, it should have the option to construct choices on the premise of needs and tackle intricacy and vagueness. Computerized reasoning (AI) is characterized as the knowledge of machines, instead of the insight of people, on other living species. Man-made intelligence can likewise be characterized as the investigation of "smart specialists"; that is, any specialist or gadget that can see and comprehend its environmental factors and in likewise manner construct a suitable move to amplify its odds of accomplishing its destinations. Computer-based intelligence likewise alludes to circumstances wherein machines can reproduce a person's thinking on learning and examination, and subsequently can work in critical thinking. This sort of insight is likewise alluded to as AI (ML). Machines modified to absolute errands conveyed to people who would require insight are said to have man-made brainpower. The logical objective of computer-based intelligence is to comprehend insight by building PC programs that display keen conduct by using representative derivation or thinking inside the machine. Computer-based intelligence definition is not time-autonomous. It gives the judgment of any framework considering time.

12.1.2   E-healthcare and electronic health records

Wellbeing documentation called electronic health record (EHR) (PCC EHR Solutions, 2014) is an electronic transformation of a forbearing's cardboard documentation. EHRs provide the potential gain of giving advice about tenacious thought in an open, secure way to different endorsed customers (Figure 12.1). Despite the fact that EHRs change according to content and assist, they are routinely planned to incorporate the clinical and treatment stories of the forbearing, such as the forbearing's discoveries, medications, immunization dates, hypersensitivities, radiology pictures, lab and test results, among other advice. EHRs can facilitate advice from different sources and give a more exhaustive viewpoint on lenient consideration, yet it has exhibited testing to achieve in genuine practice. EHRs likewise may give admittance to apparatuses like clinical choice assist updates and reports that guide medico groups in providing care dependent on the best accessible proof. As a PF, you need general advice about EHRs and the capacity to transform your practices into data on confirmed EHRs, assets for assessing and anticipating execution of an EHR, and the capacity to associate practicing individuals with

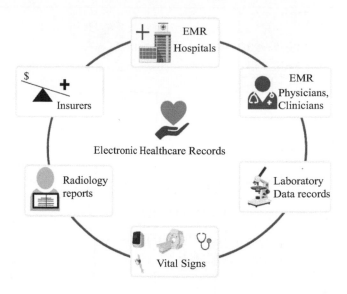

Figure 12.1 Electronic health records

specialists for proper EHR execution. For rehearses that have simply started their excursion towards computerization, furnishing them with fundamental basic EHR preparation can be useful. A thermionic wellbeing documentation is characterized as an anodic variant of a clinical past record of the forbearing as stored by the medical services supplier for quite a duration and it is comprehensive of each and every aspect. The fundamental managerial detached advice that is in line with the consideration specified to a person by a specific supplier like socioeconomics, progress reports, matters, prescriptions, significant signs, clinical history, inoculation reports, research facility advice, and radiology reports. The utilization of note as a method for documentation of wellbeing advice in the majority of medical services offices and associations has prompted a broad cardboard trail. In addition, most associations have created absorption in moving from hard copy wellbeing document to auto electronic wellbeing documentation.

12.2 AI in E-healthcare structure

12.2.1 Use of AI in E-healthcare structure

Overseeing clinical documentation and advice (Figure 12.2).

The clearest utilization of fake insights in medical services is to advice the executives. Socialize it, put it away, normalize it, and follow its parentage. It is the essential step in reforming the possible medical care frameworks [1]. As of late, the AI experimentation of the hunt monster, Google, pushed its Google Deep psyche Fitness estimate pre-owned to mine the data of clinical measurements in a

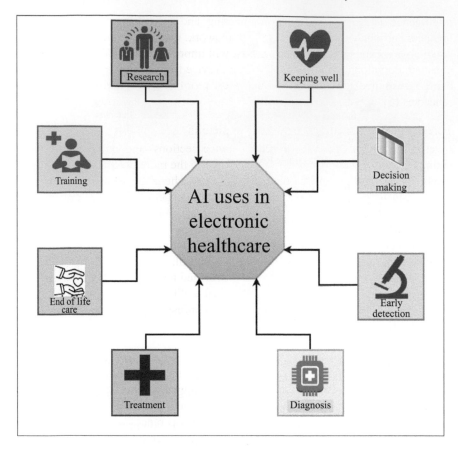

Figure 12.2   Use of artificial intelligence in e-healthcare

decent approach to provide very fast wellbeing administrations [2]. Since the fundamental step in medical safe-keeping is arranging and exploring advice, advising the board is the most comprehensively pre-owned utilization of computerized reasoning and advanced robotization. Robots gather, store, re-design, and follow advice to provide quicker, further predictable means to approach [3]. The previous decagon has perceived an emanation in the proportion of wellbeing data that is available currently [4]. In the medical services manufacturing, advice (forbearing data, determination data, latest examination discoveries, and the sky as the limit) is created in considerable volumes consistently [5]. The blend of massive advice for scientific devices has assisted associations with accomplishing the bits of knowledge fundamental to work together substantially and more productively with forbearing and undertake incredible choices, and this reliance on enormous advice and putting away is done to reduce wastage, from slicing coast to smoothing out emergency clinic staff timings; from engaging far off quiet checking to expecting pandemics, the use of swamp advice has been developing significantly. Man-made intelligence is part of software engineering and innovation adjusting with the reenactment of savvy conduct in a PC framework. Organizing the experience, data, and personal exposure of medico with AI will improve the top caliber of forbearing consideration along with curbing its price. Advice from entire forbearing populaces can be examined utilizing AI to find latest proof and decide great medical care rehearses [6].

12.2.1.1   Performing redundant positions

Investigating tests, X-rays, CT scans, advice sections, and other normal under-takings should all be made possible faster and all the more precisely through use of machines. Radiology and cardiology are areas where the measure of advice to inspect can be overpowering along with time management. Radiologists and car-diologists in the time to come should just glance at the major modern situations where personal input is useful. IBM initiated second calculation known as Clinical Sieve. It's anything but an aggressive extended haul insightful task to fabricate the cutting edge "psychological associate" with logical, thinking abilities and a broad scope of clinical advice. Clinical Sieve is qualified to assist in clinical dynamics in radiology and cardiology. The "psychological wellbeing aide" is ready to analyze radiology pictures to stamp and distinguish confusions faster and all the further reliably [7].

12.2.1.2   Treatment plan

Recreated insight is gaining momentum in clinical benefits treatments, for instance, updating the relationship of treatment methodologies, separating data to give pre-valent treatment strategies, and checking medicines. Computerized reasoning can rapidly and even more definitely see signs and appearances of disorder in clinical images, for instance, X-beam, CT scans, ultrasound, and X-rays, and along these lines permits faster diagnosis, decreasing the period of forbearing hold on for an end from weeks to just hours and quickly present any possible therapy [8]. Specialists should be able to look through data, like Modernizing Medicine, a clinical associate pre-owned to accumulate forbearing data, documentation analy-sis, order tests and remedies, and orchestrate charging advice. Moreover, the pre-ference to investigate general data sets with data from a large number of specialists and forbearing cases can assist doctors oversee better-customized medicines or find comparable cases. Simulated intelligence will empower medicos to embrace a broader procedure for disease organization, better work with care plans, and assist forbearing to all the almost-certain administer and fulfill with prolonged usage of programs [9].

12.2.1.3   Computerized meeting

Bots for medical services are majorly used for forbearing commitment. Medical care bots, which are installed in versatile informing requests, could work with forbearing rapidly and in real time just by communicating something specific, for instance Babylon and uMotif. Wellbeing discussion bots can answer to wellbeing associated inquiries and, indeed, even assist forbearing oversee prescriptions by giving advice on an assortment of prescriptions and recommended dosages [10]. Medical care monitoring devices that utilize AI strategies are currently in broad use. They can be pre-owned for remote forbearing checking for wellbeing aspects, for example, post-surgical heart activity, forbearing height and weight, etc. Wearable devices, like wristwatches, like FitBit wellness trackers, are currently very much in use. AI can be pre-owned to distantly choose tireless treatment plans, or alerts to give the customer any advice or notification. Wearable contraptions can screen data associated with wellbeing and solace, for example, the number of steps walked, or probably the amount of calories consumed. This may be important for people looking to reduce weight. Man-made intelligence would then be able to decipher this data to give individuals better advice with regard to their actual state and, consequently, provide certainty to forbearing way of existing changes.

12.2.1.4 Medication creation

AI calculations are currently being utilized with various accomplishments to decrease medicine revelation times. Creating medicines through clinical tests is incredibly dreary, as regularly as conceivable and extensively. Utilizing AI to reestablish fractions of medication disclosure cycle can be made faster, less expensive, and more secure. Simultaneously, AI cannot totally eliminate every period in medicine formation, it can assist with steps like, finding latest combinations that could be potential medications. It can likewise assist in discovering latest appeal for recently tried combinations [11]. In West Africa, during the Ebola outbreak in 2014, a plan fueled by Simulated Intelligence was utilized to examine open prescriptions that may be upgraded for effective treatment. Two medications were found to reduce toxicity in 24 hours. When such investigations require a very long time, a distinction may be implied to save considerable time. In the near future, AI stages integrated with in-recollection processing innovation will have the ability to provide accelerated medicine revelation, advancement, and convenience and furthermore assist researchers discover latest uses for medicines [12].

12.2.1.5 Recognizing psychological circumstances

A mental condition must be considered when plotting eLearning answers. To recognize these mental conditions in kids, previously a few clinical innovations centered around AI [13]. For instance, the eye-following innovation by Right Eye LLC. The innovation pioneer in late occasions set up an AI-fueled Autism trial, which grants suppliers to diagnose through eyes conditions such as beginning phases of ASD (autism spectrum disorder) in children of 12–40 months of age. Throughout the investigations, an eye-GPS beacon tested kids by introducing different pictures on the partition. Build on this innovation, medical services suppliers choose which child can hear and which child is possibly optically or mentally unbalanced or has visual problems (construct use of a lot more on different articles on display) [14].

12.2.1.6 Acknowledgement of facial side effects

Developments that allow AI structures to perceive profile in cutting-edge images at the moment hand over the relative possibility in finding real accessory in certain infirmities. Facial inclination affirmation (FER) is the main locale in the fields of PC vision; in addition, man-made mental aptitude is inferable from its considerable business potential, in reality, disregarding the way that FER can completely use construct of the various photoelectric cell [15]. To outline, think about Profile2Gene phenotyping intention that utilizes profile revelation and AI to assist clinical benefits supplier in seeing unusual inherited conditions. These requests pull out figure's centers from an image and survey it to images of forbearing from an advice index, who has moreover managed such matters. Construct use of facial affirmation is feasible to see a human being from a high-quantity media. This is done by recognizing a profile in the media and differentiating that it is anything but a database inclusive of both profile images and metadata relating the person. Our profile, similar to our fingerprints, is a digital signature, extraordinarily novel credits are removed (specifics), for profile verification, and a relative connection is pre-owned.

12.2.1.7   The leaders of diabetes
Diabetes is a determined advance metabolic disorder characterized by high blood glucose levels. Increase in blood glucose level is perceived because of damage of pancreatic β-(Type I) cells or because cells are able to produce insulin (Type II). It can lead to conditions like nephropathy, neuropathy, cardiomyopathy, and retinopathy [16]. The Avocation AI assesses or examines diabetes and can consequently determine the severity of the condition. The PC-assisted examination, conclusion-assisted structures, master structures, and implementation of programming may assist specialists in decreasing the changes. The utilization of computer-based insight redesigns interpretation of results with high precision and speed. For a case, The Diabetes Clinic's latest observational test recommends a structure dependent on top of a self- developing AI stage. The structure, named as Rhythm, guesses and supervises blood glucose levels of people with diabetes, relying on biometric photoelectric cell and AI [17].

12.2.1.8   Robot-assisted medical procedures
Computerized operation, PC-assisted operation, and moreover precisely assisted operation are terms for creative upgrades that utilize robotized structures to assist in serious procedures. Precisely assisted operation was made to vanquish the imperatives of previous unimportantly meddlesome techniques and to address the constraints of experts performing an open operation [18]. By virtue of precisely assisted unimportantly prominent operation, as opposed to directly working the implement, the expert uses one of the two strategies to command the implement; either a direct tele manipulator or through PC command. A tele manipulator is a faraway command that allows the expert to perform the normal pursuit identified with the operation. In the meantime, the robotized arms implement those upgrades and use constructs of end-effectors and regulators to perform the operation on the forbearing [4]. In PC-controlled structures the expert uses a PC to share with the robotized arms and their end-effectors, at any rate, these structures make use of tele manipulators for their advice [19]. One productive usage of

the motorized structure is that the expert shouldn't be present during the operation; however, rather they can be in a remote location and still perform the operation [20]. One such medical robot is the da Vinci Surgical Structure. Lately, Google has stated that it using a big medical robot by Johnson & Johnson [21]. They are not making use of any of lone recuperations and notwithstanding. With their AXSIS robot, Cambridge researchers look to vanquish the restriction of the da Vinci, for instance, its huge dimensions and absence of capacity to work in unbelievably distinct and sensitive conditions. Their robot decently relies upon versatile parts, nearly nothing, worm-like arms. The computer program can be used in ophthalmology, for instance, in cascade operations [22].

12.2.1.9   Impediments of artificial intelligence in medical services

The articulation "man-made thinking" could be interesting in all aspects considered as it is anything but unquestionably more advanced [23]. Best case scenario, current advancement – which implies an arrangement of AI strategies can achieve fake confined knowledge or Artificial Narrow Intelligence (ANI) in various fields. Notwithstanding, that is gaining popularity rapidly [24]. These quick systems are faster than humans at performing tasks. To do whatever it takes, not to over-exposure the development, the clinical impediments of present-day ANI additionally should be acknowledged [4]. Streamlining and normalizing clinical documentations such that computations can sort out them means another considerable limitation in familiarizing ANI with clinical center divisions for performing definitive tasks.

12.2.2   Architecture of data retrieval and data processing in electronic health records (Figure 12.3)

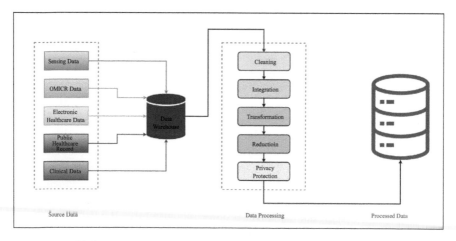

Figure 12.3   Data retrieval and processing in electronic health records

12.3   Smart devices pre-owned in electronic health documentations

12.3.1   Health documentations construct use of wearable devices

In this section, we portray the current accessible types of wearable gadgets and how they screen and foresee a person's body advice and assist for wellness. (Figure 12.4). Wearable gadgets are characterized into four classifications. with regard to their request and use.

- Way of existence and healthcare
- E-materials
- E-patches
- Adornments

This sort of wearable incorporates sports and movement screens like keen band, Lark rest photoelectric cell, and so on. Such gadgets occasionally monitor

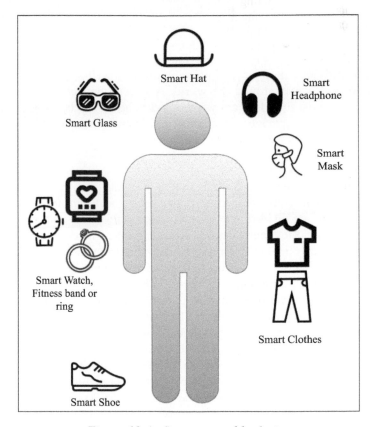

Figure 12.4   Smart wearable devices

developments during resting and determine sleep problems. Likewise, they help gather information on brewing [25].

12.3.1.1 Way of existence and healthcare

SHREWD Watches: Tracking is turning out to be more mainstream. Additionally, competitors need to gather wellbeing information during exercises. Wearable gadgets are vital in making such estimations. Smartwatches that are used to intermittently check wellness, for example, distance run, walked, calorie burnt, pulse, individual internal heat level, and nature of rest. Smartwatches are perhaps the most popular of the wearable gadgets. In view of the new Gartner report [26], smartwatch deals are auxiliary aspects as compared to Bluetooth headphones. The usefulness of smartwatches is ordered into two different methods. To begin with, it plays out certain tasks like cell phones, for example, talking, call receiving, weather reports, etc. Second, this gadget monitors individual body pursuit and transfer these gathered information to the cloud or cell phone. The optical pulse screen monitors resting pulse during the day and records continuously during exercise.

Wrist Bands: This is somewhat like smartwatches. They are available in many types such as silicone wrist bracelet and band, UV bright wrist bracelet and band, and more. Such wristbands are intended to monitor vitals during exercises. In around mid-2000s (decagon), armbands made of silicone were mainstream. They were worn to show the wearer's assist of a reason or magnanimous association, like mindfulness strips. Such wrist bracelet and bands are now called mindfulness armbands. In mid-2007 they turned into an undeniably well-known product being sold at shows and games around the world. A silicone wristband is additionally alluded to as gel wrist bracelet, jam wrist bracelet and band, elastic wrist bracelet and band, and gathering pledges wrist bracelet and band. These wrist bracelets and bands are made up of material similar to silicone.

12.3.1.2 E-materials

Called as SHREWD pieces of clothing, savvy clothing, keen materials, or keen textures, these contain computerized parts like battery and light inclusive of PCs. SHREWD materials are divided into two classes – tasteful and execution improving. It consists of light and textures that are interchangeable. The execution-improving materials are primarily intended for sports and military applications. These have accompanying benefits such as directing internal body temperature, reduce wind obstruction, and command muscle vibrations [27]. For instance, various photoelectric cell like electromyography, pulse, and respiratory photoelectric cells are joined to wellness apparels like shirts, pants, shorts. Then, at that point, the gathered advice is communicated to cell phones. Another model is wellness jeans that can gauge the beat at hips, knees, and lower legs. Likewise, this is connected with the smartphones through Bluetooth for getting extra input about developments. The GPS sports watch construct planned a polar group expert shirt basically for competitors. It's anything but a GPS detector which is situated on the front and back pocket that monitor the pulse progressively. Additionally, we can receive live advice for competitors and mentors like state and wellness quantity. The Lumo Lift tracker was planned as a keen short for running. It is a detector that can screen the ground exposure time, pulse, and step length. We can get this sort of advice through earphones, which thereby reduces the risk of injury.

12.3.1.3   E-Patches

E-patches are set on the skin to screen the particular portion of medicine through the skin. In-game, practice, and the medical services framework, there is a requirement to record a persons exercise performance. In 2016, the E-Ink operator began with LTS, a German organization that constructs conventional patches for smoking discontinuing. It is a 2-inch coin-molded battery that is utilized for forbearing execution. Numerous road accidents occur across the world. For reducing the risk, College of California San Diego fostered an adaptable wearable detector alongside a fix that is utilized to detect the concentration of alcohol in a person's body. This gadget contains a small sticker that is attached on the skin. So, we can undoubtedly determine the blood alcohol level from person's body fluid like sweat, likewise effectively we can gather the advice through Bluetooth, which is connected to a fixed detector [28]. Such wearable multi-detecting patch can intermittently measure lactate levels in a person's sweat. The wearable cathodic detector with this framework can likewise determine metabolites, electrolytes, and temperature. This framework communicates the gathered advice for constant use.

12.3.1.4   Adornments

Keen eyewear: The shrewd eyewear is a popular head-mounted gadget. First, Google Glass provided such eyewear for youngsters in chemical irregularity. The Vuzix shrewd glasses get messages and YouTube video recommendations and notify about the forecast and additionally give touchpad commands. The SOLOS empowers cyclists to get continuous advice inclusive of speed, rhythm, pulse, and force zone. Like this the Eyesight Raptor provides advice, pulse data, and other data. Another such model is ODG's R7 AR Glasses. It has a 720p focal point that shows straightforward tape [29].

12.3.2   Monitoring forbearing's construct use of smart contract

A forbearing distantly checked by a specialist is furnished with different clinical gadgets, for example, an insulin siphon or pulse screen. The crude advice is transferred to an expert "savvy gadget," ordinarily a cell phone or tablet, for conglomeration and organizing as per request. When absolute, the designed data is shipped off to the pertinent keen agreement for full examination alongside re-tried edge regards system (Figure 12.1). In the Ethereum convention, the hotspot for the data took care of the savvy contracts known as the "Prophet" [6]. Oracle is a savvy gadget that imparts straightforwardly to the shrewd agreements. The keen agreement will then, at that point, give advice and notifies through alarms to both the forbearing and medical care supplier, just as computerized therapy directions for the actuator hubs whenever wanted. No classified clinical data will be put away on the blockchain or in the keen agreements on account of HIPAA consistency reasons. We just account the way those events happened and utilizing blockchain innovation as a documentation. The actual estimations will be sent to an assigned EHR stockpiling advice base, while another exchange will be added to the blockchain expressing that the advice was effectively prepared. The framework will incorporate with EHR APIs and send advice straightforwardly to the EHR for capacity. Additionally, all treatment orders from the brilliant agreement and medical care supplier will be documented as absolute in a blockchain exchange. These blockchain exchanges would then be able to be connect to the EHR to give confirmation of the advice in the forbearing's clinical history as an exhaustive documentation of care. This verification will assist with forestalling and distinguished modifications in a forbearing's EHR, regardless of whether it be deliberately or coincidental (Figure 12.5).

This framework will have a private and consortium-driven blockchain, implying that lone approved monitors can peruse the squares and just assigned hubs can perform savvy contracts and check latest squares. Restricting the monitors to just contribute gatherings, for example, care suppliers, gadget producers, and forbearing themselves will assist with reducing abundance openness of data by expecting validation to get to the request. In the consortium style of blockchain the executives, a bunch of pre-endorsed individuals, function the hubs in the blockchain, and a substantial square should contain marks from a base number of individuals. This structure would permit diverse medical services organizations to take part in the framework while as yet keeping a proportion of decentralized administration. Moreover, by utilizing pre-approved check (mining) hubs, it will guarantee that no maverick hubs could conspire to embed bogus exchanges into the chain, just as eliminating the need to pay money for confirmation of work. All object considered, conventions like Practical Byzantine Fault Tolerance (PBFT) can be pre-owned to accomplish agreement since the hubs taking part are known and checked [5].

The shrewd agreements themselves will be measured and adjustable for every tolerant and their gadgets. The construction will be layered, with all expert gadgets calling a alike beginning shrewd agreement, which will, thus, call the important

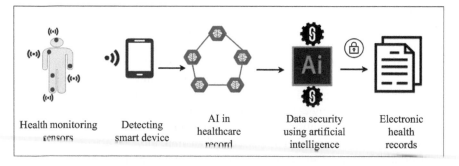

Figure 12.5   Monitoring health and security using artificial intelligence

sub-contract for the particular forbearing's gadget and pass it the info advice and custom limit esteems. This individual agreement will dissect the advice as per the limit esteems, and afterward matter any essential cautions or treatment orders dependent on its discoveries. An agreement cannot be altered after organization, yet rather should be "killed" and another agreement should be given so that this secluded design constructs it simple to supplant a gadget's agreement without influencing the activity of others.

12.4   Care and privacy of healthcare data

12.4.1   Care challenges

EHR advice is the weakest with regard to cyberthreats. The objective of fraudsters is to target medical care advice for monetary benefit. Lawbreakers sell significant advice taken from EHR to the "dark web" (dark web alludes to the substance on the web that isn't ordered via web crawlers and consequently remains stowed away from the overall population) and accomplish high monetary acquire. For the law-breakers, EHR advice is more educational than Mastercard because it contains different fixed identifiers and significant monetary data that is incredibly important in underground markets. Fixed identifiers of EHR advice cannot be reset like the ones in Mastercard. Such identifiers in EHR are the best data hotspots for the lawbreakers to get easy access to the forbearing's financial balances for getting credits or to catch their identifications and other significant archives (property, protection, and so forth) [30]. There are a few cases that show that profoundly touchy data of forbearing was effectively taken by just taking EHR advice. For instance, a latest article distributed a tale about the robbery of EHR advice (20,000 documentations) from North Carolina-based Catawba Valley Medical Center. Taken advice contained forbearing's name, date of birth, clinical advice, healthcare coverage data, and government-managed retirement numbers. Hence, the advice in EHR contains more itemized advice than different sources, accordingly, if there should be an occurrence of digital assaults (Ransomware, Distributed Denial of Service (DDoS) and so on), a major populace can be influenced without a moment's delay that can help avoid any monetary misfortunes. For instance, in the US, 4.5 million forbearing influenced by losing their advice structure through hackers' assault. Additionally, 80 million individuals were influenced since their medical services advice was lost from a healthcare coverage organization in the US.

Protection and care difficulties of the web of object begin from the specified attribute of the web of object organizations, which construct them extraordinary in their methodologies. Such trademark is the heterogeneity, unrestricted climate, compel assets, and the more noteworthy requirement for adaptability. Indeed, even the smalls processor stage by having an exceptionally secure crypto motor and adequate program recollection for carrying out important insurance tasks. Lafky and Horan recommend that care prerequisites for the Internet of Object frame-works, contingent upon their special highlights, and gathering the necessities into the accompanying positions; personality executives, network care, flexibility and belief, and ultimately protection. The creators for this situation explicitly consider various structures that have generally been proposed for the Web of Object inside the examination local area and breakdown whether a few models will, in general, meet the necessary safety norms. The basic examination shows that few protection needs are genuinely thought over; however, none of the multitudes of designs cover the entirety of the care needs. The most revealed are the belief and protection necessities. As long as there are PCs, there exists an impeccably acknowledged representation for the data innovation care dependent on the needed care highlights, generally truncated as CIA, confidentiality (e.g., attempting to forestall any type of unapproved admittance to the significant advice), belief worthiness (attempting to ensure that the advice specified isn't changed in any capacity), and in conclusion, accessibility (mass production sure that advice can be gotten to any time it is required) [31].

These belongings have been profoundly depicted in a type of set of three inside layers, which are inserted at the vertices. As years went by, the replica has been adjusted with a few conceivable principal properties; however, the fundamental properties, CIA, have stayed over the long run. An aspect highly considered is the way such three belongings can't be accomplished in a synchronous way, as they are viewed as reciprocally selective. For instance, specified similar measure of assets, it is absurd to expect to build the general accessibility, without trading off the exactness, secrecy, or even both. For the overall data preparing PC frameworks, traditional care has been centered around the general classification of the said property; however, for some of the frameworks that are implanted as the IoT, one can construct a contention that the other two angles are the most vital ones, or even a lot more fundamental than it is inside the workplace data framework. The other significant perception is that the difference in the approach in a large portion of the cases genuinely sways on collaboration, which is at the center of the quality IT frameworks and heads the command framework.

It is also affirmed that the certainty of an individual with regard to protection and care of their clinical documentations affected their resolve to build up an electronic wellbeing documentation. It affirmed that worries in regard to protection [11] adversely affected the expectations to share their wellbeing data on the web. The set up that there exists an adverse consequence of wellbeing data protection concerns on how willing the people would coordinate in giving access to individual wellbeing data [8]. Then again, Dinev *et al.* [22] discovered the presence of an assist-less connection between worries of individuals' wellbeing data care and their demeanor towards electronic wellbeing documentations. They had similar end with regard to the acknowledgment of electronic wellbeing documentation. An investigation [25] showed that worries on wellbeing data protection decreased the eagerness of forbearing to permit medical care suppliers to share their clinical advice while utilizing the distributed computing strategy. The presence of protection concerns constructs belief turn out to be more essential than, at that point, the limits while choosing medical services except for the instance of optional use. Kuo *et al.* completed an investigation whose results affirmed that there were existing concerns concerning wellbeing data care on the data protection defensive reactions (IPPR) like refusal of forbearing to give data to medical services suppliers, creating individual data of forbearing to clinical offices, mentioning evacuation of individual data of forbearing, negative expressions to their companions, grievances gave straightforwardly to the clinical offices, grievances gave in a circuitous route to an outsider association.

Rohm and Milne [18] stated that customers' interests increment if an association procured a rundown containing a person's clinical history when contrasted with a rundown containing general data. There was additionally an investigation by Zulman *et al.* that revealed that preference of people with regard to sharing of their electronic wellbeing data shift contingent upon the sort of data that is liable to go through sharing. Ruler *et al.* [12] additionally understood that matters concerning care fluctuate for explicit object of wellbeing documentations. It was affirmed that object in the wellbeing office that individuals have more worry about incorporate barrenness matters, early termination, physically communicated infections among different matters that straightforwardly influenced their household. Individuals showed a moderately low protection worry for a portion of their data on the wellbeing documentation, such as faith, date of birth, blood group, language, sexual orientation, the situation with circulatory strain, and malignancy status.

12.4.2 Care and protection highlights of current EHR frameworks

The three care-shield topics to be specific physical, specialized, moreover, authoritative have been appealed for several examinations. These topics comprise various care structures utilized by medical services organizations to give greater care to the wellbeing data that is in the electronic wellbeing documentation. The topic of regulatory security is the principal shield that involves pertinent methods like performing reviews, utilizing official accountability for data care, and thinking of alternate courses of action [30]. This subject has shielded that center around having agreeable care structures and approaches.

The other topic is actual shields that incorporate methods documentation in hierarchical protections and likewise; it centers around securing the wellbeing data actually so their product or then again, an equipment is not attacked by unapproved people or those who could abuse them. Penetrating of actual protections is among the significant donor of safety breaks positioned second. Instances of methods under actual protections incorporate having allocated care jobs [32].

Specific safeguards are third order of subjects and they manage the care of the whole advice structure found in the association of a prosperity affiliation [30]. This point is incredibly basic in ensuring the care of the affiliation in light of the fact that most use electronic media utilizing PCs and other transferrable electronic devices. This subject has care structures like the usage of firewalls besides encryption, disease checking, and measures pre-owned in approving advice. Regardless, it was stated by Lemke [33] that firewalls and cryptography were the most preferred care structures. Other care methodologies that are furthermore pre-owned included antivirus programming, supervisor advice care official likewise, dispersed processing anyway their execution is dependent on the spending plan.

From the assessment by Liu *et al.* [30], it was perceived that there is genuine safeguard, for instance, real access command that is pre-owned to hinder theft, for instance, the use of locks on PCs along with specific assurances to thwart electronic gets through the usage of firewalls and encryption. Amer [31] conducted an examination on informatics through upright use of genomic advice besides electronic prosperity documentations. He comprehended that encryption could give particular insurance while definitive safeguards pre-owned a care strategy for de-recognizing tests assembled or the examination. Particular insurance can in similar manner be performed through firewalls; encryption and translating while definitive safeguard was taken care of through executing intensive preparing and care plans and construct use of a Chief Advice Care Officer. Wikina [34] stated that administrative safeguard incorporated a manager underwriting the appearance of cardboard data containing advice of forbearing and doing pieces of planning on directions to respond to missing documentation while real safeguards incorporated the foundation of observation cameras.

There is more advantage in cutting-edge development, clinical benefits affiliations are likewise ceaselessly being centered around infiltrating care. Organizations should adapt fast to latest innovation and risks and have viewed the organization of peril appropriately, inclusive of the Clinical Engineering Advice Technology Local region; the American College of Clinical Engineering; and the Healthcare Advice and Management Structures Society among various affiliations [29]. The abovementioned documentation steps of risk assessment and the board alongside the named association's ensures that the clinical consideration affiliation are advanced in invigorating forbearing's advice inside electronic prosperity documentations. Clinical consideration foundations seeing the advantages of wellbeing care on account of applying RFID are being developed.

A couple of cases of the RFID strategies fuse the limit of data inside RFID marks, limiting the access to RFID names. These methodologies have further developed insurance and care through restrictions that grant only a few of approved individuals to get to the advice [31]. Construct use of a Chief Advice Care Officer can assist in supervising and coordinating all the care methods and drives in electronic prosperity documentation [31]. Firefox use is one of the advances that is pre-owned to provide care to the advice development structures of clinical benefits affiliations [18,19]. Firefox is effective in getting the association of an affiliation and ensuring that the prosperity advice is guaranteed on the current association. Firefox is pre-owned both inside and outside while protecting the business from risks that could interfere with its advice association. They come in different constructions [34].

The usage of a quantity doorway is the third grouping of firewalls. They expect a piece of gatekeeping for the association of the affiliation when the IP page is being separated for any threats prior to passing the page to the end customers. The external organization relationship of status audit firewalls is transparently utilizing the section so the entry of outside networks into the affiliation's intranet is prevented [34]. Convenience comparable entryways have viably gotten electronic prosperity documentations since they block developers from directly entering the structure and show up at the prosperity advice which is gotten. This social event of firewalls isn't hard to be appeal by affiliations on account of their multi-profited design and tremendous costs included and it is likewise key that both outside and inner assessment of the entire affiliation be directed to see whether the firewall is proper and appropriate for every affiliation. Finally, we have a get-together of firewalls insinuated as the association address mediator. It assists by covering the affiliation's intranet IP addresses so they are not gotten to by outside customers that could have plans to construct hurt [34]. Association address translator develops an obstruction among an affiliation's intranet a likely as the area. Despite the fact that firewalls are convincing in ensuring that the electronic prosperity documentations are secure, it is still extremely crucial that all of the four phases of its sanctuary frameworks is appeal. The solicitation for the methods joins assists command, bearing command, customer command, and direct command [31]. All around, it is critical that the affiliation does a absolute necessities examination, budgetary assessment, and threats evaluation both external and inside to the relationship prior to construct use of any sort of firewall. Frustration of a relationship to do the above assessments or lack of the four care plans can oppositely impact the care of forbearing' electronic prosperity documentations or even the entire advice course of action of the affiliation [18,19].

Cryptography has been utilized as a method of getting or securing electronic wellbeing documentations. The utilization of encryption has expanded the care of electronic wellbeing documentations during the cycle of trading wellbeing data. The way toward trading wellbeing data has persuaded details to be finished measures that ordinarily require documentation of the trading technique to be done by associations when the encryptions are either empowered or then again crippled. The Health Insurance Portability and Accountability Act (HIPAA) planned ways by which cryptography could be pre-owned to get wellbeing data. HIPAA expanded its guidelines on care in 2003 when the United States Department of Wellbeing and Person Services shaped the Concluding Rule.

The Concluding Rule empowered HIPAA to extend the associations' methods of making, getting, keeping, and sending wellbeing data that is secured (PHI) [34]. Unscrambling has assisted guarantee that the electronic wellbeing documentations of forbearing are secure. The utilization of advanced marks has tackled the matter of penetrating secured wellbeing documentations when forbearing check their data. Computerized marks have adequately been appealed to forestall care penetrates. Electronic wellbeing documentations become significantly more available and secure through shielding versatile specialists for forbearing' advice that is communicated from one office to the next [34]. The utilization of usernames is another type of cryptography. They can assist in forestalling care breaks through incorporating singular protection on passwords and supporting that secret phrase clients change these passwords now and again [35,36]. Names are generally utilized and dates must have stayed away from to forestall odds of a programmer guessing the set secret phrase. Applying username and secret word care method is valuable on account of accomplishing commands. The job-based commands perform restriction on the entrance of advice to clients through applying usernames and passwords made by framework heads [37]. This procedure doesn't provide powerful assurance of data inside electronic wellbeing documentations from inside dangers. Logging from the framework by representatives should be done once they are through in request to guarantee that the lessening well-being realities in a condition that the unapproved people can see Other ordinarily utilized care methods incorporate the establishment of antivirus programming, distributed computing, fundamental danger appraisal sequencers, work of a central data care official and radio recurrence distinguishing proof (RFID). Distant Forbearing Monitoring (RPM) is another innovation that is being pre-owned to guarantee there is protection and care of the documentations in an electronic wellbeing documentation. For this situation, various kinds of photoelectric cell are utilized to play out the observing of forbearing' significant signs while at home. They use photoelectric cell that can be worn out or embedded.

These photoelectric cells send data through remote correspondence to a neighborhood base station that is situated inside the forbearing's home. The station guarantees that the data is assessed and signals a focal checking station when there are contrasts from the put forth typical lines. The medical services supplier is then capable to construct fundamental moves once frightened in aiding the forbearing [38,39]. A portion of the conditions that the Remote Forbearing Monitoring innovation is generally reasonable for incorporate dementia, diabetes, and congestive cardiovascular breakdown. Executing these innovations can result in numerous headways in the medical care area, it can likewise meddle with the care of people despite guidelines such as the Health Insurance Portability and Accountability Act (HIPAA). The advice of electronic wellbeing documentations is conveyed electronically through the Internet or remote associations and subsequently dangers, for example, listening in, advice burglary, and advice abuse can be capable. Ultimately, difficulties like extreme social ramifications, for example, managers neglecting to recruit or terminate their workers because of their ailments and protection firms rejecting to provide protection to forbearing. The expanding utilization of innovation has prompted huge examination led on distributed computing for incorporation into the EHR frameworks [40]. The framework made by distributed computing empowers one to perform electronic tasks and data sharing the "leasing" of capacity, just as registering power. Thusly, the medical care organizations are in a situation to save on position up an EHR framework through moving proprietorship staying away from the upkeep cost, while simultaneously joining cryptography techniques. Even though the distributed computing stage looks promising, antivirus programming is an all the more ordinarily appeal care measure. Achampong additionally shows that care gives that come from IT pattern, for example, facilitating wellbeing documentations on far off serve worked by outsider cloud specialist co-ops [34,41].

12.4.3 Data innovation care episodes in medical care position

Infosec Institute announced that the development in the selection of electronic wellbeing documentation lately has not been ensured by the foundation of a network protection measure, along these lines oppressing the medical services manufacturing to a ton of harms from digital dangers [10]. This report received significantly more assistance from different reports of Advice Technology associated occurrences that were capable in clinic positions. A finding from Advice Care Media Gathering (2014), set up that in any event, one care penetrate that influences under 500 people have been accounted for in 75% of reviewed medical services associations in the US, and in any event, one episode influencing more than 500 people was accounted for by 21% of studied medical services suppliers. The Healthcare Advice and the Board Structures Society (2015) understood that 68% of studied medical services associations in the US presented that they had as of late encountered a huge care episode. These announced care episodes were from both internal threat (53.7%) as well as external threat (63.6% of medical services associations) [29].

12.5   Conclusion

The current work has laid out a writing survey identified with care and the protection of computerized wellbeing documentation frameworks. The cardboard has broken down various care and protection and matters that emerge from the utilization of EHRs and takes a gander at the likely arrangements. It is apparent from the writing that electronic health documentations permits the design of clinical advice to be shared effectively among the approved medical care suppliers to improve the general grade of the medical services administrations conveyed to the forbearing. The utilization of e-health empowers clients to have more extensive reasoning and permits wellbeing care suppliers to organize successfully. Man-made consciousness is a developing science that has applications in different fields just as restorative administration's structure. Studies exhibit that AI is a very small magnitude is creating market in the field of medical services. It has a wide assortment of uses in this field, such as advice the executives, medicine revelation, diabetes care, advanced discussions, and so on. There is some demonstrated proof that clinical AI can play a significant part in aiding the specialists and forbearing to provide and receive medical services more efficiently in the 21st century. Electronic wellbeing documentation permit the clinical data to be shared among partners effectively, and the forbearing advice is updated as the forbearing progresses with treatment. In such frameworks, notwithstanding, care and protection concerns are very much fundamental, in light of the way that the forbearing may confront serious matters if sensitive confidential data is revealed to an outsider. From the articles surveyed and dependent on the care regions analyzed, it is clear that various guidelines and norms associated to protection and care are utilized in electronic wellbeing documentations. Nonetheless, there is need for such frameworks to be orchestrated to determine potential struggles and irregularities among norms. Various encryption calculations have been proposed by different articles.

References

[1] Wukkadada B, Saiswani VP. Online healthcare system using cloud computing and artificial intelligence. *IOSR Journal of Computer Engineering* 2000;20:S40–S3.

[2] Mohammadzadeh N, Safdari R. Artificial intelligence tools in health information management. *International Journal of Hospital Research* 2012;1:71–6.

[3] Lieberman H, Mason C. Intelligent agent software for medicine. *Studies in Health Technology and Informatics* 2002;08:99–109.

[4] Maglogiannis I. Introducing intelligence in electronic healthcare systems: state of the art and future trends. *Artificial Intelligence* 1970:71–90.

[5] Mesko B. The role of artificial intelligence in precision medicine. *Expert Review of Precision Medicine and Drug Development* 2017;2:239–41.

[6] Chou S, Chang W, Cheng CY, Jehng JC, Chang C. An information retrieval system for medical records & documents. *International Conference of the IEEE Engineering in Medicine and Biology Society* 2008:1474–7.

[7] Goldman LW. Principles of CT and CT technology. *Journal of Nuclear Medicine Technology* 2007;35:115–28.

[8] Filler A. The history, development and impact of computed imaging in neurological diagnosis and neurosurgery: CT, MRI, and DTI. *Nature Precedings* 2009:1–76.

[9] Cowie J. Evaluation of a digital consultation and self-care advice tool in primary care: a multi-methods study. *International Journal of Environmental Research and Public Health.* 2018;15:E896.

[10] Horner K, Wagner E, Tufano J. Electronic consultations between primary and speciality care clinicians: early insights. *The Commonwealth Fund.* 2011;23:1–14.

[11] Sreevatsan AN, Sathish Kumar KG, Rakeshsharma S, Roomi MM. Emotion recognition from facial expression – a target oriented approach using neural network Emotion Recognition from Facial Expressions: A Target Oriented Approach Using Neural Network. Proceedings of the Indian Conference on Computer Vision, Graphics and Image Processing, 2004:1–6.

[12] Juza RM, Haluck RS, Pauli EM, Rogers AM, Lyn-sue JR. Robotic cholecystectomy: a cost comparison with historically novel laparoscopic cholecystectomy. *OA Robot Surg* 2014;2:1–4.

[13] Technion T. An Autonomous Crawling Micro-Robot. Israel: The Technology Institute. 2008.

[14] Bishara MA. New robotic hair transplantation technology provides path to the future ARTAS hair studio and ARTAS robotic system signal a paradigm shift in hair restoration. *Asthetic Guide.* 2014:1–6.

[15] Narula A, Narula NK, Khanna S, Narula R, Narula J, Narula A. Future prospects of artificial intelligence in robotics software: a healthcare perspective. *International Journal of Applied Engineering* 2014;9:10271–80.

[16] Berman D. The ARTAS Hair Studio® technology is a powerful tool integral to the patient consultation experience. *Restoration Robotics* 2015:1–4.

[17] Spector L. Evolution of artificial intelligence. *Artificial Intelligence* 2006;170:1251–53.

[18] Kye S, Lee T, Lee S, Lee K, Shin S, Lee YS. Detecting periodic limb movements in sleep using motion detector embedded wearable band, in 2017 IEEE Conference on Systems, Man and Cybernetics (SMC).

[19] Gartner Inc., "Gartner Says Worldwide Wearable Devices Sales to Grow 18.4 Percent in 2016," http://www.gartner.com, 2016.

[20] Mulligan, S. Silicone Wrist bracelet and band Explained. Wristband Bros. Sean Mulligan. Retrieved 9 September 2015.

[21] Sathis A, Ravimaran S, Jerald Nirmal Kumar SA. Well-Organized Safeguarded Access on Key Propagation by Malleable Optimization in Blend With Double Permutation, Research Anthology on Artificial Intelligence Applications in Security (pp. 806–828).

[22] Michael Sawh, https://www.wareable.com, 2017.

[23] Anastasova S, Crewther B, Bembnowicz P, *et al.* A wearable multisensing patch for continuous sweat monitoring. *Biophotoelectric Cell and Bioelectronics*, 2017;93:139–45.

[24] Achampong E. Electronic health record (EHR) and cloud security: the current issues. *IJ-CLOSER* 2014;2(6):417–20.

[25] Amer K. Informatics: ethical use of genomic information and electronic medical records. *Journal of the American Nurses Association* 2015;20(2).

[26] Collier R. New tools to improve safety of electronic health records. *CMAJ* 2014;186 (4):251. doi: https://doi.org/10.1503/cmaj.109-4715. [PMC free article].

[27] Collier R. US health information breaches up 137%. *Canadian Medical Association Journal* 2014;186(6):412. doi: https://doi.org/10.1503/cmaj.109-4731.

[28] Jerald Nirmal Kumar S, Ravimaran, Sathis A. An Efficient Security Mechanism for Cloud Data Using Elliptic Curve Digital Signature Algorithm with Wake–Sleep, https://link.springer.com/chapter/10.1007/978-981-15-2043-3_61, 2020.

[29] HIMSS. Chicago, IL: HIMSS; 2015 Jun. 2015 HIMSS Cybersecurity SurveyURL: https://www.himss.org/2015-cybersecurity-survey/full-report [accessed 2019-02-04].

[30] Jannetti MC. Safeguarding patient information in electronic health records. *AORN Journal* 2014; 100(3): C7–8. doi: https://doi.org/10.1016/S0001-2092 (14) 00873-4.

[31] Wikina SB. What caused the breach? An examination of use of information technology and health data breaches. *Perspectives in Health Information Management*; 2014:1–16.

[32] Kruse CS, Smith B, Vanderlinden H, Nealand A. Security techniques for the electronic health records. *The Journal of Medical Systems* 2017;41(8):127.

[33] Jerald Nirmal Kumar S, Ravimaran S, Gowthul Alam, MM. An effective non-commutative encryption approach with optimized genetic algorithm for ensuring data protection in cloud computing. *CMES-Computer Modeling in Engineering and Sciences*, 2020;125(2):671–697.

[34] Tejero A, de la Torre I. Advances and current state of the security and privacy in electronic health records: survey from a social perspective. *The Journal of Medical Systems* 2012;36(5):3019–27. doi: https://doi.org/10.1007/s10916-011-9779-x.

[35] Nagasubramanian G, Sankayya M. Multi-variate vocal data analysis for detection of Parkinson disease using deep learning. *Neural Computing and Applications*, 2021;33(10):4849–64. https://link.springer.com/article/10.1007/s00521-020-05233-7.

[36] Nagasubramanian G, Sankayya M, Al-Turjman F, Tsaramirsis G. Parkinson data analysis and prediction system using multi-variant stacked auto encoder. *IEEE Access*, 2020;8:127004–13, 10.1109/ACCESS.2020.3007140.

[37] Nagasubramanian G, Sakthivel RK, Patan R, Gandomi AH, Sankayya M, Balusamy B. Securing e-health records using keyless signature infrastructure blockchain technology in the cloud. *Neural Computing and Applications* 2020;32(3):639–47. https://doi.org/10.1007/s00521-018-3915-1.

[38] Kumar SR, Gayathri N, Muthuramalingam S, Balamurugan B, Ramesh C, Nallakaruppan MK. Medical big data mining and processing in e-healthcare. In *Internet of Things in Biomedical Engineering*, Academic Press, London, 2019, pp. 323–39. https://doi.org/10.1016/B978-0-12-817356-5.00016-4.

[39] Dhingra P, Gayathri N, Kumar SR, Singanamalla V, Ramesh C, Balamurugan B. Internet of Things-based pharmaceutics data analysis. In *Emergence of Pharmaceutical Industry Growth with Industrial IoT Approach*, Academic Press, London, 2020, pp. 85–131.

[40] Kavidha V, Gayathri N, Kumar SR. AI, IoT and robotics in the medical and healthcare field. *AI and IoT-Based Intelligent Automation in Robotics*, 2021:165–87.

[41] Sharma SK, Gayathri N, Modanval RK, Muthuramalingam S. Artificial intelligence-based systems for combating COVID-19. In *Applications of Artificial Intelligence in COVID-19*, Springer, Singapore, 2021, pp. 19–34.

Chapter 13

Automatic structuring on Chinese ultrasound report of Covid-19 diseases via natural language processing

K. Logu[1], T. Devi[1], N. Deepa[1], N. Gayathri[2] and S. Rakesh Kumar[2]

Abstract

Artificial intelligence (AI) technology saves human lives and reduces the risks taken by doctors. In the proposed work identification of lung sound and blood cells is automated. AI enables the extraction of de-noised lung sounds to understand the patient's health and maintain social distance between doctors and patients. The COVID-19 virus affects a large number of humans day-to-day. So doctors and caretakers are not able to maintain the social distance with the patients. In this paper, we provide intelligent interaction from patients' facial movements and sound recognition (SR) using human–robot interaction (HRI). COVID-19 attacks hemoglobin. In general, blood cells, in particular red blood cells, are counted manually using a hemocytometer along with some laboratory equipment and chemical compounds. This device detects a patient's intrusive physiological signals like whether heart rate (HR) is continuous and measures HR and SR in red blood cells using multinomial tactic regression (MTR) algorithm for better performance. Automatic lung sound extraction is done using a convolutional structural network (CSN). Natural language processing can be easily used to detect and improve the performance of the lung and for the reduction of lung sound noise.

Keywords: Augmented reality (AR); Virtual reality (VR); Sound recognition (SR); Human–robot interaction (HRI); Multinational tactic regression (MTR); Convolution structural network (CSN)

[1]Saveetha School of Engineering, Saveetha Institute of Medical and Technical Sciences, Chennai, India
[2]School of Computing Science and Engineering, Galgotias University, Uttar Pradesh

13.1   Introduction

Artificial intelligence algorithms are designed to make decisions with the regular use of real-time data. They are not like passive machines which are successful and are the simplest of mechanical or predetermined responses. Using sensors, virtual data, or far-flung inputs, AI integrates statistics from a lot of special sources, examines the cloth instantly, and acts at the insights derived from one's data. As such, they are designed by people with the intention to attain conclusions primarily based on their spontaneous analysis. AI is regularly undertaken along with gadgets study and information analytics, and the ensuing aggregate allows wise decision-making. The machine takes information that is required and searches for underlying trends. If it spots something that is applicable for a sensible problem, software program designers can take that know-how and use it with information analytics to recognize precise issues. Artificial intelligence (AI) refers back to the simulation of human intelligence in machines that are programmed to assume like people and mimic their actions. The time period can also be carried out by any device that reveals the trends related to human thoughts of getting to know and problem-solving. The best feature of synthetic intelligence is its cap potential to rationalize and make moves that have the first-class danger of accomplishing a selected goal. A subset of synthetic intelligence is device learning, which refers back to the idea that PC applications can robotically study and adapt to new statistics without being assisted via way of means of humans. Getting to know the strategies deeply permits the computer via the absorption of big quantities of unstructured records which include text, images, or video. Artificial intelligence is primarily based totally on the perception that human intelligence may be described in a manner that a gadget can without problems to mimic it and execute the tasks, from the maximum easy to the ones which are even more complex. The desire of synthetic intelligence consists of mimicking human cognitive activity. Researchers and builders within the discipline are making incredibly fast strides in mimicking sports, which includes learning, reasoning, and perception, to the volume that those may be concretely described. Some accept the fact that innovators may be capable of broadening the structures that exceed the human being's potential to examine or figure out any concern. But others continue to be skeptical about the fact that all cognitive interests are laced with free judgments which can be a concern compared to human experience. AI is constantly evolving to advantage many unique industries. Machines are developed for the use of a cross-disciplinary method primarily based on mathematics, laptop science, linguistics, psychology, and more. The applications of artificial intelligence are endless. This technology can be applied to many different sectors and industries. AI is being tested and used in the healthcare industry for dosing drugs, different treatments to patients, and surgical procedures in the operating room. AI also has its applications in the financial industry, where it is used to detect and flag activity in banking and finance, such as unusual debit card usage and large account deposits—all of which help a bank's fraud department applications. AI is also used to assist, streamline, and make buying and selling simpler. This is achieved by making the supply, demand, and pricing of securities simpler to estimate.

Natural language processing (NLP) is a department in AI that allows machines to apprehend human language. Its aim is to construct structures that could make feel of textual content and mechanically carry out obligations like translation, spellcheck, or subject–matter classification. NLP makes it feasible for computer systems to recognize the human language. Behind the scenes, NLP analyzes the grammatical shape of sentences, finds the meaning of the words/characters, makes use of algorithms to extract the meaning, and then supplies the outputs. In other words, it makes the experience of human language so that it may mechanically carry out unique tasks.

NLP, AI, and ML are sometimes used interchangeably, so you may get your wires crossed when trying to differentiate between the three. The first thing to know is that NLP and ML are both subsets of artificial intelligence. AI is an umbrella term for machines that can simulate human intelligence. It encompasses systems that mimic cognitive capabilities, like learning from examples and solving problems. This covers a wide range of applications, from self-driving cars to predictive systems.

NLP offers how computer systems recognize and translate the human language. With NLP, machines could make feel of written or spoken textual content and carry out responsibilities like translation, keyword extraction, subject–matter classification, and more. But to automate those techniques and supply correct responses, you need mastering of gadget. Machine mastering is the procedure of making use of algorithms that educate machines on the way to mechanically examine and enhance without being explicitly programmed.

Most human beings inflamed with the COVID-19 virus will reveal slight respiration contamination and gets better without requiring unique treatment. Older human beings and people with underlying scientific troubles like cardiovascular disorder, diabetes, continual respiration disorder, and cancer are more likely to be exposed to extreme contamination. The excellent manner to save you from gradual to down transmission is to be knowledgeable about the COVID-19 virus, the reasons for disorder, and the way it spreads. Protect yourself and others from contamination through washing your hands or the use of an alcohol-based sanitizer often and no longer touching your face. There are many kinds of coronaviruses. Some cause moderate illnesses, together with unusual cold. Others can have excessive acute respiration syndrome (SARS) or Middle East respiration syndrome (MERS), which may be life-threatening diseases.

13.2 Natural language processing

NLP analyzes the grammatical shape of sentences and the meaning of the character/ words, makes use of algorithms to extract the meaning, and then supplies the outputs. In other words, it realizes the human language so that it may mechanically carry out extraordinary tasks. There are many different regular apps that we use in which we have encountered NLP without even noticing, like text suggestions while writing an email, supplying translation to a Facebook put up written in a unique language, or filtering undesirable promotional emails into your unsolicited mail folder. NLP, AI, and ML are occasionally used interchangeably so that you can also additionally get your wires crossed while attempting to distinguish among the three. NLP offers how computer systems recognize and translate the human language. With NLP, machines could make feel of written or spoken textual content and carry out responsibilities like translation, keyword extraction, subject–matter classification, and more.

13.2.1   NLP techniques

NLP applies strategies to assist computer systems to apprehend the text, syntactic evaluation, and semantic evaluation.

13.2.1.1   Syntactic analysis

Syntactic analysis – or parsing – analyzes the text using basic grammar rules to identify sentence structure, how words are organized, and how words relate to each other.

(a) Tokenization: This includes breaking apart a textual content into smaller components known as tokens (which may be sentences or words) to make textual content simpler to handle.
(b) Part of speech tagging (PoS tagging): Labels tokens as a verb, adverb, adjective, noun, etc. This enables us to infer the meaning of a word (e.g., the word "book" means different if used as a verb or a noun).
(c) Lemmatization and stemming: This encompasses decreasing inflected phrases to their base shape to make them less complicated to analyze.
(d) Stop-word removal: This removes the frequently occurring words that do not add any semantic value, such as I, they, have, like, yours, etc.

13.2.1.2   Semantic analysis

Semantic evaluation makes a specialty in analyzing the meaning of a text. First, it researches the meaning of every character phrase (lexical semantics). Then, it displays the aggregate of phrases and what they suggest in context. The primary sub-responsibilities of semantic evaluation are word experience disambiguation and attempts to become aware of and experience wherein a phrase is being utilized in a given context. Relationship extraction tries to apprehend how entities (places, persons, organizations, etc.) are related to a text differently.

13.2.2   Sentiment analysis

Sentiment evaluation identifies feelings in textual content and classifies reviews as positive, negative, or neutral. You can see the way it works with the aid of using pasting textual content into this loose sentiment evaluation tool. By studying social media posts, product reviews, or online surveys, corporates and manufacturers can benefit by knowing the clients' perception and experience of products. For example, you may examine tweets citing your emblem in real time and discover remarks from irritated clients in a proper way.

Maybe you need to ship out a survey to discover how clients' experience is approximately and your stage of customer support. By studying open-ended responses to NPS surveys, you may decide which components have bad feedback or the requirement of your high-quality customer support.

13.2.3   Language translation

Machine translation has visible top-notch development in the last few years, with Facebook translations exceeding superhuman and reaching overall performance in 2019. Translation equipment permits organizations to speak in distinct languages, support them to enhance their worldwide communique, or destroy new markets. You also can teach translation equipment to recognize particular terminology in any given industry, like finance or medicine. So, you don't need to fear for misguided translations which can be unusual in places with frequent translation equipment requirement.

13.2.4   Text extraction

Text extraction allows you to tug out pre-described statistics from the textual content. If you have to address big quantities of data, this device enables you to understand and extract applicable key phrases and features (like product codes, colors, and specs) and named entities (like names of people, locations, organization names, emails, etc.). Companies can use textual content extraction to robotically discover key phrases in felony documents, pick out the principal phrases cited in customer service tickets, or pull out product specs from a paragraph of textual content, among many different applications.

13.2.5   Chatbox

Chatbots are AI structures designed to engage with human beings through textual content or speech. The use of chatbots for patron care is on the rise, because of their cap potential to provide 24/7 assistance (dashing up reaction times), deal with more than one queries simultaneously, and unfastened up human retailers from answering repetitive questions. Chatbots actively research from every interplay and get higher knowledge of person intent so that you can depend upon them to carry out repetitive and easy tasks. If they come upon a patron question that they are no longer capable of replying to, then they will skip it onto a human agent.

13.3   Machine learning for NLP

Machine mastering for NLP and textual content analytics includes hard and fast statistical strategies for figuring out elements of speech, entities, sentiment, and different factors of textual content. The strategies may be expressed as a version, which is then carried out to different textual content, additionally referred to as supervised gadget mastering. It may be a hard and fast algorithm that analyzes huge units of records to extract meaning, referred to as unsupervised device learning. It is crucial to recognize the distinction between supervised and unsupervised learning, and the way you could get excellence in every single system.

Text statistics calls for a unique method to device learning. This is due to the fact that textual content statistics may have mass heaps of dimensions (phrases), however, has a tendency to be very sparse. For example, the English language has around 100,000 phrases that are not in use. But any given tweet handle includes some dozen of them.

(A) **Part of Speech Tagging**

Part of speech tagging (PoS tagging) figures out every token's part of speech (noun, adverb, adjective, etc.), after which tags it as such. PoS tagging works on the idea of some of the crucial NLP tasks. We want to effectively perceive parts of speech for you to understand entities, extract themes, and system sentiment. Lexalytics has a high strong version that tag many PoS with >90% accuracy, even for a short, grammarly social media post.

(B) **Named Entity Recognition**

At their simplest, named entities are people, places, and things (products) stated in a textual content document. Unfortunately, entities can be hash-tags, emails, mailing addresses, telecell smartphone numbers, and Twitter handles. In fact, pretty much something may be an entity in case you examine it a proper way. And don't get us to have a say on tangential references. At lexalytics, we have educated the supervised device to gain knowledge of fashions on huge quantities of pre-tagged entities. This method allows us to optimize for accuracy and flexibility. We have additionally educated NLP algorithms to understand not well-known entities (like species of a tree, or various types of cancer).

(C) **Sentiment Analysis**

Sentiment evaluation is the manner of figuring out whether or not a chunk of writing is wonderful, bad, or neutral, after which assigning a weighted sentiment rating to every entity, theme, topic, and class withinside the document. This is an exceptionally complicated mission that varies wildly with context. For example, take the phrase, "unwell burn" In the context of video games, this could sincerely be a wonderful statement. Creating a fixed NLP guidelines to account for each viable sentiment rating for each viable phrase in each viable context might be impossible. But with the aid of using the education system on getting to know the version of pre-scored data, it is able to learn how to apprehend "unwell burn" and in what manner within the context of video gaming, as opposed to within the con-text of healthcare. Unsurprisingly, every language calls for its personal sentiment-type version.

(D) **Categorization and Classification**

The categorization method sorts out the content material into buckets to get a quick, high stage review of what is within the records. To modify the textual content class version records to various material and lightly shepherd their version till it's reached the preferred stage of accuracy.

Arrangement is an action that comprises putting things (objects, thoughts, individuals) into classifications (classes, types, list) in view of their likenesses or normal models. It permits people to coordinate things, articles, and thoughts that exist around them and improves their comprehension of the world. Order is something that people and different organic entities do: "making the best decision with the right sort of thing." The movement of classifying things can be nonverbal or verbal. For people, both substantial articles and theoretical thoughts are perceived, separated, and comprehended through an order. Articles are normally classified for some versatile or practical purposes.

13.3.1   Unsupervised machine learning

Unsupervised system mastering includes schooling a version without pre-tagging or annotating. Some of those strategies are incredibly clean to understand. Clustering way groups comparable files collectively into companies or sets. These clusters are then looked after primarily based on significance and relevancy (hierarchical clustering).

Another kind of unsupervised way of gaining knowledge is latent semantic indexing (LSI). This approach identifies the phrases and terms that often arise with every other. Data scientists use LSI for faceted searches, or for returning the effects that are not of the precise seek term.

Matrix factorization is another method used in unsupervised NLP devices to gain knowledge. This makes use of "latent elements" to interrupt a big matrix down into the aggregate of smaller matrices. Latent elements are the similarities among the items. Gaining knowledge of unsupervised is tricky, however, it has a long way, requires much less labor, and data extensive than its supervised counterpart. Lexalytics makes use of unsupervised gaining knowledge of algorithms to supply some "primary understanding" of how language works. We extract vital styles inside big units of textual content files to assist our fashions and apprehend the maximum in all likelihood interpretation.

Unsupervised getting to know, additionally referred to as unsupervised system getting to know, makes use of system getting to know algorithms to investigate and cluster unlabeled datasets. These algorithms find out hidden styles or statistics groupings without the need for human intervention. Its cap potential to find out similarities and variations, in fact, makes it an appropriate answer for exploratory statistics analysis, cross-promoting strategies, client segmentation, and photo recognition.

13.3.1.1   Clustering

Clustering is a record mining method in which organizations' unlabeled records are clustered primarily based on their similarities or differences [6]. Clustering algorithms are used to procedure raw, unclassified records gadgets into organizations represented via systems or styles within the information. Clustering algorithms may be categorized into some types, especially exclusive, overlapping, hierarchical, and probabilistic.

13.3.1.2   K-means clustering

K-means clustering is one of the clustering techniques wherein records factors are assigned into K groups. K represents the number of clusters primarily based on the gap between every group's centroid [8]. The records factors closest to a given centroid could be clustered beneath the equal category. A large K cost could be indicative of smaller groupings with extra granularity, while a smaller K cost could have large groupings and much less granularity. K-means clustering is usually utilized in marketplace segmentation, file clustering, photo segmentation, and photo compression [5].

13.3.1.3   Hierarchical clustering

(A)   **Ward's linkage:** This approach states that the space among clusters is described through the growth within the sum of squares after the clusters are merged.

(B)   **Average linkage:** This approach suggests the distance among factors in every cluster.

(C)   **Complete (or maximum) linkage**: This technique is described with the aid of using the most distance among factors in every cluster.

(D)   **Single (or minimum) linkage:** This approach is described through the minimal distance among factors in every cluster.

13.3.1.4   Probabilistic clustering

A probabilistic version is an unmanaged method that allows us to remedy density estimation or "soft" clustering problems. In probabilistic clustering, statistics factors are clustered primarily based on the chance that they belong to a specific distribution. The Gaussian mixture model (GMM) is one of the maximum used probabilistic clustering methods [15,16].

13.3.2   Concept Matrix

The Lexalytics Concept Matrix^{TM} is, in a nutshell, unsupervised getting to know system carried out on the pinnacle articles in Wikipedia^{TM}. Using unsupervised getting to know system, we constructed an internet of semantic relationships among the articles. This net lets in our textual content analytics and NLP to recognize that "apple" is near to "fruit" and is near to "tree"; however, it is a long away from "lion", and it is miles nearer to "lion" than it is miles to "linear algebra."

13.3.3   Syntax Matrix

Syntax Matrix^{TM} is an unsupervised matrix factorization applied to a massive corpus of content (many billions of sentences).

Unsupervised Matrix look at and improvement of laptop structures that may interpret speech and textual content as people certainly communicate and kind it. Human communique is frustratingly indistinct at times; all of us use colloquialisms, abbreviations, and do not frequently have trouble with accurate misspellings [1].

These inconsistencies make laptop evaluation of herbal language tough at best. But in the final decade, each NLP strategy and system gaining knowledge of algorithms has stepped forward immeasurably.

3.4 Semantic information

Semantic facts are unique. A word like "the bat flew via the air" will have a couple of meanings relying on the definition of the bat: winged mammal, wood stick, or something else totally. Knowing the applicable definition is critical for expertise in the meaning of a sentence [17].

13.3.4   Syntax information

The second key issue of textual content is a sentence or word structure, referred to as syntax information

13.3.5   Hybrid Machine Learning Systems for NLP

Each time we upload a brand new language, we start with the means of coding within the styles and regulations that the language follows. Then our supervised and unsupervised gadget studying fashions maintain one's regulations in thoughts while growing their classifiers [18,19]. We practice versions in this gadget for low-, mid-, and high-degree textual content functions.

Low-stage textual content features are preliminary methods that you run for any textual content input. These features are step one in turning unstructured textual content into based data [3]. They shape the bottom layer of records that our mid-stage features draw on. Mid-stage textual content analytic features contain extracting the actual content material of a record of textual content [2]. The high-stage feature of sentiment evaluation is the final step of figuring out and making use of sentiment at the entity, theme, and record levels.

AI (ML) for regular language preparing (NLP) and text investigation includes utilizing AI calculations and "thin" man-made consciousness (AI) to comprehend the significance of text records. These reports can be just about whatever contains text: web-based media remarks, online audits, review reactions, even monetary, clinical, legitimate, and administrative archives [9]. Fundamentally, the job of AI and AI in regular language preparation and text investigation is to improve, speed up, and mechanize the basic content examination capacities, and the NLP includes the transformation of this unstructured content into useable information and experiences.

AI for NLP and text investigation includes a bunch of measurable procedures for distinguishing grammatical forms, elements, feeling, and different parts of the text. The procedures can be communicated as a model that is then applied to other content, otherwise called directed AI [10]. It could be additionally a bunch of calculations that work across enormous arrangements of information to separate importance, which is known as unaided AI. Comprehend the contrast between directed and solo learning, and how you can defeat both in one framework [20,21].

Algorithm 1:

In N observations (with Nf features); number of variation
modes n
INITIALIZE Sk = {sk,i = (xk,i,fk,i)|i = 1, . . . , Ns(k)}
DO WHILE C(Q, Θ) decreases
Optimize model parameter (with fix Q)
DO WHILE C(Q, Θ) decreases
1. estimate variances Σ between Sk and Mk
2. optimize M⁻
3. optimize vp and λp, p = 1, . . . , n
Optimize observation parameter (with fix Θ)
DO WHILE C(Qk, Θ) decreases for each k
4. optimize Tk (and update Mk, E(Hij)k
5. optimize ωk (and update Mk, E(Hij)k
OUT Mk
OUT Θ = {M⁻ , vp, λp, n, Σ|p = 1, . . . , n}

Algorithm 2:

STEP 1: Each input unit receives the input signal x_i and transmits this signal to
all units in the above, i.e., hidden layers.
STEP 2: Each hidden unit $(z_h, h = 1, ...p)$ sums its input signals.
$(Z_{inj}, V_{oj} + \sum X_i V_{ij})$
Applying activation function
$Z_j = f(Z_{inj})$
send this signal to all units in the layer above, i.e., output units.
STEP 3: Each output unit $(Y_k, K = 1, ...m)$ sums its weighted input signals
$Y_{ink} = W_{ok} + \sum Z_j W_{ij}$
and supplies its activation function to calculate the output signals.
$Y_k = f(Y_{ink})$

13.4   Ultrasound devices

The author describes the quality of the 2D images generated by his equipment as
excellent, based on 15 years of research and expertise, and 3D as well as 4D images
are enhanced by highly sensitive transducers. He describes the quality of the 2D
images generated by his equipment as excellent, based on 15 years of research and
expertise, and 3D as well as 4D images are enhanced by highly sensitive transducers.

In addition, the spotlight is the lengthy assurance of 3 years for the devices and one-
and-a-half years for spare parts [12]. The G owns a circle of relatives fashions differentiated through a wide variety of channels. At MEDICA, Emperor provided its new G30

ultrasound a transportable device "that's extraordinarily smooth to handle", in step with Alpha Zan [11]. This multi-reason product is flawless and suitable, e.g., for emergency wards and bedside diagnostics within the context of cell rounds, and maybe to be considered for international distribution shortly. Data output is within the DICOM format [4].

Our content examination capacities depend on examples and rules. Each time we add another dialect. We start by coding the examples and decide the language that follows. Then, at that point, our managed and unaided AI models remember those standards when fostering their classifiers. We apply minor departure from this framework for low-, mid-, and undeniable level content capacities. Another sort of solo learning is latent semantic indexing (LSI). This method distinguishes words and expressions that much of the time happen with one another. Information researchers use LSI for faceted quests, or for returning indexed lists that are not the specific pursuit term.

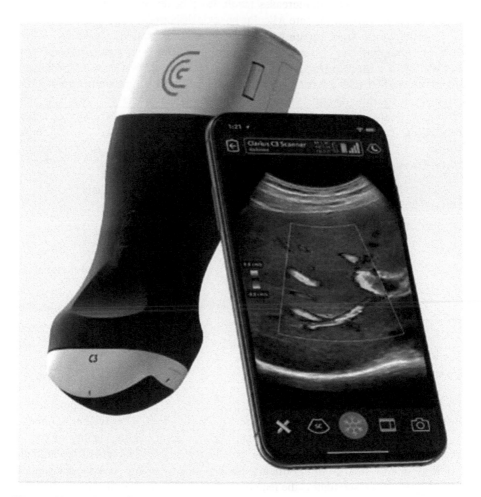

Figure 13.1   shows the portable ultrasound device in superior ultrasound imaging with a wireless scanner

Low-level content capacities are the underlying cycles through which you can run any content information. These capacities are the initial phase in transforming unstructured content into organized information. They structure the base layer of data that our mid-level capacities draw on. Mid-level content examination capacities include removing the genuine substance of an archive of text [14].

Comparably, low fee stays a key gain of the clinical era originating in China, in step with the General Manager [13]. In a unique vein, however, producers within the US have stuck up notably with reference to innovation capability, which is documented through the various patents taken out; and finally, reach a totally excessive degree during the last few years. The ultrasound marketplace serves as a super instance for this. Physicians and clients ought to hold a watch in this manufacturer, and in well-known merchandise made in China.

Reliability is a key benefit that includes this device. Important functions include, amongst others, ePure particular speckle discount era for a greater picture; eSCI spatial compound imaging; eFCI frequency compound imaging; eView panoramic imaging era; eSpeed for picture optimization; self-adaptive shade artifact clearance; trapezoid imaging to increase the visualization options; prolonged field-of-view; THI tissue harmonic imaging and TSI tissue unique imaging; MBP imaging; ergonomic design; steerage B mode; and a warm key function. The software program package deals with obstetrics and gynecology, urology, vascular, orthopedics, cardiology, and extra applications. The G30 sports a 15" high-resolution LED monitor; the weight is below 5 kg. The built-in rechargeable lithium battery allows for more than 3 hours of diagnostic activity.

13.5   Results and analysis

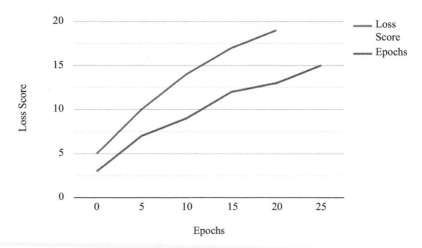

Figure 13.2   The comparison of the graph between epochs and loss score of COVID-19 ultrasound chest report

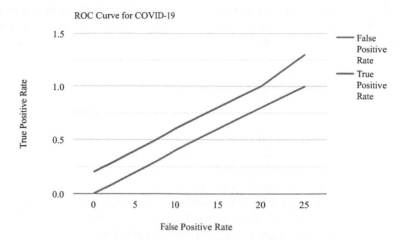

Figure 13.3 *The comparison of the graph between false positive rate and true positive rate of COVID-19 ultrasound chest report*

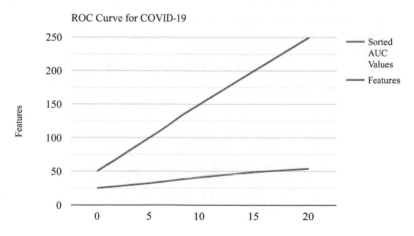

Figure 13.4 *The classifier on the automated model to assist in the diagnosis of COVID-19 through the comparison of sorted AUC values and features*

13.6 Conclusion

This chapter presented the basic work of the Chinese ultrasound report in COVID-19 to identify the disease and maintain social distance. In a portable ultrasound device it was easy to find the chest result, make a comparison between epochs and loss score of ultra chest report, predict the results accurately, and then plot better false positive and true positive rates in a ROC curve of COVID-19. In an automated model of sorted AUC, time values are improved through a comparison of sorted AUC values.

References

[1]   D. de Godoy and P. R. Kinget, "An ultra-low-power polarity-coincidence feedback time-delay-to-digital converter for sound-source localization," *IEEE Journal of Solid-State Circuits*, vol. 55, no. 6, pp. 1610–1623, 2020, doi: 10.1109/JSSC.2019.2950322.

[2]   Y. Peng, Y. Tang, S. Lee, Y. Zhu, R. M. Summers, and Z. Lu, "COVID-19-CT-CXR: a freely accessible and weakly labeled chest X-ray and CT image collection on COVID-19 from biomedical literature," *IEEE Transactions on Big Data*, vol. 7, no. 1, pp. 3–12, 2021, doi: 10.1109/TBDATA.2020.3035935.

[3]   H. Jelodar, Y. Wang, R. Orji, and S. Huang, "Deep sentiment classification and topic discovery on novel coronavirus or COVID-19 online discussions: NLP using LSTM recurrent neural network approach," *IEEE Journal of Biomedical and Health Informatics*, vol. 24, no. 10, pp. 2733–2742, 2020, doi: 10.1109/JBHI.2020.3001216.

[4]   R. Tang, L. Zhang, G. Zhang, and J. Wang, "Analysis of COVID-19 rebound based on natural language processing," 2021 6th International Conference on Intelligent Computing and Signal Processing (ICSP), 2021, pp. 333–336, doi: 10.1109/ICSP51882.2021.9408930.

[5]   S. Malo, J. Thiombiano, and Y. Traoré, "Extraction of events and qualitative data from texts for the monitoring of infectious diseases: case of meningitis and COVID-19," 2021 16th Iberian Conference on Information Systems and Technologies (CISTI), 2021, pp. 1–4, doi: 10.23919/CISTI52073.2021.9476498.

[6]   A. Abdullha and S. Abujar, "COVID-19: data analysis and the situation prediction using machine learning based on Bangladesh perspective," 2020 15th International Joint Symposium on Artificial Intelligence and Natural Language Processing (iSAI-NLP), 2020, pp. 1–8, doi: 10.1109/iSAI-NLP51646.2020.9376812.

[7]   P. Bose, S. Roy, and P. Ghosh, "A comparative NLP-based study on the current trends and future directions in COVID-19 research," *IEEE Access*, vol. 9, pp. 78341–78355, 2021, doi: 10.1109/ACCESS.2021.3082108.

[8]   A. Rajmohan, A. Ravi, K.O. Aakash, K. Adarsh, D. Anjuna, and T. Raj, Anjali, "CoV2eX: A COVID-19 website with region-wise sentiment classification using the top trending social media keywords," 2021 Sixth International Conference on Wireless Communications, Signal Processing and Networking (WiSPNET), 2021, pp. 113–117, doi: 10.1109/WiSPNET51692.2021.9419415.

[9]   Z. Irahhauten, H. Nikookar, and G. J. M. Janssen, "An overview of ultra wide band indoor channel measurements and modeling," *IEEE Microwave*

and Wireless Components Letters, vol. 14, no. 8, pp. 386–388, 2004, doi:10.1109/LMWC.2004.832620.

[10] J. Vrindavanam, R. Srinath, H. H. Shankar, and G. Nagesh, "Machine learning based COVID-19 cough classification models – a comparative analysis," 2021 5th International Conference on Computing Methodologies and Communication (ICCMC), 2021, pp. 420–426, doi: 10.1109/ICCMC51019.2021.9418358.

[11] A. Hassan, I. Shahin, and M. B. Alsabek, "COVID-19 detection system using recurrent neural networks," 2020 International Conference on Communications, Computing, Cybersecurity, and Informatics (CCCI), 2020, pp. 1–5, doi: 10.1109/CCCI49893.2020.9256562.

[12] J. Han, C. Brown, J. Chauhan, *et al.*, "Exploring automatic COVID-19 diagnosis via voice and symptoms from crowdsourced data," ICASSP 2021 – 2021 IEEE International Conference on Acoustics, Speech and Signal Processing (ICASSP), 2021, pp. 8328–8332, doi:10.1109/ICASSP39728.2021.9414576.

[13] P. K. Dutta, A. Ghosh, P. De, and M. Soltani, "A proposed model of a semi-automated sensor actuator resposcopy analyzer for 'Covid-19' patients for respiratory distress detection," 2021 11th International Conference on Cloud Computing, Data Science & Engineering (Confluence), 2021, pp. 618–623, doi: 10.1109/Confluence51648.2021.9377180.

[14] J. Andreu-Perez, SMIEEE, H. Pérez-Espinosa, E. Timonet, *et al.*, "A generic deep learning based cough analysis system from clinically validated samples for point-of-need Covid-19 test and severity levels," *IEEE Transactions on Services Computing*, 512–518, 2021, doi:10.1109/TSC.2021.3061402.

[15] G. Nagasubramanian and M. Sankayya, Multi-variate vocal data analysis for detection of Parkinson disease using deep learning. *Neural Computing and Applications*, vol. 33, no. 10. pp.4849–4864, 2021. https://link.springer.com/article/10.1007/s00521-020-05233-7.

[16] G. Nagasubramanian, M. Sankayya, F. Al-Turjman, and G. Tsaramirsis, "Parkinson Data analysis and prediction system using multi-variant stacked auto encoder," *IEEE Access*, vol. 8, pp. 127004–127013, 2020, 10.1109/ACCESS.2020.3007140.

[17] G. Nagasubramanian, R. K. Sakthivel, R. Patan, A. H. Gandomi, M. Sankayya, and B. Balusamy. Securing e-health records using keyless signature infrastructure blockchain technology in the cloud. *Neural Computing and Applications*, vol. 32(3), pp. 639–647,2020. https://doi.org/10.1007/s00521-018-3915-1

[18] S. R. Kumar, N. Gayathri, S. Muthuramalingam, B. Balamurugan, C. Ramesh, and M. K. Nallakaruppan, Medical Big Data Mining and Processing in e-Healthcare. In *Internet of Things in Biomedical Engineering*, Academic Press, London,2019, pp. 323–339. https://doi.org/10.1016/B978-0-12-817356-5.00016-4

[19] P. Dhingra, N. Gayathri, S. R. Kumar, V. Singanamalla, C. Ramesh, and B. Balamurugan, Internet of Things–based pharmaceutics data analysis. *In Emergence of Pharmaceutical Industry Growth with Industrial IoT Approach*, Academic Press, London, 2020,pp. 85–131.

[20]   S. K. Sharma, N. Gayathri, R. K. Modanval, and S. Muthuramalingam, . Artificial intelligence-based systems for combating COVID-19. In *Applications of Artificial Intelligence in COVID-19*, Springer, Singapore, 2021, pp. 19–34.

[21]   V. Kavidha, N. Gayathri, and S. R. Kumar, AI, IoT and robotics in the medical and healthcare field. In *AI and IoT-Based Intelligent Automation in Robotics,* 2021, pp. 165–187.

Index